A Short History of Chinese Art

Tao-chi (Shih-t'ao, *c*1641-*c*1717): Landscape. Album leaf; ink and slight colour on paper. Ht. 48cm. Ch'ing Dynasty.
Detail of Plate 68b.

A Short History of
CHINESE ART

Michael Sullivan

UNIVERSITY OF CALIFORNIA
Berkeley and Los Angeles

University of California Press
Berkeley and Los Angeles, California
© *1967 by Michael Sullivan*
New, revised printing, 1970

Library of Congress Card Number: 67–21260
SBN 520–01239–9

Printed in Great Britain

To KHOAN

奇文共欣賞
疑義相與析

Foreword

In this book I have, after much reflection, preserved the continuous narrative framework of my earlier *Introduction to Chinese Art*, because I feel that only a broadly historical approach, one which combines 'vertical' continuity down the ages with 'horizontal' wholeness across each period, makes it possible for the reader, perhaps approaching Chinese art for the first time, to get a glimpse of the whole pattern. Other methods — devoting separate chapters to painting and ceramics, for example, or discussing one art form under each successive dynasty — have their advantages; but the first isolates the arts from each other, while the second leaves large areas untouched. But while the shape of the book remains unchanged, the text has been extensively revised and rewritten to keep it as far as possible abreast of recent discoveries and research, and many of the illustrations are new.

I should like once more to thank my friends and colleagues to whose teaching and writing I owe so much. I should like also to express my thanks to all the private collectors and museums that have sent me photographs and permitted their reproduction, to Mr N.S.Hyslop for drawing the maps, to Mr Thomas Greeves for the drawings on pages 150 and 207, and to Mr P.L.Moldon for the care with which he has seen the book through the press.

M. S.

London
July 1966

This new printing has enabled me to make some minor revisions, and to correct errors in the text. I am particularly grateful to Max Loehr and James Cahill for their very helpful suggestions.

M.S.

London
August 1969

Foreword

Contents

Chronological Table page 26

I. BEFORE THE DAWN OF HISTORY 29

II. THE SHANG DYNASTY 39

III. THE CHOU DYNASTY 62

IV. THE PERIOD OF THE WARRING STATES 74

V. THE CH'IN AND HAN DYNASTIES 92

VI. THE SIX DYNASTIES 119

VII. SUI AND T'ANG 145

VIII. THE FIVE DYNASTIES AND SUNG 169

IX. THE YÜAN AND MING DYNASTIES 204

X. FROM 1644 TO THE PRESENT DAY 239

Books for Reference and Further Reading 266

Index 271

Monochrome Plates *at the end of the book*

Illustrations

MAPS

1. China showing Modern Political Divisions, Chief Pottery Centres, and Buddhist Monuments *page 24–25*
2. Ancient China to the End of the Han Dynasty 40
3. The spread of Buddhism into the Far East 134
4. North China in the Eleventh Century 170
5. Kiln Sites in the Hangchow Area 200

COLOUR PLATE

Tao-chi (Shih-t'ao, *c.* 1641–*c.* 1717): Landscape, Album leaf; ink and slight colour on paper. Ht. 48 cm. Ch'ing Dynasty. Detail of Plate 68b. *frontispiece*
Museum of Fine Arts, Boston

MONOCHROME PLATES
(at the end of the book)

1a. Funerary vase; pottery, painted in purple and black. From Yangshao, Honan. Ht. 42·5 cm. Neolithic.
   Museum of Far Eastern Antiquities, Stockholm
1b. Stem-dish: black Lungshan-type pottery. Neolithic.
   Private collection, Japan
2a. Anyang; tomb at Wu-kuan-ts'un after excavation. Length 10 m. Shang Dynasty.
2b. Ox-head; marble. Excavated at Hou-chia-chuang, Anyang. Length 29·2 cm. Shang Dynasty.
   Academia Sinica, Taipeh

13

3a. Jar; white stoneware with impressed decoration. From Anyang. Ht. 33 cm. Shang Dynasty.
Freer Gallery of Art, Washington, D.C.

3b. Wine container of type *kuang*; bronze. Ht. 24 cm. Late Shang Dynasty.
Fogg Art Museum, Harvard University, Cambridge

4. Vessel of type *chia*; bronze. Ht. 34·2 cm. Shang Dynasty.
William Rockhill Nelson Gallery of Art, Kansas City

5a. Dagger-axe of type *ko*; bronze haft and jade blade. From Anyang. Length 28 cm. Shang Dynasty.
A Hellström, Mölndal

5b. Executioner's axe of type *ch'i*; bronze. From Anyang. Length 23·5 cm. Shang Dynasty.
William Rockhill Nelson Gallery of Art, Kansas City

6a. Tiger; bronze. Length 75·2 cm. Chou Dynasty.
Freer Gallery of Art, Washington, D.C.

6b. Knife with animal-head handle; bronze. Length 26·3 cm. Shang Dynasty.

7a. Vessel of type *hu*; bronze. From Hsin-cheng. Ht. 52 cm. Late Middle Chou.
Kaifeng Museum, Honan

7b. *Ts'ung* (symbol of Earth); jade. Ht. 21·5 cm. Chou Dynasty.
British Museum, London

8. Vessel of type *hu*; bronze. Ht. 60·6 cm. Middle Chou period (ninth century B.C.).
M. H. de Young Memorial Museum, Avery Brundage Foundation, San Francisco

9a. Vessel of type *ting*, with cover; bronze inlaid with silver. Probably from Chin-ts'un, Loyang. Ht. 15·2 cm. Warring States.
Minneapolis Institute of Arts, Minneapolis

9b. Bell of type *chung*; bronze. Ht. 54·5 cm. Warring States.
British Museum, London

10a. Plaque depicting two animals fighting; bronze. Length 11·5 cm. Han Dynasty.
Freer Gallery of Art, Washington, D.C.

10b. Garment hook; gilt bronze, inlaid with jade and glass. Length 15·7 cm. Warring States.
Fogg Art Museum, Grenville Winthrop Collection

11a. Gong-stand formed of addorsed phoenixes and tigers; lacquered and painted wood. From Hsing-yang, Honan. Ht. 134 cm. Warring States.

11b. Top of bronze container for cowrie-shells, decorated with modelled sacrificial scene; bronze. From Shih-chai-shan, Yünnan. Diam. 34 cm. Late Warring States or early Han Dynasty.

12a. Bowl; painted lacquer. From Changsha. Diam. 25·4 cm. Warring States.
Seattle Art Museum, Eugene Fuller Memorial Collection

12b. Mirror; bronze. Diam. 14 cm. Warring States.
Museum of Far Eastern Antiquities, Stockholm

13a. *Pi* disc; jade. Diam. (of disc) 16·5 cm .Warring States.
William Rockhill Nelson Gallery of Art, Kansas City

13b. Woman, phoenix and dragon; painting on silk. Excavated at Changsha. Ht. 30 cm. Warring States.

14a. Horse trampling upon a barbarian; stone sculpture standing before the reputed tomb of Ho Ch'ü-ping (died 117 B.C.), Shensi. Ht. 188 cm. Han Dynasty.

14b. Pillar of Shen; stone sculpture. Ch'ü-hsien, Szechwan. Han Dynasty.

15a. The attempt to assassinate Ch'in Shih-huang-ti; rubbing from engraved stone in Wu family shrine at Chia-hsiang, Shantung. Ht. 23 cm. Han Dynasty (second century A.D.).

15b. Shooting birds on a lake shore; rubbing from relief on pottery tile from a tomb at Kuanghan, Szechwan. Ht. 42 cm. Han Dynasty.
Szechwan Provincial Museum, Chengtu

16a. The guests arrive for the funeral feast; wall-painting in a tomb in Liao-yang, N.E. China. Ht. 109 cm. Han Dynasty.

16b. Detail of a painted tomb tile. Ht. 19 cm. Han Dynasty.
Museum of Fine Arts, Boston

17. Hill-censer, *po-shan hsiang-lu*; bronze, inlaid with gold, silver, turquoise and carnelian. Ht. 17·9 cm. Early Han Dynasty.
Freer Gallery of Art, Washington, D.C.

18a. Paragons of filial piety; lacquer painting on basket-work box from Lolang, North Korea. Ht. (of panel) 5 cm.
National Museum, Seoul

18b. TLV-type mirror; bronze. Diam. 20·3 cm. Han Dynasty.
Raymond A. Bidwell, Springfield Mass.

19a. Head and shoulders of a horse; green jade. Ht. 18·9 cm. Han Dynasty.
Victoria and Albert Museum, London

19b. Figured silk fabric from Noin-Ula, Mongolia. Han Dynasty.
Hermitage Museum, Leningrad

20a. Model of a house; painted pottery. Ht. 132 cm. Han Dynasty.
William Rockhill Nelson Gallery of Art, Kansas City

20b. Stand for a 'coin-tree', decorated with a procession of elephants in relief; pottery. From a tomb at Neichiang, Szechwan. Ht. 33·9 cm. Han Dynasty.
Szechwan Provincial Museum, Chengtu

21a. Basin; Yüeh stoneware, covered with a grey-green glaze. Diam. 28·8 cm. Third or fourth century.
Walker Art Center, Minneapolis

21b. Seated watchdog; red-glazed pottery, from Changsha. Ht. 36·8 cm. Han Dynasty.
M. H. D. de Young Memorial Museum, Avery Brundage Foundation, San Francisco

22. After Ku K'ai-chih (c. 344–406): The bedroom scene, from the handscroll illustrating the *Admonitions of the Court Instructress* by Tso Ssu; ink and slight colour on silk. Ht. 25 cm. Ninth or tenth century?
British Museum, London

23. The story of the Filial Yüan Ku; engraved on the side of a stone sarcophagus. Ht. 56 cm. First half of sixth century.
William Rockhill Nelson Gallery of Art, Kansas City

24a. Yünkang, interior of Cave VII. Late fifth century.

24b. The Wei Empress and her attendants; restored relief panel from Pin-yang Cave, Lungmen. Ht. 198 cm. About A.D. 522.
William Rockhill Nelson Gallery of Art, Kansas City

25. Stele illustrating scenes from the Life of the Buddha and the teachings of the Lotus Sutra; stone. In Cave 133, Maichi-shan, Kansu. First half of sixth century.
Photo, Dominique Darbois

26a. Stone pagoda of Sung-yüeh-ssu, on Mount Sung, Honan. About A.D. 520.

26b. Colossal Buddha; stone. Yünkang, Cave XX. Ht. 13·7 m. Late fifth century.

27a. Standing Buddha; gilt bronze. Ht. 61 cm. Dated A.D. 536.
University Museum, Philadelphia

27b. Buddha preaching the Law; wall-painting in Cave 249 (Pelliot 101), Tunhuang. Northern Wei Dynasty.

28a. Bodhisattva; stone. Ht. 188 cm. Northern Ch'i Dynasty.
University Museum, Philadelphia

28b. Kuanyin bearing a vase; stone. Excavated at Chengtu, Szechwan. About seventh century.
Szechwan Provincial Museum, Chengtu

28c. The Buddha incarnate in a golden gazelle (the *Rūrū Jātaka*); wall-painting in Cave 257 (Pelliot 110), Tunhuang. Northern Wei Dynasty.

29. Jar; Yüeh stoneware with moulded decoration under olive-green glaze. Ht. 51·6 cm. Six Dynasties.
William Rockhill Nelson Gallery of Art, Kansas City

30a. Winged lion; stone. Length 152 cm. Sixth century.

30b. A charger and his groom; stone relief from the tomb of T'ang T'ai-tsung (died 649). Length 206 cm. T'ang Dynasty.
University Museum, Philadelphia

31a. 'Udyāna type' Buddha image; white marble. From Ch'ü-yang-hsien, Hopei. Ht. 145 cm. Seventh century.
Victoria and Albert Museum, London

31b. Nursemaid with a baby; partly glazed and painted pottery. Ht. 36·8 cm. T'ang Dynasty.
Collection of Sir Alan and Lady Barlow, Wendover

32a. The Paradise of Amitabha; detail of a wall-painting in the Kondō of Hōryūji, Nara. About A.D. 700.

32b. Yen Li-pen (died 673): The Emperor Hsüan of the Ch'en Dynasty. Detail of the handscroll of the Thirteen Emperors; ink and slight colour on silk. Ht. 51 cm. T'ang Dynasty.
Museum of Fine Arts, Boston

33. Seated Buddha; stone. From T'ien-lung-shan, Shansi. Eighth century. (Head restored.)
Fogg Art Museum, Harvard University, Cambridge

34. Sung Hui-tsung (r. 1101–25): Court Ladies preparing silk. Handscroll after Chang Hsüan; ink and colour on silk. Ht. 37 cm. Sung Dynasty.
Museum of Fine Arts, Boston

35a. Han Kan (active 740–60): 'Night White', a favourite horse of T'ang Ming Huang. Handscroll; ink on paper. Ht. 29·5 cm. (Detail.)
Lady David, London

35b. Style of Wang Wei (698–759)?: Riverside under snow. Part of a handscroll(?); ink on silk. About tenth century.
Formerly Manchu Household Collection

36. Anon: The Emperor Ming Huang's Journey to Shu. Hanging scroll; ink and colour on silk. Ht. 55·9 cm.
Palace Museum Collection, Taiwan

37. Attributed to Tung Yüan: Scenery along the Hsiao and Hsiang Rivers. Part of a handscroll; ink and slight colour on silk. Early Sung Dynasty.
Palace Museum, Peking

38a. 'Sea-horse and Grape' mirror; bronze. Diam. 24·1 cm. T'ang Dynasty.
Mr and Mrs Myron S. Falk, Jr., New York

38b. Miniature stem-cup, engraved with hunting scene; gilt bronze. Ht. 6·4 cm. T'ang Dynasty.
Royal Ontario Museum, Toronto

39a. Pottery Jar decorated with splashed polychrome glaze. Ht. 17·8 cm. T'ang Dynasty.
M. H. de Young Museum, San Francisco

39b. Ewer with stopper in the shape of a pheasant's head; white-glazed porcelain. Ht. 30·5 cm. T'ang Dynasty.
Minneapolis Institute of Arts

40a. Interior of the Buddha Hall of Upper Hua-yen-ssu, Tatung, Shansi. Dedicated 1140. Chin Dynasty.

40b. Lohan; modelled in pottery with three-colour glaze. Ht. 105 cm. Liao-Chin Dynasties.
Metropolitan Museum of Art, New York

41. Kuanyin; wood and plaster, painted and gilded. Ht. 225 cm. Sung Dynasty.
William Rockhill Nelson Gallery of Art, Kansas City

42a. After Shih K'o (active mid-tenth century); Two minds in harmony. Part of a handscroll; ink on paper. Ht. 44 cm.
Shōhōji, Kyōto

42b. Attributed to Ku Hung-chung; The night entertainments of Han Hsi-tsai. Part of a handscroll; ink and colour on silk. Ht. 29 cm. Sung Dynasty.
Palace Museum, Peking

43. Chang Tse-tuan (early twelfth century); Life along the river on the eve of the Ch'ing-ming festival. Detail of a handscroll; ink and slight colour on silk. Ht. 25·5 cm. Sung Dynasty.
Palace Museum, Peking

44. Fan K'uan (active 990–1030); Travelling amid mountains and gorges. Hanging scroll; ink and slight colour on silk. Ht. 233 cm. Sung Dynasty. (Lower half.)
Palace Museum Collection, Taiwan

45. Attributed to Su Tung-p'o (1036–1101); Bare tree, bamboo and rocks. Handscroll; ink on paper. Ht. 23·4 cm. Sung Dynasty.
Palace Museum, Peking

46. Sung Hui-tsung (r. 1101–25); The five-coloured parakeet. Handscroll; ink and colour on silk. Ht. 53 cm. Sung Dynasty.
Museum of Fine Arts, Boston

47. Hsia Kuei (c. 1180–1230); Clear distance over mountains and streams. Part of a handscroll; ink on paper. Ht. 46·5 cm. Sung Dynasty.
Palace Museum Collection, Taiwan

48. Li T'ang (c. 1050–1130); Whispering Pines in the Mountains, dated 1124. Hanging scroll; ink and colour on silk. Ht. 139·8 cm. Sung Dynasty. (Detail).
Palace Museum Collection, Taiwan

49a. Mu-ch'i (c. 1200–70); Shrike on a pine-trunk. Detail of a hanging scroll; ink on paper. Sung Dynasty.
Matsudaira Collection, Tokyo

49b. Ch'en Jung (active 1235–c. 1260); The nine dragons. Part of a handscroll; ink on paper. Ht. 46 cm. Sung Dynasty.
Museum of Fine Arts, Boston

50a. Deep bowl with incised design of ducks amid water plants; Ting ware. Diam. 20 cm. Sung Dynasty.
Museum of Fine Arts, Boston

50b. Vase with lobed sides; *ch'ing-pai* ware. Ht. 13 cm. Sung Dynasty.
The Arts Council of Great Britain, Seligman Collection

51a. *Mei-p'ing* vase; Honan black-glazed stoneware. Ht. 25·4 cm. Sung Dynasty.
Mrs Alfred Clark, Fulmer

51b. *Kinuta* vase; Lung-ch'üan celadon. Ht. 16·9 cm. Sung Dynasty.
Sir Alan and Lady Barlow, Wendover

51c. Traveller's flask, with cockscomb ornament in green enamel over white glaze. Ht. 37·5 cm. North China. Liao Dynasty.
Private collection, Japan

52a. Covered jar; stoneware decorated with black flowers on a white glaze. Tz'u-chou ware. Ht. 11·7 cm. Sung Dynasty.
Percival David Foundation, London

52b. Tea bowl; dark stoneware with black 'hare's fur' glaze. Fukien *temmoku*. Diam. 13 cm. Sung Dynasty.
Arts Council of Great Britain, Seligman Collection

53. Ni Tsan (1301–74); The Jung-hsi Studio. Dated 1372. Hanging scroll; ink on paper. Ht. 73·3 cm. Yüan Dynasty.
Palace Museum Collection, Taiwan

54. Chao Meng-fu (1254–1322); Autumn Colours on the Ch'iao and Hua Mountains. Dated 1295. Part of a handscroll; ink and slight colour on paper. Ht. 28·4 cm. Yüan Dynasty.
Palace Museum Collection, Taiwan

55. Huang Kung-wang (1269–1354); Living in the Fu-ch'un Mountains. Dated 1350. Part of a handscroll; ink on paper. Ht. 33 cm. Yüan Dynasty.
Palace Museum Collection, Taiwan

56a. Ch'ien Hsüan (c. 1235–after 1300); Sparrow on an apple-branch. Album leaf; ink and slight colour on paper. Ht. 22.2 cm. Yüan Dynasty.
University Art Museum, Princeton

56b. Wu Chen (1280–1354); Leaf from an album of studies of bamboo. Dated 1350. Ink on paper. Ht. 42·9 cm. Yüan Dynasty.
Palace Museum Collection, Taiwan

57a. Tai Chin (c. 1390–1460); Fishermen on the River. Detail of a handscroll; ink and colour on paper. Ht. 46·1 cm. Ming Dynasty.
Freer Gallery of Art, Washington D.C.

57b. Ch'iu Ying (c. 1510–51); Fisherman's flute heard over the lake. Detail of a hanging scroll; ink and slight colour on paper. Diam. 84·9 cm. Ming Dynasty.
John M. Crawford Jr., New York

58. Shen Chou (1427–1509); Returning home from the Land of the Immortals. Album-leaf mounted as a handscroll; ink and colour on paper. Ht. 38·9 cm. Ming Dynasty.
William Rockhill Nelson Gallery of Art, Kansas City

59a. Tung Ch'i-ch'ang (1555–1636); Leaf from an album dated 1601; ink and colours on paper. Ht. 42·8 cm.
Dr Franco Vannotti, Lugano

59b. Ch'en Hung-shou (1599–1652); Portrait of the poet Po Chü-i, in the manner of Li Lung-mien. Dated 1649. Part of a handscroll; ink and colours on paper. Ht. 31·6 cm. Ch'ing Dynasty.
C. A. Drenowatz, Zürich

60. Ridge-tile in the form of a guardian figure; pottery, glazed green and dark brown. Ht. 80 cm. Ming Dynasty.
William Rockhill Nelson Gallery of Art, Kansas City

61a. Peony and rock. K'o-ssu tapestry. Detail. Diam. 27 cm. Ming Dynasty.
Victoria and Albert Museum

61b. Carved lacquer cup-stand. Yung-lo mark and Ch'ien-lung inscription dated 1781. Diam. 6·5 cm. Ming Dynasty.
Lady David, London

62a. Incense-burner; cloisonné enamel. Ht. 12·7 cm. First half of fifteenth century. Ming Dynasty.
Sir Harry and Lady Garner, Beckenham

62b. Pilgrim-bottle; white porcelain decorated in underglazed blue. Ht. 30·4 cm. Hsüan-te period. Ming Dynasty.
Percival David Foundation, London

63. Kuanyin, modelled in white porcelain. Fukien Te-hua ware. Ht. 21·6 cm. Early Ch'ing Dynasty.
Sir Alan and Lady Barlow, Wendover

64a. Peking; the Ch'i-nien-tien, Hall of Annual Prayers, in the Precinct of the Altar of Heaven. Late Ch'ing Dynasty.
Photo, Hedda Morrison

64b. Peking; the Imperial Palace, looking north from the Wu-men to the T'ai-ho-men. A corner of the T'ai-ho-tien is visible beyond. Ming and Early Ch'ing Dynasties.
Photo, Hedda Morrison

65a. Covered tripod; white jade. Ht. 15·3 cm. Early Ch'ing Dynasty.
M. H. de Young Museum, Avery Brundage Foundation, San Francisco

65b. Tea-pot of enamelled porcelain. Mark and period of Ch'ien-lung. Ht. 12·9 cm. Ch'ing Dynasty.
Percival David Foundation, London

66a. Lang Shih-ning (1688–1766) (Guiseppe Castiglione): Horses in a landscape. Detail of a handscroll; ink and colour on silk. Ch'ing Dynasty.
Palace Museum Collection, Taiwan

66b. Li Yin (active about 1690–1710): Landscape, dated 1694. Detail of a hanging scroll; ink and colour on silk. Width 104·3 cm. Ch'ing Dynasty.
Freer Gallery of Art, Washington, D.C.

67a. Wang Yüan-ch'i (1642–1715): Landscape, dated 1706. Hanging scroll; ink and colour on paper. Ht. 106·4 cm. Ch'ing Dynasty.
C. A. Drenowatz, Zürich

67b. Kung Hsien (c. 1620–89): Landscape of Ch'i-hsia. Hanging scroll; ink on paper. Ht. 153 cm.
M. H. de Young Memorial Collection, San Francisco

ILLUSTRATIONS

68a. Chu Ta (Pa-ta Shan-jen, 1625–c. 1705): Two birds. Album leaf; ink on paper. Ht. 31·8 cm.
The late Sumitomo Kanichi Collection, Oiso

68b. Tao Chi (Shih-t'ao, 1641–c. 1717): Landscape. Album leaf; ink and slight colour on paper. Ht. 48 cm. Ch'ing Dynasty.
Museum of Fine Arts, Boston

69. K'un-ts'an (Shih-ch'i, c 1610–c. 1670): Autumn Landscape, dated 1666. Handscroll; ink and slight colour on paper. Ht. 31·5 cm. Ch'ing Dynasty.
British Museum, London

70a. Vase; stoneware, decorated with aubergine, yellow and blue enamels. Ht. 30·7 cm. Ming Dynasty.
British Museum, London

70b. Porcelain vase with *lang-yao* (ox-blood) glaze. Ht. 19·6 cm. Ch'ing Dynasty (K'ang-hsi period).
Percival David Foundation, London

71a. Porcelain vase, decorated in underglaze blue. Ht. 26·7 cm. Ch'ing Dynasty (K'ang-hsi period).
Victoria and Albert Museum, London

71b. Ch'i Pai-shih (1863–1957): Cabbages. Leaf from an album dated 1934; ink on paper.
Chytil Collection, Czechoslovakia

72. Li K'o-jan (born 1907): Gorges of the Yangtse. Hanging scroll, dated 1962; ink and colour on paper.
Dr Franco Vannotti, Lugano

Map of China showing Modern Political Division

.... Provincial Boundaries
○ Cities
● Pottery Centres
卍 Buddhist Monuments
ᴖᴖᴖ Great Wall
ᴉᴉᴉᴉ Grand Canal

100   200 Miles

f Pottery Centres, and Buddhist Monuments

Chronological Table

SHANG			B.C. *c.* 1550–*c.* 1030

CHOU	Western Chou	*c.* 1030– 771	
	Eastern Chou	770– 256	
	'Spring and Autumn' Period	722– 481	*c.* 1030– 256
	Warring States Period	480– 222	

CH'IN		221– 207

HAN	Former (Western) Han	B.C. 202–A.D.9	
	Hsin	9– 23	B.C. 202– 220 A.D.
	Later (Eastern) Han	25– 221	

THREE KINGDOMS	Shu (Han)	221– 263	
	Wei	220– 265	221– 265
	Wu	222– 280	

SOUTHERN (Six Dynasties)	Chin	265– 316	
	Eastern Chin	317– 420	
	Liu Sung	420– 479	
	Southern Ch'i	479– 502	
	Liang	502– 557	
and	Ch'en	557– 587	265– 581
	Northern Wei (T'o-pa)	386– 535	
	Eastern Wei (T'o-pa)	534– 543	
NORTHERN DYNASTIES	Western Wei (T'o-pa)	535– 554	
	Northern Ch'i	550– 577	
	Northern Chou (Hsien-pi)	557– 581	

SUI		581– 618
T'ANG		618– 906

FIVE DYNASTIES	Later Liang	907– 922	
	Later T'ang (Turkic)	923– 936	
	Later Chin (Turkic)	936– 948	907– 960
	Later Han (Turkic)	946– 950	
	Later Chou	951– 960	

Liao (Khitan Tartars)		907–1125
Hsi-hsia (Tangut Tibetan)		990–1227

SUNG	Northern Sung	960–1126	960–1279
	Southern Sung	1127–1279	
Chin (Jurchen Tartars)			1115–1234

YÜAN (Mongols)	1260–1368
MING	1368–1644
CH'ING (Manchus)	1644–1912
REPUBLIC	1912–

Reign Periods of Ming and Ch'ing

MING 1368–1644

Hung-wu	1368–1398
Chien-wen	1399–1402
Yung-lo	1403–1424
Hung-hsi	1425
Hsüan-te	1426–1435
Cheng-t'ung	1436–1449
Ching-t'ai	1450–1457
T'ien-shun	1457–1464
Ch'eng-hua	1465–1487
Hung-chih	1488–1505
Cheng-te	1506–1521
Chia-ching	1522–1566
Lung-ch'ing	1567–1572
Wan-li	1573–1620
T'ai-ch'ang	1620
T'ien-ch'i	1621–1627
Ch'ung-chen	1628–1644

CH'ING 1644–1912

Shun-chih	1644–1661
K'ang-hsi	1662–1722
Yung-cheng	1723–1735
Ch'ien-lung	1736–1795
Chia-ch'ing	1796–1821
Tao-kuang	1821–1850
Hsien-feng	1851–1861
T'ung-chih	1862–1873
Kuang-hsü	1874–1908
Hsüan-t'ung	1909–1912

NOTE

The earliest exactly known date in Chinese history is 841 B.C. According to calculations made by a number of scholars on the basis of probable reign lengths, the date of the founding of the Shang Dynasty has been put between 1766 and 1523 B.C., that of the Chou conquest between 1122 and 1018 B.C.

CHAPTER ONE

Before the Dawn of History

In far off times the Universe, according to a popular Chinese legend, was an enormous egg. One day the egg split open; its upper half became the sky, its lower half the earth, and from it emerged P'an Ku, primordial man. Every day he grew ten feet taller, the sky ten feet higher, the earth ten feet thicker. After eighteen thousand years P'an Ku died. His head split and became the sun and moon, while his blood filled the rivers and seas. His hair became the forests and meadows, his perspiration the rain, his breath the wind, his voice the thunder — and his fleas our ancestors.

A people's legends of its origins generally give a clue as to what they think most important. This one is no exception, for it expresses a typically Chinese viewpoint — namely that man is not the culminating achievement of the creation, but a relatively insignificant part in the scheme of things; hardly more than an afterthought, in fact. By comparison with the beauty and splendour of the world itself, the mountains and valleys, the clouds and waterfalls, the trees and flowers, which are the visible manifestations of the workings of the *Tao*, he counts for very little. In no other civilization — unless it be, in far smaller compass, in that of Britain — do the forms and patterns of nature, and man's humble devotion and response to it, play so big a part. We can, moreover, trace the germs of this attitude back into the remote past, when in North China nature was a kinder master than she is now. Half a million years ago, in the time of Peking Man, that region was comparatively warm and wet; elephants and rhinoceros roamed a more luxuriant countryside than today's barren hills and wind-

29

swept plains. Within this now inhospitable area, forming the modern provinces of Honan, Hopei, Shensi and Shansi, was born a uniquely Chinese feeling of oneness with nature which, in course of time, was to find its highest expression in philosophy, poetry and painting. This sense of communion was not merely philosophical and artistic; it had a practical value as well. For the farmer's prosperity, and hence that of society as a whole, depended upon his knowing the seasons and attuning himself to the 'will of Heaven', as he called it. Agriculture in course of time became a ritual over which the emperor himself presided, and when at the spring sowing he ceremonially ploughed the first furrow, not only did he hope to ensure a good harvest thereby, but his office was itself further ennobled by this act of homage to the forces of nature.

This sense of 'attunement' is fundamental in Chinese thinking. Man must attune himself not only to nature but also to his fellow men, in ever-widening circles starting from his family and friends. Thus his highest ideal has always in the past been to discover the order of things and to act in accordance with it. As in the following pages the history of Chinese art unfolds, we will find that its characteristic and unique beauty lies in the fact that it is an expression of this very sense of attunement. Is that one reason why Westerners, often with no other interest in Chinese civilization, collect and admire Chinese art with such enthusiasm? Do they sense, perhaps, that the forms which the Chinese artist and craftsman have created are *natural* forms — forms which seem to have evolved inevitably by the movement of the maker's hand, in response to an intuitive awareness of a natural rhythm? Chinese art does not demand of us, as does Indian art, the effort to bridge what often seems an unbridgeable gulf between extremes of physical form and metaphysical content; nor will we find in it that pre-occupation with formal and intellectual considerations which so often makes western art difficult for the Asian mind to accept. The forms of Chinese art are beautiful because they are in the widest and deepest sense harmonious, and we can appreciate them because we too feel their rhythms all around us in nature, and instinctively respond to them. These rhythms, moreover, this sense of inner life expressed in line and contour, are present in Chinese art from its earliest beginnings.

Every lover of Chinese art today is familiar with the magnificent painted pottery of the Neolithic period, and we are apt to forget that fifty years ago this stage in the evolution of Chinese civilization, and all that went before it, was completely unknown. It was not until 1921 that positive evidence was found that China had actually passed through a Stone Age at all. In that year the Swedish geologist J. Gunnar Andersson and his Chinese assistants made two discoveries of immense importance. The first was at Chouk'ou-tien, northwest of Peking, where in a cleft in the hillside Andersson picked up a number of flint tools, indicating that it had been occupied by very early man. He himself did not excavate, but his find led to further excavations and to the eventual discovery by Dr P'ei Wen-chung of fossil bones which, with the exception of late Java Man, *Pithecanthropus erectus*, were the oldest human remains yet discovered. The bones were those of a hominid, *Sinanthropus pekinensis*, who lived in the middle Pleistocene period, about half a million years ago. The remains in the deep cleft, fifty metres thick, represent many thousands of years of occupation. Peking Man had tools of quartz, flint and limestone, made either from pebbles chipped to shape or from flakes struck off a large pebble. He was a cannibal who broke open the bones of his victims to suck out the marrow; he had fire, ate grain, and probably knew some very primitive form of speech. In 1964, in deposits on an open hillside in Lan-t'ien County, Shensi, palaeontologists discovered the skull of a hominid believed, from related fossil remains, to be at least 100,000 years older than Peking Man, and so roughly the same age as early Java Man, *Pithecanthropus robustus*.

In 1935 and 1939 Dr G. H. R. von Koenigswald, examining some 'dragon bones' in a chemist's shop in Kwangsi, found three teeth of a giant apelike creature which he named *Gigantopithecus*. In a cave at Holung, also in Kwangsi, were discovered remains of late Palaeolithic man (200,000 years ago) and of *Homo sapiens* of the Mesolithic period (10,000–7000 B.C.). Thus in Kwangsi alone it is now possible to study every stage of human development from the oldest hominid up to modern man. Some idea of the speed with which discoveries are now being made can be gained from the fact that within the last nine years more teeth and bones of Peking Man have been discovered at Chou-k'ou-tien; at Ting-ts'un in Shansi teeth and tools of a later stage of early man have been found (200,000 years old); while the remains of a girl of Neanderthal type of 80,000 years ago have been unearthed at Tze-yang in Szechwan.

The deposits in another cave at Chou-k'ou-tien reveal a much more advanced culture than that enjoyed by Peking Man. 'Upper Cave Man' (*c.* 25,000 B.C.) had a wider range of tools; he wore coarsely-woven clothing, and his wife adorned herself with stone beads, drilled and painted red with hematite. Similar sites have been found in Shensi, Ninghsia and Suiyuan, the latter including many beautifully-shaped microliths — stone knives and arrowheads only a few centimetres long. By 10,000 B.C., sites in Manchuria such as Djalai-nor show a further advance; a fragment of a basket (possibly a fish-trap), wooden tools, microliths and, for the first time, artefacts decorated with geometric designs.

The men who inhabited the earliest Neolithic sites in Manchuria and Mongolia, such as Ang-ang-hsi, differed chiefly from their Mesolithic forebears of Djalai-nor in knowing the art of making pottery. It is crude stuff: a coarse greyish-brown ware, sometimes adorned with rough comb-marked geometrical designs. In the next stage, represented by Lin-hsi in north Jehol, we find a finer, light brown pottery crudely painted with red and grey stains and decorated with textile impressions. These were a sedentary agricultural people, with a wider range of stone tools. At Hungshan-hou, also in Jehol, Japanese archaeologists unearthed in addition to the grey pottery, a fine red ware with designs painted in black, and well-polished stone axes.

The first definite evidence of the existence of a Neolithic culture in China was found in 1921 by Andersson and his assistants, who located at Yang-shao-ts'un in Honan an extensive deposit of Neolithic tools and beautiful red pottery painted with designs in black. Before long more sites had been discovered in Honan. In 1923 Andersson went to Kansu to attempt to trace the connecting links which he suspected existed between this painted pottery and that of the Near East, and there found more than fifty pre-historic sites representing a gradual development from about the third millennium B.C. to the Late Chou. Some of the features of this Neo-lithic culture are common to all early civilizations and belong to a culture-complex that extends from the Nile Valley to Mesopotamia, from the Indus Valley to the Tarim Basin, linked to China by the 'Corridor of the Steppes', a natural mig-ration route. In all these areas there developed at about the same time the use of polished stone tools and of the bow and arrow, the domes-tication of animals, the cultivation of cereals and the making of pottery. At first it was thought that in China

Neolithic painted pottery from Anau (*left*) and China (*right*) compared. (After Andersson.)

this culture was concentrated in two areas only — Honan and Kansu, where Andersson made his finds; but more recent excavations by Chinese archaeologists — particularly those that have followed in the wake of the huge reconstruction schemes that have been in progress since 1950 — reveal that it was widely diffused through-out China.

For many years we had to visualize Chinese Neolithic culture in terms of the rather poor sites found by Andersson — notably the single grave at Pan-shan in Kansu, and the extensive but imprecise deposits at Yang-shao in Honan. This picture was dramatically revised in 1953 by the discovery of a complete Neolithic village at Pan-p'o, east of Sian on the right bank of the Chan River. The village covers two and a half acres; four separate layers of houses have been found in a cultural deposit three metres thick, representing several centuries of occupation between about 2500 and 2000 B.C. The earliest inhabitants lived in round wattle-and-daub huts with reed roof and plaster floor and an oven in the centre, the design perhaps copied from an earlier tent or yurt. Their descendants built rectangular or square houses with a framework of wooden planking, sunk a metre below ground level and approached by a flight of steps. The roof of one particularly large building over twelve metres long was supported on three rows of posts. In the village were found no less than six pottery kilns, of two types: a simple pocket-shaped pit with a perforated floor, and a cylindrical tunnel with forced draft, leading to a beehive-shaped chamber. In these kilns the Pan-p'o potters made both a coarse grey or red pottery and a fine red ware burnished and then painted in black with geometric designs and occasionally with fishes and human faces. They seem not to have known the potter's wheel, but made their vessels by coiling long strips of clay. From clay they also made spindle-whorls and even hairpins, but the finer objects such as needles, fish hooks, spoons and arrow-heads were made of bone. Part of the village of Pan-p'o has been roofed over and preserved as a museum of Chinese Neolithic culture.

The painted pottery first discovered at Pan-shan in Kansu has not been matched in quality and beauty by any Neolithic wares discovered since. It consists chiefly of mortuary urns, wide and deep bowls and tall vases, often with loop-handles set low on the body (Plate 1a). Though the walls are thin, the forms are robust, their generous contours beautifully enhanced by the decoration in black pigment which was clearly executed with a crude form of brush. Some of the designs are geometric, consisting of parallel bands or lozenges containing concentric squares, crosses or diamonds. The lower half of the body is always left undecorated, perhaps because it may have been set in the sandy ground to prevent it overturning. Many vessels are adorned with magnificent sweeping wave-like bands which gather into a kind of whirlpool; others make use of the stylized figures of men, frogs, fishes and birds, while a human face with some sort of ceremonial headdress found at Pan-p'o perhaps represented a shaman. Shards found at Ma-chia-yao in Kansu reveal a quite sophisticated brush technique, in one case depicting plants each of whose leaves ends in a sharp point with a flick of the brush — the same technique that was to be used by the Sung artist, three thousand years later, in painting bamboo. The naturalistic motifs however are rare, and the vast majority are decorated with geometric or stylized patterns whose significance is still a mystery. In point of technique, shape and even to some extent in the motifs themselves, the Yang-shao pottery seems to be influenced by that of Western Asia, for the very similar painted red ware found at Anau in Russian Turkestan is at least one to two thousand years older (page 33). But the Kansu vases reveal in their lively, uplifted forms, and still more in the dynamic linear movement of their brush decoration, a quality that is uniquely Chinese.

In 1928 Dr Wu Chin-ting of the Academia Sinica discovered at Ch'eng-tzu-yai, near Lung-shan in western Shantung, a quite different type of prehistoric pottery. It was made on the wheel of black clay fired in a reducing atmosphere, sometimes built up in thin sheets laminated together. Many of the shapes are elegant and somewhat metallic; while the decoration, consisting chiefly of raised bands, grooves and milled rings, gives it a rather machine-made look. Several of the Lung-shan shapes, notably the wide dish, beaker and dish on a tall stem (Plate 1b) resemble vessels in use from one to two thousand years earlier in Western Asian sites such as Tepe Hissar, Anau and Susa; while in East Asia it has been found in a huge arc stretching from Northeast China down to Thailand and northern Malaya. At some sites, such as Miao-ti-kou, it lies over a painted pottery stratum going back to about 3000 B.C. while in its later phases, as at Hu-shu near Nanking, it continued down to about 500 B.C., and hence well into the late Bronze Age.

Among the black pottery types one vessel, the *li* tripod, was destined to have a special significance in early Chinese culture. This vessel, which is found also in the grey wares, appears to be

derived from the joining together of three tall ovoid jars with pointed bottoms. Perhaps three such vessels had stood together over a fire, and some practical housewife had the idea of combining them into one, the hollow legs (whose mammiform shape cannot have been accidental) both supporting the body and presenting a greater surface to the fire. This shape, which in Kansu only appears in the latest Neolithic sites such as Hsin-tien, seems to be uniquely Chinese. It was trans-mitted into the bronze culture of the Shang

Hsien steamer from Chengchow. (After *Kaogu Xuebao*, 1957.)

Dynasty, where it gave the form to the most important and characteristic of the early ritual vessels. When supporting a pot with a perforated base, it becomes the *hsien* steamer, the pictograph for which meant 'to sacrifice'.

Some of the precision and symmetry of the black Lung-shan ware appears also in the thin wheel-made, grey pottery found by Andersson, and later by Hsia Nai, at Ch'i-chia-p'ing in Kansu. The elegance of its vases and pitchers with their long thin handles also suggests an origin in metal forms, and it is perhaps this rather than archaeological findings which has led scholars to date the Ch'i-chia wares between 1500 and 500 B.C.[1] Indeed it seems that

---

[1] A distant descendant of the Ch'i-chia-p'ing pottery has been found in the bronze age slate tombs of the Lifan district of Szechwan, which have been dated approximately between 500 and 1 B.C. Most remarkable among the Lifan wares are the burnished dark grey amphorae with bold volutes curling over the body, which are unique in the history of Chinese ceramics, and of which there is a fine specimen in the British Museum. It is illustrated (though wrongly dated) in Leigh Ashton and Basil Gray, *Chinese Art* (London, 1951), Plate 1b.

Neolithic culture persisted in outlying regions long after the beginning of the Bronze Age in North China. Painted pottery of Yangshao type, for example, has been found in South China, Formosa and Szechwan, while in Ning-yang District, Shantung, has been found a Lung-shan type ware decorated with triangles, circles and scrolls in black and white which seem to show links with the Yang-shao tradition. Other and more important sites in North China, notably Chengchow and Anyang, were in continuous occupation from late Neolithic times well into the Bronze Age. These will be dealt with in the next chapter.[1]

Some of the stone weapons and artifacts used in prehistoric China are common to all the Neolithic peoples of Asia, others are of purely Chinese origin. Among the latter we find a wide-bladed hoe and the *ko* type dagger-axe (which was later to be translated into bronze and iron), and a broad rectangular chopping knife bound to the handle by thongs passed through two holes bored in the upper part. Some of these tools are beautifully polished, the finest being made in jade which, because of its hardness, fine texture and purity of colour has been an object of special veneration from ancient times until today. In the Kansu hills, Andersson found beautifully worked jade axes, knives, ornaments and rings. The latter included the circle (*huan*) and flat disc (*pi*), while elsewhere was found a ring, square outside and circular inside, possibly the ancestor of the *ts'ung* (page 71). By the Chou Dynasty the *pi* and the *ts'ung* had acquired an almost sacred place in court ritual as symbols of Heaven and of Earth. Whether or not these, or indeed any, symbolic meanings were already attached to

---

[1] Excavation in China since 1950 has proceeded at such a pace that the archaeological picture is constantly becoming out of date. New sites are continually being discovered and, until the Cultural Revolution began in 1966, were published within a commendably short time in such journals as *Wen-wu*, *K'ao-ku Hsüeh-pao* and *Kaogu* (*K'ao-ku*), while brief English summaries of recent developments appeared from time to time in *China Reconstructs*. A useful summary of findings up to 1960 is given by William Watson in his *China Before the Han Dynasty*, (London, 1961). Cheng Te-k'un's 'Archaeology in Communist China' (*The China Quarterly*, July–Sept. 1965, 67–77) describes how the archaeological service is organized.

them in the Late Neolithic period it is impossible to say.

Into this short chapter we have compressed half a million years of human history in China. Although the picture is enormously oversimplified (particularly in regard to the Neolithic) it shows that before the dawn of recorded history there had already emerged many of those characteristics which we consider essentially Chinese: a highly organized social life centred on agriculture and bound together by ritual, high standards of craftsmanship, the flexible brush as an instrument of artistic expression, the ceremonial use of jade, and pre-occupation with man's fate after death. This primitive culture lingered on in South and West China long after the coming of bronze had opened a new and incomparably richer chapter in Chinese history.

CHAPTER TWO

The Shang Dynasty

For centuries, farmers living in the village of Hsiao-t'un near Anyang in Honan have been picking up peculiar bones which they found lying in the fields after rain or while they were ploughing. Some were polished and shone like glass; most had rows of oval notches in their backs and T-shaped cracks; a few had marks on them that looked like primitive writing. The farmers would take these bones to apothecaries in Anyang and neighbouring towns, who often ground off the marks before selling them as 'dragon bones', a potent ingredient in restoratives. In 1899 some of the inscribed bones fell into the hands of the noted scholar and collector Tuan Fang, who recognized the writing as a still older form of the archaic script of the Chou ritual bronzes. Soon other scholars, notably Lo Chen-yü and Wang Kuo-wei, took up the study of what were, in fact, fragments of the archives of the royal house of Shang, the actual existence of which had hitherto not been proved, though Chinese historians had never doubted it.

The bones were traced to Anyang. The farmers began to dig deeper, and before long there began to appear on the antique market in Peking and Shanghai magnificent bronze vessels, jades and other objects, whose exact place of origin was kept secret. For nearly thirty years the farmers and dealers' agents, working at night or during the idle winter months, continued their indiscriminate pillaging of Shang tombs. Finally, in 1928, the Chinese National Research Institute (Academia Sinica) began at Anyang an important series of excavations which were to provide the first definite archaeological evidence that the Shang Dynasty had

ANCIENT CHINA
To the end of the Han Dynasty

× } • Prehistoric Sites (chiefly Neolithic)
× } × Bronze Age Sites (Shang & Chou)
□ } □ Han Sites
• Modern Cities
ᴖᴖᴖ Great Wall
W.EI Feudal States at end of Chou
⠿ Land over 1500 ft.

Ang-ang-hsi

ORDOS
DESERT

Lin-hsi
Hung-shan-hou
Sha-kuo-t'un

Chu-chia-chai

Li-yü
Peking
Chou-kou-tien
Pi-tzu-wo
Lolang

CHAO

YEN

Ma-ch'ang
Lanchow
Hsin-tien
Pan-shan
Ch'i-chia-p'ing

Ting-ts'un
Anyang
Tsinan
Ch'eng-tzu-yai
(Lung-shan)
CH'I
Shih-chia-chuang
LU
Liang-ch'eng-shan

WEI
Hui-hsien
Chin-ts'un
Hsün-hsien
SUNG

CH'IN
Yang-shao-ts'un
Loyang
Kaifeng
Chengchow

HAN
Pan-p'o
Sian
(Chang-an)
Lan-t'ien
Hsin-cheng
Huai River
Shou-chow

Lifan
SHU
Han-chow
PA
CH'U
Nanking
Liang-chu

Chengtu
Tzeyang
Chiating
Yangtse River

Shih-chai-shan
Changsha
Ch'ing-chiang
Kuang-tse
Shao-wu

Ch'ang-t'ing
Foochow

Wu-p'ing
Amoy

Laipin (Holung)
Canton
Hoifung

Hong Kong
Lamma Is.

Dong-son

0   100   200   300   400 Miles

actually existed and was not, as some western writers had come to suspect, a pious fabrication of the backward-looking Chinese. By 1935 more than three hundred graves had been discovered, ten of which, of enormous size, were undoubtedly royal tombs.

These discoveries posed more problems than they solved. Who were the Shang people, and where did they come from? How was it that their earliest remains revealed a culture of such sophistication, particularly in their bronze techniques? If the Shang existed, then perhaps remains would be found of the even earlier Hsia Dynasty.

The Chinese traditionally believe that they are descended from Huang Ti, the Yellow Emperor, who lived for a hundred years. After him came Fu Hsi, who first drew the magical diagram *pa kua* (the 'eight trigrams') from which the art of writing is descended. Shen Nung, the Divine Farmer, invented agriculture and discovered the use of medicinal herbs. Then came Yao and the filial Shun, the ideal rulers, and finally Yü the Great, who founded the Hsia Dynasty. In these legendary figures the Chinese personified all that they held most sacred: agriculture, good government, filial piety, and the art of writing. Now it is believed that all these personages were invented or took on these rôles at a much later date. Yü, Yao and Shun appeared first in late Chou literature. Huang Ti was probably invented by the Taoists. As for the Hsia, although the character appears on the Shang oracle bones, it is never used there to refer to a Dynasty, which may simply have been invented by the Chou people to legitimatize their conquest of the Shang, whom they chose to consider as usurpers. Before the rise of Shang there were, as we saw in the first chapter, many primitive communities, and one of those conquered by the first Shang ruler may have been called Hsia. Such communities form a connecting link between the Late Neolithic and the full flowering of the Bronze Age.

As early Chinese culture coalesced it came to incorporate elements characteristic of several distinct regions. The people of North China practised shamanism and elaborate burial rites; some authorities believe that they were originally matriarchal; they had timber houses partly sunk in the ground, and ate dry grains such as wheat and barley. By the second millennium B.C. they were being influenced by the northwestern 'proto-turkic' peoples, who bridged the huge empty spaces between them and the cultures of Central and Western Asia, and who brought to China itself a patriarchal nomadism, horses and horse-sacrifice, the worship of the heavenly bodies, tumulus graves and the use of earthen drums. At a somewhat later stage, and especially in the Chou period, North China felt the impact of the Yüeh group of peoples from the southeast and south, whose ethnic links were as much with Southeast Asia and Oceania as with China proper. They lived by the sea and on the rivers, had longboats and fought naval battles, worshipped the forces of the rain and rivers in serpents and crocodiles ('dragons'), used bronze drums, tattooed themselves, perhaps lived in long houses, cultivated wet rice, and decorated their pottery with stamped designs.

Until 1950 our knowledge of Shang culture was derived almost wholly from the ruins of the Shang capital at Anyang, founded by King P'an-keng about 1300 B.C., and finally conquered by the armies of the Chou at a date which most authorities on this highly controversial question put between 1122 and 1027 B.C. At Anyang the bronze culture was at its height; the metal-workers were producing sacrificial vessels of a quality that has been equalled nowhere in the world — the culmination, clearly, of centuries of development. The oracle bones gave the names of eighteen kings before P'an-keng and, according to tradition, the Shang had moved their capital five times before finally settling at Anyang. If traces of these earlier capitals could be found, the gap between the Late Neolithic and the mature bronze culture of Anyang might be closed.

When the new régime came to power in 1949, there was some fear that the authorities would have no time or funds for archaeological excavation, and that the pioneer work of the Academia Sinica would be forgotten. Happily the position has, on the contrary, greatly improved. Popular education and the fostering of pride in China's cultural heritage have combined to arouse the interest of the poorest peasant, while the work of the Institute of Archaeology of the Chinese Academy of Sciences and of various regional organizations is rapidly altering the whole archaeological picture. One result of this activity has been that, since 1952, well over a hundred Shang sites have been discovered, in an area embracing the whole of central and eastern China, from Shensi in the northwest to Kiangsi and Kiangsu in the southeast. Just how closely these areas were related to the centre of Shang power in Shansi and Honan is not yet clear, but the view that bronze culture began in Honan and spread outwards has now been abandoned in favour of a picture of primitive metal-working cultures evolving in a number of centres more or less simultaneously.

Some of these sites are contemporary with Anyang, and therefore late. The most remarkable discoveries have been made at Liu-li-ko near Huihsien, where fifty-three Shang tombs have been unearthed, and at Chengchow, which it was suggested might have been the site of the ancient city of Ao, founded by Cheng-ting, the tenth ruler of Shang. Thus, under and beyond the confines of modern Chengchow lie the probable remains of one of those earlier capitals for which Chinese archaeologists have been searching for the past thirty years. The city was more than a mile square, surrounded by a wall more than sixty feet thick at the base. Houses, tombs and drains have been unearthed, as well as bronze-foundries, pottery kilns and bone-carving workshops. Four distinct levels have been identified. The lowest represents a Late Neolithic culture in occupation before the city became a Shang capital, with grey and black pottery, stone and bone implements, and no oracle bones. Above it lie three stages in the development of bronze culture. The first and second appear to be earlier than the earliest Bronze Age remains at Anyang, while the third phase has been tentatively placed as contemporary with the second Anyang stage. Taken together, therefore, the successive strata at

Chengchow and Anyang present a continuous archaeological sequence from Neolithic times to the end of the Shang Dynasty.

The inscriptions on the oracle bones tell much about the beliefs, social organization and activities of the Shang — or Yin, as the Chou people called them. Shang society was probably feudal, though this cannot be said as positively of the Shang as it is of the Chou. Successful generals, sons and even wives of the Shang rulers were enfeoffed, while small neighbouring 'states' paid regular tribute. Prominent among the officials was the *chen-jen* who, as a scribe, composed and probably wrote the inscriptions on the oracle bones, and, as a diviner, interpreted the cracks which appeared in them when a hot metal rod was applied to one of the holes bored into the back. These inscriptions were generally engraved, though a few were written with a brush and some sort of ink. About three thousand characters have been identified, rather less than half of which have been deciphered; they were written in vertical columns, moving either to the left or to the right, apparently according to the dictates of symmetry. In the early stages at Chengchow the oracle bones were mainly scapulae of pig, ox or sheep; in the final phase at Anyang tortoise-shells were used almost exclusively, fastened together with thongs passed through holes at each end, as is shown in the pictograph for a book, *ts'e*.

The inscriptions on the bones are either declarations of fact or of the ruler's intentions, or questions about the future which could be answered with a simple yes or no. They relate chiefly to agriculture, war and hunting, the weather, journeys and the all-important sacrifices by means of which the ruler attuned himself to the will of Heaven. They reveal that the Shang people had some knowledge of astronomy, knew precisely the length of the year, had invented the intercalary month, and divided the day into periods. Their religious belief centred in a supreme deity (*Ti*) who controlled the rain, wind, and human affairs, and in lesser deities of the heavenly bodies, of the soil, of rivers, mountains and special places (the *genius loci*); special respect was paid to the ancestral spirits, who lived with *Ti* and could affect the destinies of men for good or ill, but whose benevolent concern in the affairs of their descendants could be ensured by elaborate sacrificial rites.

Many years' work at Anyang have given us a fairly clear picture of the later phases of Shang architecture. The Shang people built chiefly in wood and tamped earth. Remains have been found of several large buildings; one of them, over ninety feet long, was raised on a high plinth, its presumably thatched roof supported on rows of wooden pillars, of which the stone socles remain. Another was laid out axially with steps in the centre of the south side, and but for its roof would not have looked so very different from any large building in North China today. Some of the more important buildings were adorned with formalized animal heads carved in stone, and their beams were painted with designs similar to those on the ritual bronzes. The most popular method of construction — presumably because it was cheap and provided good protection against the piercing cold of the North China winter — was the *pan-chu* 'plank building' technique, in which the earth was stamped between vertical boards with a pole: the smaller the diameter of the pole, the stronger the wall. Chou texts relate that the common people lived in 'burrows and nests'. The 'nests' may refer to little huts raised, as in Southeast Asia, several feet above the ground. The 'burrows' were either caves in the loess terraces, still inhabited today by millions of North China peasants, or dwellings sunk below the surface of the ground, a custom inherited from Neolithic times. Many of these dwelling pits have been found at Anyang. They had plaster floors and walls, while as in Neolithic times rows of timber posts supported a thatched roof, probably with a hole in the centre through which the smoke from the central hearth escaped. Often a deep storage pit was sunk in the floor of the house. We can imagine ancient Anyang as a cluster of these lowly dwellings, with here and there a large timber building raised on a platform, the whole city surrounded by a mud wall with gates at intervals surmounted by watch towers.

The most spectacular of Shang remains, however, are not the buildings but the tombs. The Chinese belief that the spirit of the departed must be provided with all he possessed (or, indeed, would have liked to possess) in his earthly life led to immolation and human sacrifice on a gigantic scale. Later the more frightful practices were abandoned, but until the Ming Dynasty the custom persisted of placing in the tomb pottery models not only of furniture, farms and houses, but also of servants, guards and domestic animals. At the same time the corpse was decked out with the richest clothing, jewellery and jades that his family or the state could afford. Collectors are even known to have been buried with their favourite paintings. However much one may deplore this custom, it has ensured the preservation of many beautiful things that would otherwise have been irretrievably lost.

The Shang tombs throw a brilliant, even lurid, light upon early Chinese civilization. Some of them were of enormous size, and rich with superb bronze vessels, jade objects and pottery. One royal personage, apparently an animal lover, had his pets, including an elephant, buried near him in separate graves. The tomb recently excavated at Wu-kuan-ts'un (Plate 2a) had only two sloping ramps, north and south, but contained the remains of an elaborate canopy of painted leather, wood-bark and bamboo; here both the ramps and main chamber were crammed with the complete skeletons of no less than twenty-two men (one beneath the tomb chamber) and twenty-four women, and in addition the skulls of a further fifty men were buried in adjacent pits. In some cases the bodies lie quietly with no signs of violence — the result, perhaps, of voluntary self-immolation by relations or retainers of the dead man — while the decapitated victims may have been criminals or prisoners of war. Other excavations at Hsiao-t'un and Ta-ssu-kung-ts'un have revealed chariot burials in which the complete chariot with horses and driver were buried in specially prepared pits with channels dug out for the wheels. The wood has of course perished, but impressions in the earth have made it possible to reconstruct the chariot itself, and thus to determine the position and function of many of its beautiful bronze fittings. It is disconcerting for us when we admire the marvellous refinement and craftsmanship of the ritual bronzes to be reminded of the ferocious rites with which they are associated. Mass immolation was not practised officially by the Chou, though it appears to have been revived from time to time, on a more modest scale, by later rulers.

One of the biggest surprises at Anyang was the discovery of Shang marble sculpture in the round, a notable example of which is the head of an ox illustrated in Plate 2b. Previously nothing of the sort earlier than the Han Dynasty was known, and even today only a handful of Chou stone carvings have been unearthed and those so small as hardly to deserve the name of sculpture. Other figures include tigers, buffaloes, birds, tortoises, a kneeling captive (or sacrificial victim) with his hands tied behind his back, two sitting figures, one headless and clasping his knees, the other complete, leaning back on his arms, his head thrown back. A few of the larger pieces have slots in the back suggesting that they might have had some function in the structure and decoration of a building, perhaps in a sacrificial hall — for there is a close similarity in theme and style between many of these figures and those depicted on the ritual bronzes. They are carved four-square out of the block, rigidly frontal, and have something of the formality and compactness of Egyptian art. Their impressiveness derives from their solid, monumental feeling of weight, and from the engraved geometric and zoomorphic designs which play over their surface, rather than from the tension over the surface itself which enlivens Egyptian sculpture.

While we still had only the evidence of Anyang before us, it seemed that the Bronze Age appeared with startling suddenness in Chinese history, and that there was little visible connection between it and Late Neolithic culture. That gap, however, is being bridged by recent discoveries. Certain types of Neolithic pottery of the grey family can now be traced into the Shang Dynasty, where we see them existing side by side with the same shapes in bronze, and we can observe how an originally coarse and inelegant form becomes in the hands of the metal-worker an object of beauty. We have already encountered the *li* tripod in Neolithic pottery, while finds at Chengchow reveal the ceramic origin of several other vessels previously thought to be peculiar to bronze — notably the *kuei*, a bowl on a high foot-rim, but lacking the prominent handles found on the bronze *kuei*. Some of the grey vessels are cord-marked; some are decorated with horizontal bands and fillets, or with incised lozenges and chevrons (a clear adaptation of designs found on the painted pottery), while on others the decoration consists of repeated stamped or incised motifs ranging from squares and coils, the ancestor of the 'thunder pattern' (*lei-wen*), to simple versions of the zoomorphic masks which appear on the bronzes. Pottery decorated by stamping or carving geometric designs in the wet clay has been found in a number of Neolithic sites in the southeast, notably in Fukien (Kuang-tse) and Kwangsi (Ch'ing-chiang). In South China, this technique persisted into the Han Dynasty and was carried thence to Southeast Asia — if, indeed, it had not originated there. It is very seldom found in the Neolithic pottery of North China (Hou-chia-chuang is an exception), and its appearance on vessels at Chengchow and Anyang suggests that by the Shang Dynasty the culture of the southern peoples was already beginning to make its influence felt. At Anyang there has been found a beautiful white ware which is unique in the history of Chinese ceramics. So fine is it that it has been taken for porcelain, but it is in fact a very brittle stoneware made from almost pure kaolin, finished on the wheel, and fired at about 1000° centigrade. Many writers have remarked how closely its decoration echoes that of the bronzes, but, as Basil Gray has pointed out, there is no proof that this style in fact originated in bronze. As we have seen in the preceding paragraph, southeast China had already evolved a technique for stamping designs in the wet clay, which in turn influenced bronze design; the magnificent white stoneware urn in the Freer Gallery illustrated in Plate 3a is indeed very close in design and decoration to a bronze vessel in the

Hellström collection. The Chengchow finds suggest that the motifs decorating both the white ware and the bronzes originated, at least in part, in the earlier stamped grey pottery. The techniques and designs used in wood-carving suggest another possible source. Some of the grey and buff ware found in Shang sites in Honan is glazed. While in some cases the glaze was produced accidentally when wood-ash fell on the heated pottery in the kiln, in others it is a true felspathic glaze, generally reddish-brown or greenish-yellow, applied very thinly and evenly to both inner and outer surfaces of the vessel.

According to tradition, when the great Emperor Yü of the Hsia divided the empire, he ordered nine *li* tripods to be cast in metal brought as tribute from each of the nine provinces, and decorated with representations of the remarkable things characteristic of each region. These tripods were credited with magical powers; they could ward off noxious influences, for example, and cook food without fire. From dynasty to dynasty they were handed down as the palladia of empire, but at the end of the Chou they were lost. The unsuccessful efforts of the first Ch'in emperor, Shih-huang-ti, to recover one of them from the bed of a river are mocked in several delightfully humorous Han reliefs, though one of the Han emperors tried to accomplish the same thing by means of sacrifices and was just as unsuccessful. But so strong was the tradition of the nine tripods that as late as the T'ang Dynasty the Empress Wu caused a set to be cast in order to bolster up her own dubious claim to the throne.

Long before any archaeological evidence of the Shang Dynasty had been unearthed, the ritual bronzes bore witness to the power and vitality of this remote epoch in Chinese history. Bronze vessels have been treasured by Chinese connoisseurs for centuries: that great collector and savant, the Sung Emperor Hui-tsung, is even said to have sent agents to the Anyang region to search out specimens for his collection. These vessels which, as Hansford has aptly observed, formed a kind of 'communion plate', were made for the offerings of food and wine to ancestral spirits which formed

THE SHANG DYNASTY

the core of the sacrificial rites performed by the ruler and the aristocracy. Some of them bear very short inscriptions, generally consisting of two or three characters forming a clan name. Often this inscription is enclosed within a square device known as the *ya-hsing*, from its resemblance to the character *ya*. A number of theories as to its meaning have been advanced. The recent discovery at Anyang of bronze seals leaving an impression of precisely this shape suggests that it was in some way connected with the clan name.

Chemical analysis shows that the bronze vessels were composed of five to thirty per cent tin, two to three per cent lead, the rest (apart from impurities) being copper. In course of time many of

Ritual bronzes excavated at Chengchow:
1. *li*; 2. *tsun*; 3. *chia*; 4. *hu*; 5. *chüeh*; 6. *ku*.

them have acquired a beautiful patina, much valued by connoisseurs, which ranges from malachite green and kingfisher blue to yellow or even red, according to the composition of the metal and the conditions under which the vessel was buried. Forgers have gone to enormous trouble to imitate these effects, and Yetts records the case of one family of which each generation buried fakes in specially treated soil, to be dug up and sold by the next generation but one. It was long thought that the Shang and Chou bronzes were made by the cire-perdue method; for how, it was argued, could such exquisite detail have been modelled except in wax? However, while the technique was probably used in the later periods, large numbers of outer and inner clay moulds and crucibles have been found at Anyang and Chengchow, and it is probable that most of the vessels were cast in such sectional moulds assembled round a solid central core, and that legs and handles were cast separately and soldered on. Many vessels still show ridges or rough places where two mould sections were imperfectly joined.

There are at least thirty main types of ritual vessels, which range in size from a few inches in height to a gigantic *ting* unearthed at Anyang in 1939 which was cast by a Shang king in memory of his mother; it is over four feet high and weighs 1950 lb. They can most simply be grouped according to their use in the sacrifices. For cooking food (of which the essence only was extracted by the spirits, the participants later consuming the residual matter), the chief vessels were the *li* tripod and the *yen* (or *hsien*) steamer consisting of a *li* with a vessel having a perforated base resting on it. Both of these types, as we have seen, were common in Neolithic pottery and may then already have had a more-than-utilitarian function in some primitive rite. The *ting*, which has three or four straight legs, is a variant of the *li*, and like it generally has fairly large handles or 'ears' to enable it to be lifted off the fire. Vessels made for serving food included the two-handled *kuei*, the *yü* (basin) and *p'an* (wide flat dish). Among those for fluids (chiefly wine) were the *hu* (a vase or jar with a cover), the *yu* (similar but with a swing or chain handle and sometimes fitted with a spout), the *chih* (a cup with a bulbous body and spreading lip), the *ho* (kettle), the tall and elegant trumpet-mouthed *ku* for pouring libations, and its fatter variant, the *tsun* — both derived from pottery prototypes, the *chia* and the *chio* for pouring and probably also for heating wine, and the *kuang*, for mixing wine (Plate 3b), shaped like a gravy boat, generally with a cover and provided with a ladle. Other vessels such as the *i* and *lien* were presumably made for ritual ablutions.

During the fifteen hundred years that bronze-casting was a major art form in China, the style of decoration went through a series of changes which make it possible to date vessels within a century or less. In 1953 Professor Max Loehr proposed five phases for the Shang which have since been largely confirmed by excavation: Shang I, vessels with thin relief decoration, simple forms, and a light, airy effect. Shang II, decoration in ribbon relief and forms that tend to be harsh and heavy. Shang III, dense fluent curvilinear designs. (In fact, II and III are not always distinguishable, and may have been contemporaneous). In Shang IV, main motifs and spiral background first become separated, though in the same plane. In Shang V motifs rise in bold relief and background spirals may disappear altogether. Phases I, II and III have been found at Chengchow (see p. 50); Phases IV and V evolved after the move to Anyang. Our Plate 3b is an example of the transition from IV to V, Plate 4 of fully developed Phase V.

The Chou took over the arts and styles of late Shang, but introduced new motifs of their own, notably jutting flanges and a rich repertory of stylized birds. In the 'Middle Chou' style, animals and masks break down into meander and scale patterns, and contours become heavy and sagging (Plate 8). Then, after a period of extreme intricacy and restless ornament in the VII and VI centuries (Plate 7a), the bronze art moves into the final elegant Late Chou or Warring States phase (Plate 9a).[1]

The bronze vessels found in the early levels at Chengchow have not yet been adequately published, but from the photographs available they appear to be much what one would expect — simpler, cruder versions of the magnificent bronzes of the Anyang period. The *chüeh* libation cup, for example, which at Anyang is tall and elegant, with rounded bottom, gracefully curving spout, a

[1] For a detailed analysis see Max Loehr, *Ritual Vessels of Bronze Age China* (New York, 1968).

Ritual bronzes of Late Shang and Early Chou: 1. *li*; 2. *tsun*; 3. *hsien*; 4. *ting*; 5. *chia*; 6. *chüeh*; 7. *tsun*; 8. *fang-i*; 9. *ku*; 10. *yu*; 11. *kuang*; 12. *kuei*. (After Mizuno.)

handle at one side and prominent 'horns', at Chengchow is squat and clumsy, with a flat bottom, no handle, and thinly cast in a poor-quality alloy. The decoration, which at Anyang is subtle and refined, is here crude and, with the exception of the protuberant eye, all in one plane of relief. It is too soon to assess fully the significance of Chengchow, but these discoveries are sure to throw light on the vexed question of the connection between Shang China and the bronze cultures of Southern Siberia, Russia and the Near East. In point of time, the oldest bronze objects found at Chengchow can hardly be much earlier than 1500 B.C.; this, coupled with the fact that certain types of tools and weapons have western affinities, suggests that both the craft itself and some types of artefacts may have been imported into China from the Near East between 2000 and 1500 B.C.

At Anyang, the bronze art is fully mature, the reflection of a stable and prosperous society. In the perfection of their craftsmanship and the immense power of their form and decoration, the Shang bronzes must rank as one of the great artistic triumphs of early civilization. The zoomorphic motifs which adorn them and give them their intense vitality may seem to be innumerable, but are for the most part variations and combinations of the same few elements — notably the tiger, the water-buffalo, elephant, hare, deer, owl, parrot, fish, cicada, and possibly the silkworm. Occasionally in a frieze around an otherwise plain vessel these creatures may be represented naturalistically, but far more often they are so stylized as to be barely recognizable: their bodies dissolve, their limbs break down or take on a life of their own, sprouting other creatures. The *k'uei* dragon, for example, may appear with gaping jaws, with a beak, with a trunk, wings or horns, or he may form the eyebrow of that most impressive and mysterious of all mythical creatures, the *t'ao-t'ieh*. This formidable mask, which often appears to be split open on either side of a flange and laid out flat on the belly of the vessel, is the dominating element in the decoration of bronzes of the first phase. There has been much speculation as to precisely what it signified. Sung antiquarians named it *t'ao-t'ieh* in deference to a passage in a third-century B.C. text, the *Lü Shih Ch'un-ch'iu*, which runs, 'On the *ting* of the Chou there is applied the *t'ao-t'ieh*: having a head but no body he ate people, but before he had swallowed them, harm came to his body.' Thus by the end of Chou, the *t'ao-t'ieh* was considered as a monster; later it came to be called 'the glutton', and was interpreted as a warning against overeating. Modern scholars have claimed that it represents a tiger or a bull; sometimes it has the characteristics of the one, sometimes of the other. Mizuno has drawn attention to a passage in the *Ch'un-ch'iu Tso-chuan* describing the *t'ao-t'ieh* as one of the four devils driven away by the Emperor Shun, and subsequently made defenders of the land from evil spirits.[1] Like the grotesque characters in the Tibetan 'devil dance', the more terrifying the *t'ao-t'ieh*, the greater his protective power.

Two examples will show how effectively the various elements can be combined and integrated with the shape of the vessel itself. The lid of the *kuang* in Plate 3b terminates in a tiger's head at one end and an owl's at the other; the tiger's legs can clearly be seen on the front of the vessel, the owl's wing at the back. Between them a serpent coils up onto the lid, ending in a dragon's head at the crown of the dorsal flange. The main decoration of the magnificent *chia* in Kansas City (Plate 4) consists of *t'ao-t'ieh* masks divided down the centre by a low flange and standing out against a background of spirals, called *lei-wen* by Chinese antiquarians from their supposed resemblance to the archaic form of the character *lei*, 'thunder'. However, like the endless spirals painted on the Yangshao pottery, their meaning (if any) is lost. The *t'ao-t'ieh* has large 'eyebrows' or horns; a frieze of long-tailed birds fills the upper zone while under the lip is a continuous band of 'rising blades' containing the formalized bodies of the cicada, a common symbol of regeneration in Chinese art. The vessel is crowned with a squatting heraldic beast and two large knobs for lifting it off the fire with tongs, while the tapering legs are decorated with a complex system of antithetical *k'uei* dragons.

[1]Mizuno Sei-ichi, *Bronzes and Jades of Ancient China* (1959), 8–9.

Several distinct bronze styles appear to have existed simultaneously. The *ku* libation vessel, for example, may be decorated all over, its motifs divided by high serrated vertical flanges which add considerably to its elegance; or the decoration may be confined to the 'collar' and the base, or, in the plainest examples, to the collar alone. The *tsun* — a fatter and heavier relation to the *ku* — is often treated in the same way. In vessels of the *li* and *yu* types the zoomorphic designs may be confined to a narrow frieze below the lip, while the body of the *kuei* is generally rather severely treated with vertical flutings like a Georgian teapot — although its high handles, like those of most Shang bronzes, are vigorously modelled in the form of elephants, bulls, tigers, or more fabulous creatures. Occasionally the effect is too bizarre and extravagant to be altogether pleasing, but in the finest vessels the main decorative elements play over the surface like a dominant theme in music against a subtle 'ground bass' of *lei-wen*; indeed, to pursue the analogy further, these motifs seem to interpenetrate one another like the parts in a fugue, and at the same time to pulsate with a powerful rhythm. Already in the sweeping decoration of the Yangshao painted pottery we saw a hint of that uniquely Chinese faculty of conveying formal energy through the medium of dynamic linear rhythms; here in the bronzes that faculty is even more powerfully evident, while many centuries later it will find its supreme expression in the language of the brush.

The bronze weapons used by the Shang people show several aspects of this many-faceted culture. Most purely Chinese was a form of dagger-axe known as the *ko* (Plate 5a), with pointed blade and a tang which was passed through a hole in the shaft and lashed to it, or, more rarely, shaped like a collar to fit round the shaft. The *ko* probably originates in a Neolithic weapon and seems to have had a ritual significance, for some of the most beautiful Shang specimens have blades of jade, while the handle is often inlaid with a mosaic of turquoise. The *ch'i* axe, which also originated in a stone tool, has a broad curving blade like that of a mediaeval executioner's axe, while its flanged tang is generally

decorated with *t'ao-t'ieh* and other motifs. A fine example of a
ch'i axe, now in Kansas City, is illustrated in Plate 5b. On one side
of the tang is the archaic character *fa* ('to kill a victim for sacrifice')
depicting a man being struck by a *ko*; the other side has a graph of
a *hsien* steamer, which also has the meaning 'to sacrifice'. Less
exclusively Chinese are the bronze daggers and knives, simple
forms of which have been found at Chengchow. At Anyang they
become more elaborate, the handle often terminating in a ring, or
in the head of a horse, ram, deer, or elk (Plate 6b). These have
their counterparts in the 'animal style' of the Ordos Desert, Inner
Mongolia and Southern Siberia.

The problem as to whether China or Central Asia was the
source of this style has long been debated. Much turns upon the
date of the South Siberian sites such as Karasuk where it also
appears, and until this is established the question of priority
cannot be finally settled. It seems that an animal style existed
simultaneously in Western Asia (Luristan third phase), Siberia
(Karasuk) and China (Anyang) roughly between 1500 and 1000
B.C., and that China drew upon this style from her western
neighbours and at the same time contributed from her own
increasingly rich repertoire of animal forms. Elements of the
animal style appear also in the bronze fittings made for chariots,
furniture and weapons. Recent excavations at Anyang have made
it possible to reconstruct the Shang chariot and to assign to their
correct place such objects as hub-caps, jingles, pole-ends, awning-
fittings and the V-shaped sheaths for horses' yokes.

The origin of the decoration on the bronzes presents a difficult
problem. The most striking element in it is the profusion of
animal motifs, not one of which appears in Chinese Neolithic art.
The Shang people, the contents of whose tombs reveal this
extraordinary passion for animals, had cultural affinities with the
steppe and forest folk of Siberia and, more remotely, with the
peoples of Alaska, British Columbia, and Central America. The
similarities between certain Shang designs and those, for example,
in the art of the West Coast Indians of North America are too

close to be accidental. Li Chi has suggested that the richly-decorated square-section bronze vessels with straight sides are a translation into metal of a northern wood-carving art, and Carl Hentze has amassed a considerable amount of evidence for the stylistic similarity between the décor of these bronzes and the art of the northern nomadic peoples. On the other hand, the art of carving formalized animal masks on wood or gourd is native to Southeast Asia and the Archipelago, and still practised today. Also native to Southeast Asia is the technique of stamping designs in the wet clay, which survived in the Neolithic pottery of South China until well into the Iron Age, and may have contributed the repeated circles, spirals and volutes to bronze ornament. Clearly the sources of the decorative language of the Shang bronzes are more numerous and complex than was once supposed.

Whatever the origins of this language, we must not think of it as confined solely to the sacrificial bronzes. Only they have survived intact, but could we but transport ourselves to the home of some rich Anyang nobleman we would have seen *t'ao-t'ieh* and beaked dragons, cicadas and tigers, painted on the beams of his house and applied to hangings of leather and matting about his rooms, and, very probably, woven into his silk robes. That this was likely we know from the contents of the tombs, and it tends to reinforce the view that these motifs are not tied to the form or function of any individual bronze vessel, but belong to the whole repertoire, part decorative, part magical, of Shang art.

Already in certain Neolithic sites we have encountered jade, selected, it appears, for objects of more than purely utilitarian purpose by virtue of its hardness, strength and purity. In the Shang Dynasty the craft of jade carving progresses a further step forward, and we must briefly consider the sources of this stone, the technique of carving it, and the unique place it occupies in early Chinese culture. Although early Chinese texts speak of jade from several places in China, for many centuries the chief source has been the river-beds of the Khotan region in Central Asia, and Western scholars had come to the conclusion that jade did not exist in its true state in China proper. Recent discoveries, however, seem to lend some support to the ancient texts, for a jadeitic stone used today by Peking jade-smiths has been traced to Nanyang in Honan. However, the true jade (*chen-yü*) prized throughout history by the Chinese is nephrite, a crystalline stone harder than steel and of peculiar toughness. In theory it is pure white, but even small amounts of impurities will produce a wide range of colours from green and blue to brown, red, grey, yellow and even black. In the eighteenth century Chinese jade carvers discovered in Burma a source of another mineral, jadeite, whose brilliant apple and emerald green have made it deservedly popular for jewellery both in China and abroad. Because of its unique qualities, jade has since ancient times been regarded by the Chinese with special reverence. In his great dictionary the *Shuo-wen Chieh-tzu* the Han scholar Hsü Shen described it in words now well known to every student of Chinese art: 'Jade is the fairest of stones,' he wrote. 'It is endowed with five virtues. Charity is typified by its lustre, bright yet warm; rectitude by its translucency, revealing the colour and markings within; wisdom by the purity and penetrating quality of its note when the stone is struck; courage, in that it may be broken, but cannot be bent; equity, in that it has sharp angles, which yet injure none.'[1]

The extraordinary hardness of jade makes it very difficult to carve. No other stone or metal alone can cut it, and to do so one must use an abrasive. Hansford has demonstrated that it is possible, given time, to drill a hole in a slab of jade using only a bamboo bow-drill and builder's sand. It has recently been suggested that metal tools were already employed at Anyang, and there is evidence that the Shang lapidary may also have used a drill-point harder than modern carborundum. Some small pieces carved in the round have been found in Shang sites, but the vast majority consist of weapons, ritual and decorative objects carved from thin slabs seldom more than half an inch thick. The jades from Chengchow include long beautifully shaped knives and axe

[1] *Cf.* S. H. Hansford, *Chinese Jade Carving* (London, 1950), 31.

blades (*ko*), circles, sections of discs, a figure of a tortoise, flat plaques in the shape of birds and other creatures pierced at each end for use as clothing ornaments or pendants. A particularly interesting find was a perforated disc called *hsüan-chi* with three 'teeth' like a ratchet which is believed to have been used together with a long sighting tube for astronomical observations.

The finds at Anyang have been incomparably richer in beauty, workmanship and range of types than those at Chengchow, and

recent discoveries make it likely that the great numbers of jade objects labelled 'probably from Anyang' which have reached western collections as a result of the indiscriminate digging of the last fifty years must have come from that site. The excavations at the Anyang village of Ta-ssu-kung-ts'un in 1953, for example, yielded plaques carved in the shape of birds, fishes, silkworms and tigers; *pi*, *ts'ung*, *yüan* and other ritual objects; beads, knife-handles and *ko* axes. The most impressive recent find at Anyang was a huge sonorous stone found lying on the floor of the grave-pit at Wu-kuan-ts'un (Plate 2a); cut from a thin slab of marble thirty-three inches long and pierced for suspension, it is decorated on one side with a magnificent design of a tiger executed in thread relief.

Carved bone handle from Hsiao-t'un. (After Li Chi.)

Not all carving was done in such intractable materials as jade and marble. Some of the most beautiful of all Shang designs were carved in bone and ivory. Elephants roamed North China in prehistoric times and probably were still to be found north of the Yangtse in the Shang Dynasty. We know that at least one Shang emperor kept one as a pet, possibly sent as tribute from Yüeh, while a plentiful supply of ivory could be had from China's southern neighbours. On plaques of ivory and bone a few inches square, made presumably as ornaments for chariots, furniture or boxes, were carved *t'ao-t'ieh* and other designs of extraordinary intricacy and beauty, sometimes inlaid with turquoise. Like the bronzes, these bone and ivory carvings show striking similarities with the art of the West Coast Indians of North America. For years scholars have toyed with the fascinating possibilities that these similarities have opened up, but as yet no archaeological connecting links have been found to account for them.

T'ao-t'ieh mask decorating a bronze vessel of type *fang-i*. Early Chou Dynasty. *Freer Gallery, Washington.*

CHAPTER THREE

The Chou Dynasty

During the last years of the decline of Shang, the vassal state of Chou on her western frontier had grown so powerful that its ruler Wen was virtually in control of two-thirds of the Shang territories. Finally in 1027 B.C. (Ch'en Meng-chia's chronology) Wen's son Wu, the Martial King, captured Anyang and the last Shang ruler committed suicide. Under Wu's young successor Ch'eng Wang a powerful regent known to history as the Duke of Chou (Chou Kung) consolidated the empire, set up feudal states and parcelled out the Shang domains among other vassals, though he took care to permit the descendants of Shang to rule in the little state of Sung so that they could keep up the hereditary sacrifices to their ancestral spirits. Chou Kung was chief architect of a dynasty which was to have the longest rule in China's history, and even though its later centuries were clouded by incessant civil wars in which the royal house was crushed and finally engulfed, the Chou Dynasty, more than any other, gave to China her most characteristic and enduring institutions.

There was no abrupt break with Shang traditions; rather were many of them developed and perfected. Feudalism, court ritual and ancestor worship became more elaborate and effective instruments in welding the state together: so effective indeed that from the time of confusion at the end of the dynasty many people, Confucius among them, came to look back upon the reigns of Wen, Wu and Duke Chou as a golden age. Religious life was still centred in worship of Shang Ti, though the concept of 'Heaven' (*T'ien*) now begins to appear and eventually replaces the cruder notions embodied in Shang Ti. Bronze inscriptions and early texts indicate the beginnings of a moral code centred in adherence to the will of Heaven and in respect for *te* (virtue), both of which will be fundamental in the teachings of Confucius. The Chou court became the focus of an elaborate ritual in which music, art, literature and pageantry all combined under the direction of the master of ceremonies (*pin-hsiang*) to give moral and aesthetic dignity to the concept of the state. The king held audiences at dawn and dusk (a custom that survived until 1912); orders for the day were written on bamboo slips, read out by the court historian and then handed out to officials for execution. From the time of Mu Wang (947–928 B.C.) onwards it became the custom to preserve these orders by casting them on the bronze ritual vessels. These inscriptions, which became longer as time went on, are one of the main sources for the study of early Chou history, the other chief documents being the *Book of Songs* (*Shih-ching*) an anthology of ancient court odes, ballads and love songs said to have been compiled by Confucius, and the authentic chapters of the *Classic of History* (*Shu-ching*) which tell of the fall of Shang and the early years of the Chou. These documents bear witness to that sense of history which is one of the most striking features of Chinese civilization, and, as a corollary, to the almost sacred place held in Chinese life by the written word.

The first phase of Chou history ended in 771 with the death of Yu Wang and the shift of the capital eastwards from Shensi to Loyang. The art of this period, in so far as it has survived, is generally considered as forming a single entity. By this time the feudal states were growing more and more powerful, and P'ing Wang, the first ruler of Eastern Chou, was helped to power by two of them — Chin and Ch'eng. Before long the Chou state was declining still further, till eventually it became a mere shadow of its former self, kept artificially alive by the powerful states that surrounded it solely in order to maintain the prestige of the royal house, from which the 'mandate of Heaven' had not yet been withdrawn. The period from 722 to 481 is often known as the *Ch'un-ch'iu* (Spring and Autumn) because the events of the greater part of it are recorded in the *Spring and Autumn* Annals of the State of Lu, while for the rest we have the stories in another classic, the *Tso-chuan*. The feudal chiefs spent their time, it appears, in making aggressive and defensive alliances with other states, in keeping the northern barbarians at bay, and in honouring the shrunken Chou, which survived, a pale shadow of its former glory, till its destruction in 256 B.C. at the hands of Ch'in.

Although the historical documents on the Chou Dynasty are voluminous, the archaeological picture is still by no means clear. Since 1950, however, it has begun to fill out. Early Chou ritual vessels, sent no doubt to the rulers of feudal dependencies, have been found as far afield as Kiangsu, Anhui and Liaoning. At Chang-chia-p'o, west of Sian, the traditional site of the Western Chou capital is now being excavated. Remains of all periods have been found at Lo-yang; a tomb of a prince of the obscure state of Kuo (near the San-men Gorge dam site in Honan) has been dated about 650 B.C.; outside the west gate of Shou-hsien (Anhui) an important tomb has been found of a Ts'ai prince, dateable by its inscribed bronzes as between 518 and 491 B.C.; while a tomb of the reign of Mu Wang (947–928) has been found at P'u-tu-ts'un, Ch'ang-an, containing bronzes with long inscriptions, jades and a single specimen of glazed pottery. In addition to these scientific-ally-conducted excavations great quantities of bronzes and jades have been dug up over a long period of years at Chin-ts'un and Hsin-cheng near Loyang, Li-yü in Shansi, and Shou-hsien (Anhui) and Ch'ang-sha (Hunan), both in the ancient state of Ch'u. But we must not suppose that all of China had reached the same stage of a mature bronze culture. It is likely that in the Western Chou period the inhabitants of large areas of South and West China were still living in the Stone Age.

At the moment, more is known about Shang architecture than about that of the early Chou, for which we have to rely largely on the evidence of the written word. One of the chief sources for the study of Chou institutions and customs is the *Chou-li*, a manual of ritual and government compiled, it is believed, in the former Han

Dynasty. Its authors, looking back through the mists of time to the remote golden age, present a somewhat idealized picture of Chou ritual and life, but the *Chou-li* is not without significance, for its descriptions were taken as canonical by later dynasties who strove always to follow the ancient institutions and forms as the *Chou-li* presented them. Writing of the ancient Chou city, the *Chou-li* says, 'The architects who laid out a capital made it a square nine *li* (about three miles) on a side, each side having three gateways. Within the capital there were nine lengthwise and nine crosswise avenues, each nine chariot tracks wide. On the left was the Ancestral Temple, on the right the Altar of the Soil; in front lay the Court of State, at the rear the market-place.' The western Chou capital has been located, and the capital of the state of Ch'i, in Lin-tzu-hsien, Shantung, has been superficially explored; it was a mile from east to west and two-and-a-half miles from north to south; the palace area lay in the southwest corner and the whole city was surrounded by a stamped earth wall over thirty feet high. The capital of the state of Yen, discovered in I-hsien, Hopei, was even larger. Almost all that remains of these cities above ground are the thousands of roof-tiles with stamped designs which litter the fields.

The *Book of Songs* contains several vivid descriptions of ancestral halls and palaces. Here is a part of one of them, translated by Arthur Waley:

> To give continuance to foremothers and forefathers
> We build a house, many hundred cubits of wall;
> To south and east its doors.
> Here shall we live, here rest,
> Here laugh, here talk.
> We bind the frames, creak, creak;
> We hammer the mud, tap, tap,
> That it may be a place where wind and rain cannot enter,
> Nor birds and rats get in,
> But where our lord may dwell.
> As a halberd, even so plumed,

As an arrow, even so sharp,
As a bird, even so soaring,
As wings, even so flying
Are the halls to which our lord ascends.
Well levelled is the courtyard,
Firm are the pillars,
Cheerful are the rooms by day,
Softly gloaming by night,
A place where our lord can be at peace.
Below, the rush-mats; over them the bamboo-mats.
Comfortably he sleeps,
He sleeps and wakes
And interprets his dreams. . . .[1]

In this and other ballads we get a picture of large buildings with rammed earth walls standing on a high platform, of strong timber pillars supporting a roof whose eaves, though not yet curving, spread like wings, of floors covered with thick matting like the Japanese *tatami*, of warmth, light and comfort. While the most monumental buildings were the ancestral halls, the palaces and private houses were often large, and may well have had several successive courtyards as they do today. Chou texts are full of warnings against those who build too extravagantly, and above all against the usurper of royal prerogatives. Confucius, for example, rebuked a contemporary who kept a tortoise (presumably for divination) in a pavilion adorned with the hill-pattern on its capitals and the duckweed pattern on its kingposts, insignia reserved exclusively for the emperor. Duke Chuang of Lu in 670 B.C. infringed the sumptuary laws by painting the pillars of his father's shrine bright red and carving his rafters. By comparison the authors of these texts extol the simplicity of ancient times, when a virtuous ruler roofed his ancestral shrine with thatch, when King Ho-lu of Wu never 'sat on double mats. His apartments were not lofty . . . his palaces had no belvederes, and his boats and carriages were plain.'

[1] Arthur Waley, *The Book of Songs* (1937), 282–3.

The most conspicuous of Chou buildings, apart from palaces and ancestral halls, must have been the *ming-t'ang* ('Bright Hall'), a ritual edifice of which detailed but conflicting accounts are given in early texts, and the towers (*t'ai*) constructed of timber on a high platform of rammed earth. Passages in the *Tso-chuan* show that the princes used them as fortresses, for feasting or simply as look-outs. Perhaps they survived in the tall storage and look-out towers that were, till recently, a feature of villages and farms in South China.

No trace of the kind of decorative stone sculpture that adorned Shang interiors has yet been discovered in Chou sites. But the Chou craftsmen were certainly capable of modelling a figure in the round and endowing it with extraordinary vitality, even when, as in the famous pair of tigers in the Freer Gallery (Plate 6a), its limbs and features are stylized. Indeed, here the rhythmic movement of the semi-abstract decoration over the surface gives these creatures a curious animation different from, but no less intense than, that which a more naturalistic treatment would have achieved. Although they have been tentatively dated as early as the tenth century B.C., the coarseness of the modelling and the all-over 'baroque' decoration seem to herald the style of the Middle Chou period.

In the earliest Western Chou ritual bronzes the Shang tradition is carried on without a break, one of the more significant differences being in the inscriptions, which are no longer a simple record of ownership but become valuable historical documents, often setting out in some detail the circumstances in which that vessel was bestowed. A vessel of the reign of Ch'eng Wang (1024–1005), for instance, recently excavated in Tan-t'u, Kiangsu, had an inscription of 120 characters, that on a *ting* of the reign of his successor K'ang Wang runs to 291 characters. Later they became even longer. The typical short early Chou inscription on a *kuei* in the Alfred Pillsbury Collection shows the function of the vessel quite clearly: 'The King attacked Ch'i-yü and went out and attacked Nao-hei. When he came back, he made *liao*-sacrifice (burnt offering) in Tsung-chou and presented to me, Kuo Pao X, ten double strings of cowries. I presume in response to extol the King's grace, and so I have made my accomplished dead father's *kuei* vessel. May for a myriad years sons and grandsons forever treasure and use it.'[1]

For perhaps a century after the Chou conquest Shang bronze styles survived, though increasingly modified by the taste of the Chou invaders from the West. By the tenth century the *ku, chüeh, kuang, yu* and square *i* had disappeared, along with such ubiquitous Shang motifs as the *t'ao-t'ieh*, cicada, 'rising blades', and long-tailed bird. The *ting* had become a wide, shallow bowl on three cabriole legs, and the *li*, when it appears at all, has a curiously arched contour. The *p'an*, a wide flat dish, has become more common, while the *kuei* may have four handles and stand on a square base. Bronzes in the Chou style generally show a certain exaggeration and coarseness of modelling, while shapes become increasingly slack and sagging. Flanges tend to be large and spiky, and new creatures make their appearance, among them the gaping monster with spiral tail and a bird with head turned back and frills of quill-like feathers along its body. By the ninth century birds and beasts are dissolving into a variety of vertical and horizontal scales, and broad, flat meander patterns that cover the whole surface (Plate 8). The bronzes of late Western Chou, often called the Middle Chou style (Yetts' 'Second Phase', ninth and eighth centuries) have none of the dynamic tension and unity of design that marks the vessels of late Shang and the first decades of the Chou.

The stylistic change was given a further impetus in the eighth and seventh centuries first by foreign ideas and techniques brought back by the Chou kings from their northern campaigns, and later by increasing pressure from the northern barbarians themselves. The most striking new feature which this contact introduced is the

[1] Slightly adapted from Bernhard Karlgren, *A Catalogue of the Chinese Bronzes in the Collection of Alfred F. Pillsbury* (Minneapolis, 1952), 105. The last sentence, a common formula in the inscriptions, makes it clear that the bronzes were made for ritual use rather than for burial.

Left: Ritual bronzes of Middle Chou: 1. *li*; 2. *hu*; 3. *fu*; 4. *p'an*. *Right*: Ritual
bronzes of the Warring States: 5. *ting*; 6. *hu*; 7. *t'ui*; 8. *tou*; 9. *chien*.
(After Mizuno.)

69

art of interlacing animal forms into intricate patterns. This first appears in Chinese art in the bronzes excavated from seventh-century graves at Hsin-cheng and Shang-ts'un-ling in Honan. A more highly developed example is the Hsin-cheng *hu*, dateable around 650 B.C. which is illustrated in Plate 7a. It stands on two tigers; two more tigers with huge horns and twisting bodies curl up the sides to form handles, while smaller tigers play at their feet. The body is covered with an all-over pattern of flat, rope-like interlaced dragons. The lid is surrounded with flaring leaf-shaped flanges, while in the centre a crane with spreading wings seems about to take flight. Gone is the wonderfully integrated quality of the early bronzes, which achieved so perfect a fusion of form and decoration. Gone too is the coarse but imposing strength of the early Middle Chou. Now the shape is often ungainly, the surface treatment flat and monotonous, while as if to compensate, the vessel sprouts extravagant creatures who tend to obscure rather than to enhance its form. These Hsin-cheng bronzes represent a restless period of transition before the flowering of the refined art of the Warring States.

Reliable archaeological evidence on the jade of the Early and Middle Chou is very scanty. Before the Second World War archaeologists working at Hsin-ts'un in Hsün-hsien (Honan) discovered a number of jade objects which were for the most part rather cruder versions of Shang types, with the relief carving often confined to shallow incisions on a flat surface. Since 1950 excavations of graves at Loyang and at P'u-tu-ts'un, Ch'ang-an, have tended to confirm the impression that there was a decline in the craft in the early Western Chou. But the Chou jades excavated under controlled conditions represent a minute proportion of the total number; this, combined with the likelihood that the traditional forms must have persisted for long periods without change, makes the dating of individual pieces on grounds of style alone extremely difficult.

There is less doubt, fortunately, about the meaning and function of the ritual and funerary jades. According to the *Chou-li*, and there is no reason to doubt its reliability, certain shapes were appropriate to particular ranks. The king in audience, for example, held a *chen-kuei*, a broad, flat perforated sceptre; a duke held a *huan* (ridged sceptre); a prince a *hsin* (elongated sceptre); an earl a *kung* (curved sceptre); while the lower ranks of viscount and baron held *pi* discs decorated with the little bosses known as the 'grain

Some ritual and funerary jades: 1. *kuei*; 2. *pi*; 3. *ts'ung*; 4. *ya-chang*; 5. *yen-kuei*; 6. *huang*; 7. *chang*; 8. *han*.

pattern'. Proclamations were issued with jade objects to indicate the royal authority — as for instance the *ya-chang* (a long knife) for mobilizing the imperial garrison, a *hu* (tiger) in two halves for transmitting military secrets, a *yen-kuei* (sceptre with concave butt) for protecting official envoys, and so on. Equally specific were the jades used to protect the body at burial, numbers of which have been found in their original positions in the grave. Generally the corpse lay on his back (a change from Shang practice). On his chest was placed a *pi* disc, symbol of Heaven; beneath his body a *ts'ung*, symbol of earth (Plate 7b); to the east of the body was placed a *kuei* sceptre, to the west a tiger, to the north (at his feet) a *huang* (half circle), to the south a *chang* (a short stubby *kuei*); the seven orifices of the body were sealed with jade plugs, while a flat plaque, *han*, generally in the shape of a cicada, was placed in the mouth. Thus was the body protected from all harm without, and sealed lest any evil influences should escape from within. In addition the early Chou lapidaries carved many kinds of pendants and ornaments, as in the Shang Dynasty, but as these were to be far more beautiful and refined in the late Chou period we will defer discussion of them to the next chapter.

By comparison with the bronzes, the pottery of Western and early Eastern Chou is sober stuff. Many of the finest pieces are crude imitations of bronze vessels, though generally only the shape is copied, such bronze-like decoration as there is being confined to bulls' heads or *t'ao-t'ieh* masks attached to the sides. Although a few specimens of plain red ware have been found, most Western Chou pottery consists of a coarse grey ware, the most popular purely ceramic shape being a round-bottomed, wide-mouthed storage jar which is often cord-marked. In the upper stratum of the famous black-pottery site at Lung-shan in Shantung, imitations of bronze shapes were excavated together with elegant tall *tou* reminiscent of the earlier black Lung-shan wares. *Hu*-type vessels found in Hsün-hsien repeat the dragon feet and dragon handles on the extraordinary bronzes unearthed in the same district.

Recent discoveries show that in addition to this mass of unglazed wares a much more sophisticated ceramic art was beginning to develop. Dr Hsia Nai has gone so far as to say that very early in the Chou Dynasty pottery 'had been perfected almost to the level of proto-porcelain by high-temperature firing'.[1] The important tomb of the reign of Mu Wang (947–928) at P'u-tu-ts'un near Sian contained vessels decorated with horizontal grooves and covered with a thin bluish-green glaze quite different

[1] Hsia Nai, 'Tracing the Thread of the Past', *China Reconstructs* 8.10 (October, 1959), 46.

from the blackish or yellowish Shang glazes. Other glazed wares, dateable by bronze inscriptions to the eleventh and tenth centuries, have been found in graves in Honan, Kiangsu and Anhui.

CHAPTER FOUR

The Period of the Warring States

A map of China in the sixth century B.C. would show a tiny and impotent state of Chou, somewhat like modern Canberra, surrounded by powerful principalities constantly forming and breaking alliances and attacking each other, condescending to consult the royal house only on matters of legitimacy and inheritance. In the north, Chin kept the desert hordes at bay until she was destroyed in 403 and parcelled out among the three states of Chao, Han and Wei: at one time these three states formed an alliance with Yen and Ch'i in the northeast against the power of the semi-barbarian Ch'in, now looming dangerously on the western horizon. The smaller states of Sung and Lu, which occupied the lower Yellow River valley, were not militarily powerful — though they are famous in Chinese history as the home of the great philosophers. In the region of modern Kiangsu and Chekiang, Wu and Yüeh were emerging into the full light of Chinese culture, while a huge area of central China was under the domination of the southward-looking and only partly sinicized state of Ch'u. Gradually Ch'u and Ch'in grew stronger. In 473 Wu fell to Yüeh, then Yüeh to Ch'u. Ch'in was even more successful. In 256 she obliterated the pathetic remnant of the great state of Chou; twenty-three years later she defeated her great rival Ch'u then rapidly turned on the remaining states of Wei, Chao and Yen. In 221 B.C. she defeated Ch'i, and all China lay prostrate at her feet.

As often happens in history, these centuries of ever-increasing political chaos were accompanied by social and economic reform, intellectual ferment and great achievement in the arts. Iron tools and weapons were coming into use. Now for the first time private individuals could own land, and trade was developing, much aided by the invention of currency — bronze 'spade' money in Central China, knife-shaped coins in the North and East. This was the age of the 'Hundred Schools', when roving philosophers known as *shui-k'e* ('persuading guests') offered their council to any ruler who chose to listen to them. The most enlightened patronage was that offered by King Hsüan of Ch'i who welcomed brilliant scholars and philosophers of every school to his 'Academy of the Chi Gate'. But this was exceptional. Confucius, the greatest of them, was ill-used in the state of Lu, for in those chaotic times few rulers saw any immediate advantage in the Sage's emphasis upon the moral and social virtues, upon *jen* ('human-heartedness'), or upon the value of knowledge and self-cultivation. Wanting power at home and victory over their enemies abroad, they were often more attracted by the Machiavellian doctrines of Lord Shang and the Legalists, which were to find their ultimate justification in the ruthless rise of the state of Ch'in.

Against the social commitment of Confucius and his follower Mencius on the one hand and the amoral doctrines of the Legalists on the other, the Taoists offered a third solution — a submission not to society or the state but to the universal principle, *tao*. Lao Tzu taught that discipline and control only distort or repress one's natural instinct to flow with the vast stream of existence. In part this was a reaction against the rigidity of the other schools, but it was also a way of escape from the hazards and uncertainties of the times into the world of the imagination. It was, in fact, through Taoism, with its intuitive awareness of things that cannot be measured or learned out of books, that the Chinese poets and painters were to rise to the highest imaginative flights. The state of Ch'u was the heart of this new liberating movement. The great mystical philosopher-poet Chuang Tzu (*c.* 350–275 B.C.) belonged in fact to the neighbouring state of Sung, but, as Fung Yu-lan has observed, his thought is closer to that of Ch'u, while Ch'ü Yüan and Sung Yü, who in their rhapsodic poems known as *sao* poured out a flood of such passionate feeling, were both natives of Ch'u. It is perhaps no accident that not only the finest poetry of this period, but also the earliest surviving paintings on silk, should have been produced within its boundaries.[1]

During the early Warring States period, however, the region covered by modern Honan was still the heart of Chinese civilization, protected by the defensive walls which were being constructed at intervals along China's northern frontiers. The most ancient section of wall was built about 353 B.C. across modern Shensi, not only to keep the marauding nomads out, but equally to keep the Chinese in, and to attempt to prevent that 'desinicization' which in the Six Dynasties was to prepare the way for the foreign occupation of large areas of North China.

Until recently archaeologists had given much less attention to the remains of the Chou Dynasty than had been devoted to the Shang. Before the Second World War, only one important late Chou site had been scientifically excavated, at Hsin-cheng in Honan, where were found tombs containing bronzes that span the years from the baroque extravagances of Middle Chou to the simpler forms and more intricate decoration of the Early Warring States. At the same time the local farmers living between Loyang and Chengchow had for some years been robbing tombs at Chin-ts'un. Bronzes believed to have come from these tombs range in style from late, and rather subdued, versions of the Hsin-cheng manner to magnificent examples of the mature style of the fourth and third centuries B.C. Since 1950, however, controlled excavations have been carried out extensively in the region of Hui-hsien,

---

[1] It was Arthur Waley in his *Introduction to the Study of Chinese Painting* (21–23) who first pointed out the importance of Ch'u in the emergence in ancient China both of creative art and of a consciousness of the power of the artistic imagination. More recently David Hawkes has discussed the contribution of Ch'u in his *Ch'u Tz'u, The Songs of the South* (Oxford, 1959). He ends his General Introduction (p. 19) with these words: 'As we begin to learn from the archaeologists something of the art of that great but ill-fated Kingdom of Ch'u, it becomes apparent that what we have in the earlier poems of *Ch'u Tz'u* is not an isolated and unaccountable literary phenomenon, but the full flowering of a remarkable and fascinating culture.'

which like Chin-ts'un lay within the state of Wei. At Liu-li-ko just outside Hui-hsien a pit was found containing nineteen chariots, with the horses buried separately — a late survival of the Shang custom. At Ku-wei-ts'un huge tomb pits have been found containing magnificent bronzes inlaid with gold and silver, jades and other precious objects; while a tomb at Chao-ku-chen yielded a number of copper and bronze vessels one of which bears an engraved picture of a house — perhaps the earliest representation of architecture yet found in China. All these Hui-hsien sites may be dated in the late fourth or early third century B.C.

Excavations have also been proceeding continuously at Loyang, the Late Chou capital. Between 1950 and 1954 it was reported that over six hundred tombs (of various periods) had been opened, yielding over ten thousand objects. It would be very surprising if all of them had received the attention of trained archaeologists, and in fact very few of them have yet been published. Just how widely late Chou culture was diffused is shown by recent important discoveries not only in Central China but also at Li-yü in north-western Shansi, at T'ang-shan, east of Peking, and at Yang-tzu-shan just outside Chengtu, capital of the far western state of Shu. All reflect to varying degrees the artistic developments that were taking place in the Loyang — Hui-hsien region.

Already in the seventh century a change was beginning to become apparent in the bronze style. The huge extravagance of the Middle Chou décor seems to have exhausted itself. Ungainly excrescences are shorn off, the surface is smoothed away to produce an unbroken, almost severe silhouette. The decoration becomes ever more strictly confined and, as though it sought to hide itself, is often sunk below the surface, or inlaid in gold or silver. Hints of archaism appear in the emphasis upon the *ting* tripod and in the discreet application of *t'ao-t'ieh* masks which now make their reappearance as the clasps for ring-handles. But this stylistic revolution was not accomplished all at once. The vessels unearthed at Li-yü, for example, represent a transitional stage. Their décor of flat interlocking bands of dragons looks forward to the restless, intricate decoration of the mature Huai style; but in their robust forms, in the tiger masks which top their legs and the realistic birds and other creatures which adorn their lids, they recall the vigour of an earlier age.

This 'decrescendo' from the coarse vigour of the Middle Chou style continues in the later bronzes from Hsin-cheng and in the new style associated with Chin-ts'un and Li-yü. The typical broad three-legged *ting* from Li-yü, for example, is decorated with bands

Bronze flask inlaid with silver, from Chin-ts'un, Honan. Warring States.
Tenri Museum, Japan.

of flat interlocked dragons separated by plait-like fillets. The tendency to imitate other materials is carried even further in a *hu* from Li-yü on which knotted cords are modelled in relief in the bronze — perhaps reproducing the flask carried by the northern nomads. Another flask from Chin-ts'un is flat with a circular silhouette, the surface covered with plain bars imitating leather straps, between which the intricate pattern which Karlgren has called 'teeming hooks' seems to suggest, perhaps accidentally, some coarse stuff or animal pelt.

The earliest of the vessels found at Chin-ts'un are sober in decoration, though their ungainly flanged lids are clearly a survival from Middle Chou. However in a square *lien* now in Toronto we can see a further stage: the main body has an all-over pattern in which the interlaced dragons have almost completely broken down into 'teeming hooks', typical of the sixth century B.C., but the upper part is decorated with a flat band of geometric decoration inlaid with malachite and gold. As time goes on this motif, which at first consists of modest rectangular elements divided diagonally and set about with small curls and volutes, gradually grows until it dominates the decoration not only of bronzes but also of lacquer and jade. The final evolution of this tradition can be seen in the beautiful bronzes from the later phase at Chin-ts'un (Plate 9a). The simple shapes recall pottery; except for the masks and ring-handles the surface is flat, giving full play to the inlaid decoration which is sometimes geometric, sometimes

Rhinoceros; bronze, inlaid with gold. L. 57·8 cm. Found in Hsing-p'ing County, Shensi. 3rd century B.C.

sweeps in great curves over the contour of the vessel. Gold had been used at Anyang, but now the goldsmith's art comes into its own, and in form, decoration and craftsmanship the finest of the inlaid Warring States bronzes from the Loyang region are unsurpassed. The bronze *ts'un* in the form of a rhinoceros illustrated on this page was unearthed in Hsing-p'ing County, west of Sian.

in 1963. Inlaid with gold, it is a remarkable example of the ability of the Chinese craftsman to combine the decorative arabesque with a vigorous naturalism.

With the decline of the ancient rituals and the emergence of a wealthy upper middle class, the metal-worker's art was diverted, so to speak, from 'communion plate' to 'family plate'. A rich man would give his daughter inlaid vessels as part of her dowry, while for himself he could adorn his furniture and carriages with bronze fittings inlaid with gold, silver and malachite, and when he died, take them with him into the next world. If anyone criticized him for his extravagance, he might well quote in self-defence this advice from the philosophical and economical treatise *Kuan Tzu*, much of which was probably written at about this time: 'Lengthen the mourning period so as to occupy people's time, and elaborate the funeral so as to spend their money. . . . To have large pits for burial is to provide work for poor people; to have magnificent tombs is to provide work for artisans. To have inner and outer coffins is to encourage carpenters, and to have many pieces for the enshrouding is to encourage seamstresses.'

The value of music as a moral force in society was recognized by Confucius as it was by his contemporary Pythagoras. Ballads were sung at the feudal courts not merely as entertainment but as admonition and example; the stately measure of the classical modes was an aid to right thinking and harmonious action, and it is not surprising that some of the finest of the bronzes of the Middle and Late Chou should be the bells (*chung*) made in sets, either with a loop for suspension (*po*) from a wooden frame, or with a long handle so that they could be rung by hand. The rubbing from a relief in a third-century tomb in Shantung, illustrated on the facing page, shows how the performer struck these bells with a heavy wooden beam suspended from the ceiling. Bells of the *po* type decorated on the side with magnificent *t'ao-t'ieh* masks have recently been unearthed at Anyang, together with hand-bells (*chih-chung*) and harness jingles. In the Western Chou period *chung* bells became larger and more elaborate. Oval in section, the lower part was decorated with an animal mask or interlaced dragons; the upper part consisted of three bands of projecting knobs alternating with a dragon or *k'uei* motif on either side of a vertical panel which often contained an inscription. In the Warring States these knobs were flattened into serpent coils with feline heads, and the loop handle was often beautifully modelled in the form of back-to-back creatures, real or fabulous (Plate 9b). In the tombs at Chin-ts'un nearly fifty bells were found from thirteen different sets, one of

Striking the bells. From a rubbing of a third-century stone relief in the tomb at I-nan illustrated on page 101.

which, according to its inscriptions, was made for the Piao clan in 404 B.C. Another bell, in the British Museum, bearing a long inscription, was made for the Duke of Lu.

While the aristocracy of metropolitan China were indulging in music, dancing and other delights in the comfort and security of their great houses, less fortunate areas were fighting a desperate and often losing battle against the savage tribes who harried the northern frontiers. Mounted on horseback and using the compound bow, the nomads were more than a match for the Chinese troops, who were finally forced to abandon the chariot and copy both their methods and their weapons of war. Their influence on the Chinese did not end with warfare. Their arts were few but vigorous. For centuries they and their western neighbours of the Central Asiatic Steppe had been decorating their knives, daggers and harness with animal carvings — first in wood, and later in bronze cast for them, it is believed, by slaves and prisoners of war. This 'animal style' as it is called was totally unlike the abstract yet fanciful style of the Chinese bronzes. It was intensely realistic, formalized only to the degree necessary to adapt it to small utilitarian objects. With barbaric vigour the nomads of the Ordos desert and the wild regions to north and west of it modelled elk and reindeer, oxen and horses; they loved also to depict with compact savagery a tiger or eagle leaping on the back of some terrified game beast — a scene they often witnessed, and the representation of which probably was intended to bring success to their own hunting expeditions (Plate 10a). Hints of this animal style appeared, as we have seen, on some of the knives at Anyang. During the late Chou and Han, when the impact on China of the Hsiung-nu and other northern tribes was at its height, its influence can be seen in the design of some of the inlaid bronzes, on which hunting scenes are modelled with a curiously un-Chinese angularity and harshness of form.

The widest variety of animal designs is found on the bronze garment or belt hooks. Many of these hooks indeed are purely Chinese in style, being carried out in the exquisite inlaid technique of Chin-ts'un and Shou-chou. Court dancers wore them, as we know from the *Chao Hun*:

Two rows of eight, in perfect time, perform a dance of Cheng;
Their *hsi-pi* buckles of Chin workmanship glitter like bright
    suns. . . .[1]

The beautiful specimen illustrated in Plate 10b is fashioned in gilt bronze, inlaid with a dragon in jade and multicoloured balls

[1] David Hawkes, *Ch'u Tz'u*, 108. The phrase *hsi-pi* indicates their western origin.

of glass. Some, representing the creatures of the steppes singly or in mortal combat, are almost purely 'Ordos'. Yet others are in a mixed style: a magnificent garment hook recently excavated at Hui-hsien, for example, is decorated with three penannular jade rings in a setting formed of two intertwined dragons in silver overlaid with gold. The dragons are Chinese, but the sweeping angular planes in which they are modelled come from the northern steppes.

No such barbarian influences appear in the pottery of North China at this time. (The nomads indeed had little use for pottery and no facilities for making it.) The grey tradition continues, but the coarse cord-marked wares of the early Chou are left behind. Shapes become more elegant, often imitating bronze — the most popular forms being the *tsun*, the three-legged *ting*, the tall covered *tou* (stem-cup) and an egg-shaped covered *tui* on three feet. Generally they are heavy and plain; but some of those found at Chin-ts'un bear animals and hunting scenes stamped or incised with great verve in the wet clay before firing. Sometimes the potter even attempted to imitate the original metal by giving his vessel a lustrous black surface. Some of the most remarkable vessels were found in the big graves at Ku-wei-ts'un, Hui-hsien. Obviously intended as substitutes for bronzes, they are painted in bright colours either with slightly stylized birds and animals, or with geometric designs in rather clumsy imitation of the later Chin-ts'un style.

During the early nineteen-forties a group of miniature pottery vessels and figurines, claimed to have come from late Chou tombs in the Hui-hsien region, began to appear on the Peking antique market. Very heavily potted and beautifully finished, the vessels included miniature *hu*, covered *ting*, *p'an*, and a garment hook and mirror, on the burnished black surface of which the inlaid geometric decoration of the Chin-ts'un bronzes was imitated in red pigment. Among animals were a tiger, an owl and several horses. The figurines were, however, the most striking; simply and compactly modelled with flat, schematic faces, they nevertheless convey a remarkable feeling of life and movement by the way in which their twisting bodies and wide-flung arms express the movements of the dance. These are indications that many, if not all, of these pieces are modern forgeries. It seems hardly possible that a forger could have completely invented this type, however, and excavations have in fact produced two possible sources of inspiration for them. Small pottery figurines, with simplified bodies, incised features and red pigment, were discovered in 1954

Miniature pottery vessels excavated at Ch'ang-p'ing, near Peking. Warring States.

in a small tomb at Ch'ang-chih in south Shansi (as works of art they are in every way inferior to the 'Hui-hsien' pieces); while as a possible source for the ritual vessels we have a group of rather similar miniature pottery vessels unearthed in 1959 in a Warring States tomb at Ch'ang-p'ing near Peking, three of which are illustrated on this page.[1]

While what might be called the 'classical' tradition was developing in the Honan-Shensi region, a quite different style of

[1] See Su T'ien-chun, 'Report on the Excavation of a Warring States tomb at Sung-yüan-ts'un, Ch'ang-p'ing District, Peking', Wen Wu 9, 1959, 53–55 (in Chinese).

art was maturing in the large area of Central China dominated by the state of Ch'u. It is not known precisely how widely her boundaries extended (particularly in a southward direction), but they included the city of Shouchou on the Huai River in modern Anhui, while the influence of the art of Ch'u can be traced in the bronzes of Hui-hsein, Honan and even northern Hopei. Until Ch'in rose menacing in the West, Ch'u had been secure, and in the lush valleys of the Yangtse and its tributaries had developed a rich culture in which poetry and the visual arts flourished exceedingly. The air of leisure, wealth and refinement that her arts exude no doubt was partly responsible for her downfall, which was finally accomplished when Ch'in sacked the city of Shouchou, whither the Ch'u court had fled from Changsha three years before.

In the late sixth century B.C. Shouchou was still under the state of Ts'ai. A grave of this period recently excavated in Shou-hsien contained bronzes most of which were rather restrained versions of the Hsin-cheng style, and the art of Shouchou, even after its absorption into the expanding state of Ch'u, always retained some of its northern flavour. It must also have been an important ceramic centre at this time, if we are to judge by the beauty and vigour of the pottery excavated there. The body is of grey stoneware with incised decoration under a thin olive-green glaze, the immediate predecessor of the Yüeh type wares of the Han Dynasty, and the ancestor of the celadons of the Sung.

It is only in recent years that archaeological excavation in the Changsha region has revealed both the wealth and the essentially southern character of Ch'u art. Indeed, it is interesting to speculate on the course that Chinese culture would have taken if the victory in 221 B.C. had gone, not to the Ch'in savages from the western marches, but to this sophisticated and enlightened people.

Since the replanning of Changsha started in 1950 many large tombs have been brought to light. They were dug through a hard white clay which has in some mysterious way acted as a preservative of their contents, although they have for the most part been under water for the past two thousand years. The deep shafts are lined with timber; at the centre of each chamber stands the coffin — or rather the multiple layers of inner and outer coffins which *Kuan Tzu* recommended as giving employment to worthy artisans. The

Sketch of a reconstructed Warring States tomb at Changsha, showing the *ming-ch'i* crammed between the inner and outer coffins.
(After *Ch'ang-sha fa-chüeh pao-kao.*)

space between the outer coffin and the chamber wall is often crammed with funerary furniture (*ming-ch'i*). Sometimes the body lay on a long wooden plank carved with exquisite pierced scroll patterns, while about it were set discs of jade, stone and glass (excavations have yielded glass beads as early as Western Chou), bronze weapons and vessels, pottery and lacquer ware. The waterlogged ground, with its 'filter' of white clay, has even preserved fragments of silk and linen, documents written with a brush on slips of bamboo and beautifully painted shields of lacquered leather.

Here for the first time we find large numbers of wooden figurines of attendants and slaves. Confucius is said to have condemned this practice as he thought it would lead people on, or back, to burying the living with the dead. He thought straw figures were safer. In the succeeding Han Dynasty pottery cast in moulds was found to be both cheaper and more enduring than wood, and perhaps more acceptable to Confucians. The Changsha figures, carved and painted, give useful information about Late Chou costume. More spectacular are the cult objects, consisting of grotesque monster heads, sometimes sprouting antlers and a long tongue, and the drum- or gong-stands formed of birds standing back-to-back on tigers or entwined serpents, decorated in yellow, red and black lacquer. The gong-stand in Plate 11a, found in 1957 in a tomb in the Ch'u city of Hsin-yang in Honan, reflects her contacts with the south: similar stands are engraved on a number of bronze vessels from Ch'u sites, while bronze drums found in the Dongson region of northern Indochina also bear snake and bird designs, believed to be connected with rain-magic.

A remarkable offshoot of the Ch'u culture has recently been unearthed at Shih-chai-shan, about sixty miles south of Kunming, capital of Yunnan. A score of tombs have been opened there, containing a wealth of bronze weapons and ritual objects, gold and jade ornaments. Most extraordinary are the bronze drums and drum-shaped containers filled with cowrie-shells, the top of one of which is illustrated in Plate 11b. The figures who crowd it are evidently taking part in some sacrificial rite. Prominent are the ceremonial drums, some of which seem to be of enormous size, while a set of smaller drums stands on a platform under a wagon roof of a type still common in southeast Asia today.

From Chinese sources we know that these are the tombs of the rulers of the state of Tien, which had been conquered by a Ch'u general in the third century B.C., and continued to flourish in remote independence well into the Han Dynasty. As would seem natural from its geographical position, the Shih-chai-shan culture contains elements of Chinese and Dongson art, and of the animal style of the western nomads. Struck by its extraordinary vigour, a recent Chinese writer has suggested that Dongson is the debtor, and in fact, 'No more than a pale reflection of the high bronze culture of the Tien people in ancient Yunnan.' The unadulterated realism of Shih-chai-shan art, however, while no doubt gratifying to present Chinese taste, hardly justifies such extravagant claims. Indeed, its very 'stylelessness' suggests that it was produced in almost total isolation from the main stream of Chinese culture.

Whether it be the accident of preservation or that the Ch'u people actually did develop pictorial art at an earlier stage than North China is an open question, but it is the Changsha graves that have yielded the oldest painting on silk yet discovered (Plate 13b). Swiftly sketched with deft strokes of the brush, it shows a woman in a full-skirted dress tied with a sash at the waist, standing in profile attended by a strutting phoenix and a sinuous dragon, whose reptilian origin is vividly suggested. A bamboo brush with rabbit's-fur tip has also been found at Changsha, together with other writing and painting materials. Much of the most beautiful painting, however, appears on the lacquer-ware for which Ch'u was famous — the lacquer bowls, dishes, toilet boxes, trays and low tables which, though made for daily use, in due course were placed in their owner's tomb. In black lacquer on a red ground, or red on glossy black (Plate 12a), the swirling volutes may transform themselves into tigers, phoenixes or dragons. Common vessels were lacquered over a core of wood or woven bamboo, but the finest were built up of alternate layers of cloth and lacquer without a wood core, and are of incredible lightness and delicacy.

Also to be classed with the pictorial arts are the lively scenes cast on the surface of a remarkable bronze *hu* in the Palace

Museum, Peking. In separate panels we see an attack on a city wall, a fight between long-boats, shooting wild duck with arrows on the end of long cords, mulberry-picking and other domestic arts, all carried out in silhouette with extraordinary vitality, elegance and humour. The free treatment of this and other

Designs engraved on an inlaid bronze *hu*. Late Warring States. Peking.

engraved and inlaid vessels, considered together with the miniature lacquer paintings, suggests that the source of the pictorial naturalism of Han art is to be found not so much in metropolitan Loyang and Changan as in Changsha and Shouchou.

Large numbers of bronze mirrors have been found both in the north and within the confines of Ch'u state. At first, and always to some degree, their purpose was not to reflect one's face only, but one's very heart and soul. An entry in the *Tso-chuan* under the year 658 B.C., for instance, says of a certain individual, 'Heaven has robbed him of his mirror' — i.e. made him blind to his own faults. The mirror too is that in which all knowledge is reflected —

as it was to the mediaeval encyclopaedist St Vincent of Beauvais: 'The heart of the sage is quiet', wrote Chuang Tzu, 'it is a mirror of Heaven and Earth, a mirror of all things.' The mirror also holds and reflects the rays of the sun, lighting the eternal darkness of the tomb and warding off evil.

A bronze disc with a loop handle and dragon and snake decoration, believed to be a mirror, was found in a Shang tomb at Anyang. Perhaps the earliest true mirrors are those of the Ch'un-ch'iu period from Shang-ts'un-ling in Honan. Thereafter they are plentiful at Loyang. The face is polished, all decoration being confined to the back. Round the central loop (for the tassel) a mass of *lei-wen* or dragon-like creatures writhe within a confining border of ropes or twisted cowrie strings. A slightly later group (sixth–fifth centuries B.C.) most of which come from the Chin-ts'un tombs, are decorated with *t'ao-t'ieh* masks within a broad flat rim. The earliest mirrors from Ch'u were nearly all found in the Shouchou region. Their boss rises from a bare ring of bronze; over a background of comma patterns appear either quatrefoil petals or large staggered ⊿⊿-shaped motifs resembling the character *shan* (mountain), or swirling dragons or other semi-stylized creatures reminiscent of those on the lacquer vessels. Some of the most beautiful of all were made in the Loyang region in the fourth and third centuries B.C. (Plate 12b). Upon an intricate interlocked geometric or lozenge design picked out in minute granulations, superb creatures stride or whirl around the plain central ring. The contrast in texture between the background and the dynamic yet simple forms of the dragons make these mirrors a triumph of design.

This power to unite in one object the most exquisite and intricate refinement of detail with a dynamic rhythm and boldness of silhouette is present also in the carved jades of the late Chou period, which must surely be among the great achievements of the Chinese craftsman. Now jade was no longer reserved for worship of Heaven and Earth or for the use of the dead; it became at last a source of delight for the living. Indeed, as the ritual objects such as the *pi* and *ts'ung* lost their original symbolic power they too became ornaments, while jade was now used for sword fittings, hairpins, pendants, garment hooks, in fact wherever its qualities could show to best advantage. Until recently very few jades had been found in controlled excavations, and dating on purely stylistic grounds is, in view of the Chinese love of copying the antique, extremely unreliable. But the jade objects found in 1953 in a tomb at Yang-tzu-shan outside Chengtu confirm the impression that at this time the quality of carving rises to new heights; the stones are chosen for their rich, unctuous texture; the cutting is flawless and the finish beautiful. A chain of four discs in the British Museum, connected by links and carved from a single pebble less than nine inches long, is a technical *tour-de-force* which suggests that the iron drill and cutting disc were already in use. Few of the *pi* of the period are left plain; their surface is generally decorated with a row of spirals, either engraved or raised to form the popular 'grain pattern', and sometimes confined within an outer geometric border. Magnificent flat plaques in the form of dragons, tigers, birds and fishes combine an arresting silhouette with a surface treatment of extraordinary delicacy. One of the most beautiful early Chinese jades yet discovered is the celebrated disc in Kansas City ornamented with magnificent heraldic dragons, two on the outer rim, a third crawling round a small inner disc in the centre (Plate 13a).

As we survey the inlaid bronzes of Chin-ts'un, the mirrors of Shouchou, the marvellous lacquer-ware of Changsha, the jades and the minor arts, we become aware that the period between 500 and 200 B.C. was one of the great epochs in the history of Chinese art. Moreover, the forms perfected during these restless years, the vocabulary and syntax, as it were, of Chinese decorative art, were to remain the characteristic modes of artistic expression throughout her later history.

CHAPTER FIVE

The Ch'in and Han Dynasties

B y 221 B.C. the inexorable steamroller of the Ch'in armies
had crushed the remnants of the ancient feudal order. Now
all China was united under the iron rule of King Cheng,
who set up his capital in Hsien-yang and proclaimed himself
Ch'in Shih-huang-ti — First Emperor of the Ch'in Dynasty.
Aided by his Minister Li Ssu, an ardent Legalist, he proceeded to
consolidate the new state. He strengthened the northern frontiers
against the Huns and, at the cost of a million lives, linked up the
sections of wall built by the previous kings of Chao and Yen into a
continuous rampart 1,400 miles long. The boundaries of the
Empire were greatly extended, bringing South China and Tonkin
for the first time under Chinese rule. The feudal aristocracy were
dispossessed and forcibly moved in tens of thousands to Shensi;
rigid standardization of the written language, of weights and
measures and of wagon axles (important in the soft loess roads of
North China) was enforced, and over it all Shih-huang-ti set a
centralized bureaucracy controlled by the watchful eye of censors.
All that recalled the ancient glory of Chou was to be obliterated
from men's minds; copies of the classical texts were burned, and
the death penalty imposed on anyone found reading or even discussing the *Book of Songs* or the *Classic of History*. Many scholars
were martyred for attempting to protest. But while these measures
imposed an intolerable burden on the educated minority, they
unified the scattered tribes and principalities, and now for the
first time we can speak of China as a political and cultural entity.
This unity survived and was consolidated on more humane lines
in the Han Dynasty, so that the Chinese of today still look back on

this epoch with pride and call themselves 'men of Han'.

The megalomania of the First Emperor drove him to build at Hsien-yang vast palaces the like of which had never been seen before. One series, ranged along the riverside, copied the apartments of each of the feudal lords whom he had defeated. The climax was the O-p'ang or O-fang Kung; he never lived to complete it, and it was destroyed in the holocaust which, as so often in Chinese history, marked the fall of his Dynasty. The Emperor lived in constant fear of assassination, and the roads connecting his many palaces were protected by high walls. So great was his dread of even a natural death, that he was forever seeking through Taoist practitioners the secret of immortality. In his search for the elixir, tradition has it that he sent a company of aristocratic youths and girls across the Eastern Sea to where the fabulous Mount P'eng-lai rises amid the waves — ever receding as one approaches it. They never returned, and it is thought that they may have reached the shores of Japan.

Shih-huang-ti died in 210 B.C. The reign of his son Hu Hai was short and bitter. His assassination in 207 was the signal for a rebellion led by Hsiang Yü, a general of Ch'u, and Liu Pang, who had started his life as a bandit. In 206 the Ch'in capital was sacked; Hsiang Yü proclaimed himself King (Wang) of Ch'u, while Liu Pang took the crown of Han. For four years the two rival kings fought for supremacy, till finally in 202, when defeat seemed inevitable, Hsiang Yü committed suicide and Liu Pang, after the customary refusals, accepted the title of Emperor of the Han with the reign name Kao-tsu. He established his capital at Changan, and there inaugurated one of the longest dynasties in Chinese history.

So sharp was the popular reaction against the despotism of the Ch'in that the early Han rulers wisely adopted a policy of *laissez-faire* in domestic matters and even restored the old feudal order in a limited way. At first there was chaos and disunion, but Wen Ti (179–157 B.C.) brought the scattered empire together and began to revive classical learning and to restore to court life some of the dignity and order that had attended it under the Chou. The early Han emperors were constantly either fighting or bribing the Hsiung-nu, who had taken advantage of the fall of Ch'in to drive their arch-enemy the Yüeh-chih westwards across the deserts of Central Asia and invade North China. Finally, in 138 B.C. the Emperor Wu (140–87 B.C.) sent out a mission under General Chang Ch'ien to make contact with the Yüeh-chih and form an alliance with them against the Hsiung-nu. The Yüeh-chih were no longer interested in their old and now distant enemy and the mission failed; but Chang Ch'ien spent twelve years in the far western regions, where he found Chinese silk and bamboo brought there, he was told, by way of India. He returned to Changan with a report which must have stirred the public imagination as did the travels of Marco Polo or Vasco da Gama. Henceforth, China's eyes were turned westwards. Further expeditions, sent into distant Ferghana to obtain the famous 'blood-sweating' horses for the imperial stables, opened up a trade route which was to carry Chinese silk and lacquer to Rome, Egypt and Bactria. Travellers told of great snow-capped ranges reaching to the clouds, of fierce nomadic tribes and of the excitement of hunting wild game among the mountains. Somewhere beyond the horizon lay Mount K'un-lun, the axis of the world and home of Hsi Wang Mu, Queen Mother of the West, and the counterpart of the foam-washed P'eng-lai on which dwelt Tung Wang Kung, the immortal king of the East. During these first two centuries of the Han, indeed, the popular mind, from the Emperor down, was filled with fantastic lore, much of which is preserved in pseudo-classical texts such as the *Huai Nan Tzu* and *Shan-hai-ching* (Classic of Hills and Seas), which are invaluable sources for the interpretation of the more fabulous themes in Han art. With the unification of the Empire many of these cults and superstitions found their way to the capital, where were to be found shamans, magicians and oracles from all over China. Meanwhile the 'Taoists' were roaming the hillsides in search of the magical *ling-chih* (spirit fungus) which, if properly gathered and prepared, would guarantee one immortality, or at least a span of five hundred years. Yet, at the same time, Confucian ceremonies had been introduced at court, scholars and encyclopaedists had reinstated the classical texts, and Wu Ti, in spite of his private leanings towards Taoism, deliberately gave Confucian scholars precedence in his entourage.

It is these diverse elements in Han culture — native and foreign, Confucian and Taoist, courtly and popular — that give to Han art both its vigour and the immense variety of its styles and subject-matter.

When Wu Ti died, China was at one of the highest points of power in her history. The empire was secure; her arms were feared across the northern steppes, Chinese colonies were flourishing in Tonkin (Katigara), Manchuria, Korea and Central Asia. But Wu Ti's successors were weak and the administration crippled by palace intrigues and the power of the eunuchs, a new force in Chinese politics. In A.D. 9 a usurper named Wang Mang seized the throne and under the cloak of Confucian orthodoxy embarked upon a series of radical reforms which, had he been served by an honest and loyal administration, might have achieved a revolution in Chinese social and economic life. But by antagonizing the privileged class Wang Mang ensured his own downfall. He was murdered by a merchant and the brief Hsin Dynasty came to an end in A.D. 25. The Han house was restored and at once began the long task of reconstruction. From their new capital at Loyang they reached out once more into Central Asia, consolidated their hold on Annam and Tonkin, and for the first time made contact with Japan. By the end of the century so great was their prestige that for a time even the distant Yüeh-chih, now established as the Kushan Dynasty in Afghanistan and Northwest India, paid them tribute.

The Kushans, the only power in the history of Asia to straddle the Pamirs, brought Indian culture and religion into Central Asia. This region became a melting-pot of Indian, Sasanian and provincial Roman art and culture, which in turn travelled eastwards to China by way of the oases to north and south of the Tarim Basin. Buddhism must have been known by repute at least in the

Former Han — the mythical mount K'un-lun was very likely a Chinese version of the Buddhist Meru, or the Hindu Kailas, the axis of the universe — but now it finally took root on Chinese soil. The well-known story of the Emperor Ming who in A.D. 67 dreamed of a 'golden man' (i.e. a Buddhist image) in the far west and sent emissaries to fetch it is a late fabrication, but already two years earlier a certain Liu Ying, Prince of Ch'u, had held a great feast for monks (*śramana*) and lay brethren, which indicates that at

Seated Buddha in *abhaya-mudrā*. Rubbing of a relief in a Later Han shaft a Chiating, Szechwan. (After *Ssu-ch'uan Han-tai hua-hsiang hsüan-chi*.)

least one monastic community was in existence in Central China by that date, while there are several references to Buddhism in the *Hsi-ching-fu*, 'Rhapsody (or "Rhyme-prose")' on the Western Capital' (Ch'ang-an) by Chang Heng (A.D. 78–139). During the second century there was also flourishing a Buddhist community in Katigara (modern Vietnam), whence the new faith spread northwards into South China and Szechwan.

Until the time of troubles that accompanied the downfall of the Han, however, Buddhism was merely one among many popular cults. Officially, Confucianism still reigned supreme, and the

Later Han saw the enormous expansion of a scholarly and official class nurtured in the Confucian doctrines. Many of these men had been trained in the Imperial Academy, founded by Wu Ti in 136 B.C. From its graduates, selected by competitive examination in the Classics, were drawn recruits for that remarkable civil service which was to serve China for the next two thousand years. Unswerving loyalty to the Emperor, respect for scholarship, and a rigid conservatism which sought for every measure the sanction of antiquity — these became the guiding principles of Chinese social and political life. Such ideals, however, offer no stimulus to the imagination, and it was not until Confucianism was enriched by Buddhist metaphysics in the Sung Dynasty that it became a thesource of highest inspiration to painters and poets.

Already in the Former Han, those who possessed skills useful to the Emperor were organized under a bureau known as the Yellow Gate (*huang-men*), which was based on the somewhat idealized picture of Chou institutions set out in the *Chou-li*. The highest ranks in this professional hierarchy were known as *tai-chao*, officials in attendance on the Emperor. These included not only painters, Confucian scholars and astrologers, but also jugglers, wrestlers, and fire-swallowers, who might be called upon at any time to display their various skills in the imperial presence. The lower ranks of artists and artisans, those who made and decorated furniture and utensils for court use, for example, were known as *hua-kung*. This organization was not confined to the court, however: each commandery — in theory — had its own agency (*kung-kuan*) for the production and decoration of such things as ritual vessels, robes, weapons and lacquer ware, for which latter Ch'u and Shu (Szechwan) were especially famous. Gradually, however, this system was relaxed. Under the Later Han, the emergence of the scholar-official class, the decline of the rigid Confucian order at court, and the corresponding rise of Taoist individualism, all combined to reduce the importance and activity of these largely anonymous professionals. By the end of the dynasty there had come into being a gulf between the intellectual aristocracy on the one hand and the unlettered craftsmen on the other which was to have a profound influence on the character of later Chinese art.

The wonders of Changan and Loyang are vividly described in the *fu* rhapsodies on the Han capitals by Chang Heng and Ssu-ma Hsiang-ju, and though their beauties may have been somewhat exaggerated, some idea of the scale of the palace and government buildings can be gauged from the fact that the audience hall of the Wei-yang Palace at Changan was over 400 feet long — considerably longer than the T'ai-ho-tien, its counterpart in latter-day Peking. To the west of the capital Han Wu Ti built a pleasure palace, linked to the Wei-yang Palace within the city by a covered two-storey gallery ten miles long. At Loyang the palace lay in the centre of the city with a park behind it, built up with artificial lakes and hills into a fairy landscape in which the Emperor could indulge his Taoist fancies. Other parks further from the capital and likewise landscaped on a colossal scale were stocked with all manner of game birds and beasts — some brought as tribute from remote corners of the empire. From time to time a vast imperial hunt, or rather slaughter, was organized, followed by lavish feasting and entertainments. The *fu* poems describe these extraordinary spectacles, in which by some Leonardesque device P'eng-lai and K'un-lun, with wild animals fighting on their slopes, might be made to appear out of a cloud of smoke while attendants in galleries over-

Han pottery watch-tower

head crashed great stones together to simulate thunder. These hunts among mountains and the wild, extravagant orgies that followed them were to become favourite subjects in Han art.

The palace gateways were marked by pairs of tall watch-towers (*ch'üeh*), while within its precincts stood multi-storey pavilions (*lou*) or towers (*t'ai*) which were used for entertainment, for admiring the view, or simply for storage. When Loyang burned in A.D. 185 the Cloud Tower (*Yün-t'ai*) went up in flames, and with it a huge collection of paintings, books, records and *objets-d'art* — to say nothing of the portraits of thirty-two distinguished generals which Wu Ti had had painted on the walls of the tower itself. This was but one of the many occasions in Chinese history when the art treasures accumulated through a whole dynasty were destroyed in a few hours. Palaces, mansions, ancestral halls were built of timber, their straight-tiled roofs supported by a simple system of brackets resting on wooden pillars (Plate 20a). Their timberwork was picked out in rich colours and their inner walls, like those of the Yün-t'ai, were often decorated with wall paintings.

These great mansions come vividly before our eyes as we read such poems as the *Chao Hun*, a passionate appeal addressed by an unknown Han author to the soul of a King which, in his illness, has left his body and gone wandering to the edge of the world. To lure it back, the poet describes the delights that await it in the palace:

'O soul, come back! Return to your old abode.
All the quarters of the world are full of harm and evil.
Hear while I describe for you your quiet and reposeful home.
High halls and deep chambers, with railings and tiered balconies;
Stepped terraces, storeyed pavilions, whose tops look on the high mountains;
Lattice doors with scarlet interstices, and carving on the square lintels;

Draughtless rooms for winter; galleries cool in summer;

Streams and gullies wind in and out, purling prettily;

A warm breeze bends the melilotus and sets the tall orchids swaying.

Crossing the hall into the apartments, the ceilings and floors are vermilion,

The chambers of polished stone, with kingfisher hangings on jasper hooks;

Bedspreads of kingfisher seeded with pearls, all dazzling in brightness;

Arras of fine silk covers the walls; damask canopies stretch overhead,

Braids and ribbons, brocades and satins, fastened with rings of precious stone,

Many a rare and precious thing is to be seen in the furnishings of the chamber.

Bright candles of orchid-perfumed fat light up flower-like faces that await you;

Twice eight handmaids to serve your bed, each night alternating in duty,

The lovely daughters of noble families, far excelling common maidens. . . .

O soul, come back!'[1]

Much of our knowledge of Han architecture is derived from the reliefs and engravings or the stone slabs lining tombs and tomb shrines. In crude perspective, they show two-storeyed gateways flanked with towers and often surmounted by a strutting phoenix, symbol of peace and of the south. An engraved stone from I-nan, Shantung, depicts a large country house with two courtyards, double doors with mask-handles and flanking storage towers. The reliefs from the Wu family shrines, also in Shantung, show a two-storeyed house in whose kitchens on the ground floor a banquet is

[1] David Hawkes, *Ch'u Tz'u*, 105–7. Hawkes suggests (p. 103) that this poem may have been written in 208 or 207 B.C.

in preparation, while the host entertains his guests on the *piano nobile* above. The humbler dwellings — farm houses, granaries, even pig-sties and watchmen's huts — survive in the rough and lively pottery models made to be placed in the tombs.

Never in Chinese history, indeed, was so much care lavished on the tomb and its contents as in the Han Dynasty. Huge numbers have survived and every day more are revealed. They are interesting not only for their contents but also for their structure, which varies considerably in different areas and provides us with almost the only surviving remains of Han architecture. They are not, of

Isometric sketch of a third-century stone tomb at I-nan, Shantung.
(After *I-nan ku-hua-hsiang shih-mu fa-chüeh pao-kao.*)

course, representative of Han building as a whole, nearly all of which was carried out in timber; the more adventurous techniques of the dome and vault in brick or stone were reserved almost exclusively for the permanent mansions of the dead. In the Chinese colonies in Korea and Manchuria tombs were square or rectangular with flat roofs of stone slabs supported on stone pillars, or shaped like clusters of beehives with corbelled brick vaults. Tombs in Shantung were also of stone, sunk in the ground, while before them stood stone shrines for offerings to the spirits of the departed. A magnificent example, discovered at I-nan, is shown in the sketch on this page. At Nanyang in southern Honan they were brick-vaulted, long and narrow, lined with stone panels carved in relief. Sometimes the walls were plastered and painted. In Szechwan most of the tombs are small barrel-vaulted structures built of bricks on the inner face of which a lively scene was stamped in relief, though at Chiating deep tomb shafts were cut into the cliffs in groups with a common vestibule carved out to suggest a timber building. The tombs of the Ch'u people of Central China, whose culture underwent a considerable revival during the Han, were large rectangular chambers up to seventy feet long vaulted in brick and, as in the Late Chou, lined with timber. But elaborate as some of them were, they were nothing to the tombs of the Ch'in and Han emperors, whose stone passages and vaults were enclosed in the heart of an enormous artificial hill approached by a 'spirit way' lined with colossal guardian figures carved in stone, and guarded by booby-traps. All the imperial tombs were desecrated during the rebellions at the end of the Han Dynasty.

It is in the Han Dynasty that we encounter the earliest monumental sculpture in stone. Its appearance at a time when China was highly receptive to western ideas and forms, combined with the style of the sculpture itself, are more than suggestive of foreign origins. Near Hsienyang in Shensi is a mound believed to be the grave of General Ho Ch'ü-ping who died in 117 B.C. after a lifetime of successful campaigning against the western barbarians. Before the tomb a life-size stone figure of a horse stands with majestic indifference over a fallen barbarian soldier who is attempting to kill him with his bow. The modelling is massive but shallow, giving the impression more of two reliefs back to back than of carving in the round, and indeed in its heavy, flat and somewhat coarse treatment this piece is from the technical point of view more reminiscent of the Sasanian rock-cut reliefs at Tak-i Bustan in Persia than of anything in early Chinese art (Plate 14a). Many writers have pointed out how appropriate such a monument would be to a Chinese general whose victories over the western nomads were due to the very horses which China had acquired from their enemy and used so effectively against them. Clearly, however, the Chinese sculptors had not yet mastered the art of carving in the round on a big scale, and the other figures before the tomb — a buffalo and a recumbent horse — are disengaged from the original boulder only to the degree necessary to indicate their form, and no more.

While the idea of executing stone sculpture in relief was probably derived from Western Asia, it had been thoroughly assimilated by the Later Han. Stone reliefs have been found in almost every part of China. The most truly sculptural are the animals and figures carved on a pair of funerary pillars standing before the tomb of an official named Shen who was buried at Ch'ü-hsien in Szechwan during the second century A.D. The pillars themselves are timber towers translated into stone (Plate 14b). In high relief between the beam-ends is a monster like a gargoyle; at the corners crouching Atlantean figures — perhaps representing barbarian prisoners — support the beams, while above on each main face stand a beautifully-modelled deer and rider. The only figures in flat relief are the directional symbols: on the east the dragon, on the west the tiger, to north the 'dark warrior' (snake and tortoise), to south the phoenix.

Nearly all of what passes for 'relief sculpture' in the Han period, however, is not really sculpture at all, so much engraving in the flat surface of a stone slab, or flat relief with the background cut back and striated to give a contrasting texture. These slabs preserve the subject matter — and something even of the composition — of the lost mural paintings of the Han Dynasty. They not only give a vivid picture of daily life in this far-off time, but also show clear regional differences in style, so that we can without much difficulty identify the elegant dignity of some of the Shantung reliefs, the luxuriance of the stones from Nanyang in Honan, the wild, extravagant manner of the reliefs from distant Szechwan. After the Han Dynasty China becomes ever more of a single cultural entity, and these regional styles will very largely disappear.

The stone shrines standing before the tombs were often decorated with engraved designs, the best known series being those at the Hsiao-t'ang-shan (Hill of the Hall of Filial Piety) near Fei-ch'eng in Shantung, and the slabs from four now-demolished shrines of the Wu family near Chia-hsiang in southwestern Shantung, which are dated by their inscriptions between A.D. 145 and 168. The scenes, which are left in silhouette on the flat surface of the stone while the background is cut away, give a remarkable picture of the syncretic nature of Han art, in which Confucian ideals, historical events (real and legendary), and 'Taoist' mythology and folklore are all brought together. On the shallow end gables of two of the shrines to east and west we find Tung Wang Kung and Hsi Wang Mu respectively. Below we see the legendary meetings of Confucius and Lao Tzu, or ancient kings, filial sons and virtuous women. The attempted assassination of Ch'in Shih-huang-ti (Plate 15a), and his effort to raise one of the tripods of the Emperor Yü, are favourite themes. The central recess and most of the remaining space is devoted to a magnificent banqueting scene. Below, all the preparations for the feast are shown with great precision and no little humour, while above, the host (presumably the deceased) welcomes his guests in a pavilion flanked by towers. We see the ponderous officials in their voluminous robes, the short deep-chested horses of Central Asian stock who trot with high-stepping precision while the air above them is filled with swirling clouds and loud with the clamour of a fantastic assortment of winged creatures come to do honour to the dead. In this fabulous setting, the soul of the deceased can pass easily from the world of men to the world of the spirits.

There can be little doubt that both the style and the subject-matter owe much to the great cycles of wall-paintings in halls and palaces, all trace of which has long since disappeared. Only a few miles away from the Wu family tombs lay the Ling-kuang Palace built by a brother of Han Wu-ti. The fame of its wall-paintings is celebrated in a poem by Wang Yen-shou, written a few years before the Wu shrines were erected, which exactly describes the subject-matter of their reliefs:

Upon the great walls
Flickering in a dim semblance glint and hover
The Spirits of the Dead.
And here all Heaven and Earth is painted, all living things
After their tribes, and all wild marryings
Of sort with sort; strange spirits of the sea,
Gods of the hills. To all their thousand guises
Had the painter formed
His reds and blues, and all the wonders of life
Had he shaped truthfully and coloured after their kinds. . . .[1]

By contrast with these lost wall-paintings, the reliefs from
vaulted brick tombs in distant Szechwan show an easy naturalism
far in advance of the pictorial art of the rest of China at this period.
One of these moulded panels shows salt mines set in a landscape
of wooded hills, with towers for hoists, pipe-lines of bamboo
carrying the brine to the evaporating pans, methods still in use in
Szechwan in the twentieth century. Another, divided horizontally,
shows in the lower half men harvesting and threshing in the rice-
fields, while another brings their lunch; above, two hunters kneel
at the shore of a lake, shooting up at the rising ducks with arrows
trailing long cords (Plate 15b).

The Wu Liang reliefs are in one plane, the only concession to
the third dimension being to twist a chariot slightly sideways to
show both wheels, while its three horses are drawn in echelon as
on an early Greek vase. A more advanced treatment of architecture
is seen in the I-nan reliefs where buildings are boldly placed on a
diagonal and we are able to see over roofs and into courtyards. It
is in Szechwan, however, that we first encounter a convincing
landscape in three dimensions. In the hunting scene (Plate 15b),
for example, the border of the lake winds back, seeming almost to
lose itself in the mist, while behind the hunters stand two bare
trees. On the surface of the water are fishes and lotus flowers, and

[1] Translated by Arthur Waley in his *Introduction to the Study of Chinese Painting*,
30–31.

ducks swimming away towards the upper border of the panel as fast as they can go. It shows that already in the Later Han artists in Szechwan — perhaps because it was furthest removed from the formal 'court style' of Honan and Shantung — were beginning to solve the problem of *continuous* recession in depth which, three hundred years later, was still to defeat the engraver of the famous sarcophagus in the Nelson Gallery.

Landscape must however have played a very subordinate part in the great fresco cycles which decorated the palaces and ancestral halls. The themes were most often Confucian, as illustrated by a passage from the *Han-shu*: 'The Mother of Jih Ti in teaching her sons had very high standards: the Emperor (Wu Ti) heard of it and was pleased. When she fell ill and died, he ordered her portrait to be painted on the walls of the Kan-ch'üan Palace in Shensi. . . . Every time Jih Ti saw the portrait he did obeisance to it and wept before he passed on.' A rough provincial echo of this kind of painting survives in the large figures of civil and military officials paying their respects to the deceased, painted on the walls of a tomb at Wang-tu in Hopei. Other passages in the *Han-shu* bear witness to the Taoist predilections of the Han Emperors. Wu Ti for example, had a tower in the Kan-ch'üan Palace where were depicted 'the demons and deities of Heaven, Earth, and the Supreme Unity. Sacrificial utensils were set out, by which the divine beings were to be addressed.'

The finest Han wall-paintings yet discovered line the plastered walls of a stone tomb at Liao-yang in Manchuria. Their theme is the most popular one in Han funerary art — a splendid entertainment given by the deceased for his friends and fellow officials. We find him ensconced in a pavilion receiving two guests, while beneath a three-storey tower the entertainment is in progress, with feasting, juggling, acrobatic feats, a dance round a great revolving drum, and a group of four girl musicians seated on a mat, with clappers, *p'i-p'a* (guitar), *hsiao* (straight flute) and *ch'in* (lute). On one wall gentlemen in covered carriages pass across the scene at a smart pace, accompanied by others on horseback (Plate 16a). These too are stock subjects in Han funerary art. The only deliberate perspective device is the placing of the carriages at a slight angle so that the dashboard, both occupants, both wheels and horses are clearly visible. Other horsemen gallop along near the top of the panel, one partly concealed by his horse's head which is turned right back to see who is following. There is no ground, no hint of any setting, and yet we seem to be looking down from above on a rolling plain across which these horsemen are dashing with tremendous speed. Indeed the invention of aerial perspective in the Han Dynasty, which puts everything into its proper position and yet preserves the sense of limitless space, was to render unnecessary for the Chinese artist the scientific treatment of perspective which was to present such a challenge to the western painter.

This subtle sense of space appears too in the relationship between the figures painted on a celebrated series of tiles from the gables of a tomb-shrine now in the Boston Museum of Fine Arts. One scene depicts an animal combat; another may represent, as Sickman has suggested, an incident in the life of the virtuous Empress Chiang of the ninth century B.C. who took off her jewels and demanded to be incarcerated in the jail for court ladies as a protest against the Emperor's dissipation — a threat which soon brought him to his senses. The figures, drawn in long sweeping lines with a sensitive, pliant brush, stand and move with wonderful ease and grace; the men discuss the affair in dignified agitation (Plate 16b) while the women, elegant and playful, seem to find the whole incident rather amusing. Happy the man whose tomb was adorned with such charming figures!

The power of the Chinese craftsmen to impart life and movement to his subjects is vividly shown in the decoration of the lacquer objects for which Szechwan province was especially famous. That the output of her factories — especially those of Shu and Kuang-han — must have been considerable we know from the first century *Discourses on Salt and Iron*, whose author protests that the wealthy classes were spending five million cash annually on lacquer alone. A number of Szechwan lacquer bowls, cups and boxes, bearing dates between 85 B.C. and A.D. 71, have been found in tombs in the vicinity of Pyongyang in North Korea. Most famous, though undated, is the 'painted basket' (actually a box) found in a tomb at Lolang.

On its lid and sides are ninety-four figures of filial sons, virtuous and wicked rulers and ancient worthies. All are sitting on the floor, but monotony is avoided by the skill and inventiveness with which they turn to one side or the other, gesticulate or engage in lively conversation (Plate 18a). Even in this crowded space we find the same sense of individuality, of interval and

Detail of decoration on an inlaid bronze tube in the Hosokawa collection. Han Dynasty.

psychological relationship between the figures as we encountered on the Boston tiles. Other lacquer objects such as bowls and trays, of which many beautiful examples have been preserved in the waterlogged soil of Changsha, are adorned with sweeping scrolls and volutes evolved out of the décor of the lacquers and inlaid bronzes of the Warring States. Now, however, these whirls erupt into flame-like tongues. The presence of a flying phoenix turns these tongues into clouds; when set about with tigers, deer and hunters they are magically transformed into hills; sometimes the transformation is aided — as on a beautiful inlaid bronze tube in the Hosokawa collection — by vertical striations suggesting grass, or by little trees which grow from the volutes on some of the painted pottery *hu*. There is no attempt to depict a real landscape; rather has the craftsman taken the sweeping volute as the essential form common to all things in nature, and by means of a few accessories transformed it into clouds, waves or mountains without robbing it of any of its rhythmic force. Because its forms follow the natural sweep and movement of the artist's hand they express the rhythms of nature itself.

From the kind of pictorial art that I have been describing, rough and provincial as most of it is, we may imagine what the finest Han paintings must have been like. Although paper had been invented by the end of the Western Han, it is likely that paintings were still executed chiefly on long rolls of silk, in which the pictures alternated with blocks of text. Figure subjects included illustrations to the Classics and other more fanciful works such as the *Huai Nan Tzu* and *Shan-hai-ching*; while for landscape themes there were illustrations to the *fu* rhapsodies describing the royal palaces and hunting parks, and the wonders of the northern and southern capitals. Some of the most interesting attempts at landscape must have been the pictorial maps made for strategic purposes or for flood control, of which the most ambitious was probably the huge sectional relief map of China made by the cartographer Hsieh Chuang in the fifth century. Not one of these paintings has survived, however. Most of the imperial collection was destroyed in the sack of the capital in A.D. 190. Seventy cartloads — all that remained — were sent westwards for safety, but half was lost on the way, and remnants were used by the soldiers to patch their tents.

With the fall of the Chou the traditional rituals were forgotten, and consequently Han bronzes, while many were no doubt used in domestic rites of various sorts, are generally more utilitarian or decorative than those of Shang and Chou. Shapes are simple and functional, the commonest being the deep dish and the wine-jar (*hu*) which were often decorated with inlaid designs in gold or silver. One object with definite ritual associations was the *po-shan hsiang-lu*, a censer in the shape of a fairy mountain often covered with animals, hunters and trees modelled in relief. Its base is lapped by the waves of the Eastern Sea, while a hole behind each little peak emits the incense smoke symbolizing the cloud-vapour (*yün-ch'i*) which is the exhalation of the fairy mountain — and indeed of all mountains, for, according to traditional Chinese belief, all nature is alive and 'breathing' (Plate 17). In Han tombs there have been found great quantities of bronze objects, including harness and carriage fittings, swords and knives, utensils and belt buckles, many of which are inlaid with gold or silver, turquoise or jade. Even the trigger mechanism of a crossbow was often so cunningly inlaid as to make it an object of beauty. Some of these show the powerful impact of the 'animal style' of the Ordos region which in turn was influenced by that curious mixture of stylization and brutal realism characteristic of the art of the northern steppes.

The bronze mirrors of the Han Dynasty continue the traditions developed at Loyang and Shouchou during the Warring States. The Shouchou coiled dragon design becomes more complex and crowded, the dragon's body being drawn in double or triple lines, while the background is generally cross-hatched. Another group, also chiefly from Shouchou, has an all-over design of spirals on which a scallopped many-pointed device is sometimes superimposed; its significance may be astronomical. Most interesting and most pregnant with symbolic meaning are the so-called TLV mirrors, of which the finest were produced in the Loyang region between 100 B.C. and A.D. 100, although the design was already being used on mirror-backs in the second century B.C.

A typical TLV mirror (Plate 18b) has a large central boss surrounded by a square panel with twelve smaller bosses separating the characters of the twelve Earthly Branches. The T's, L's and V's protrude into a circular zone adorned with animals which, taken together with the fifth, central zone, symbolize the five elements, a system of cosmology first set down by Tsou Yen (*c.* 350–270 B.C.) and very popular in Han times. According to this system, the great ultimate (*t'ai-i*) produces the positive-negative dualism of *yang* and *yin*, the interaction of which in turn gives birth to the five elements (*wu-hsing*) from which all events and objects are derived. The way in which the five elements work upon each other and are symbolized is as follows:

element	function	colour	direction	season	symbol
WATER	puts out fire	black	north	winter	'black warrior' (snake and tortoise)
FIRE	melts metal	red	south	summer	bird (phoenix)
METAL	destroys wood	white	west	autumn	tiger
WOOD	overcomes earth	green	east	spring	dragon
EARTH	absorbs water	yellow	centre		*ts'ung*

On the TLV mirror, the central circle within a square represents the earth symbol, *ts'ung*, while the four directions, seasons and colours are symbolized by their animals in the appropriate quarters. Many bear inscriptions which clearly set out the meaning and purpose of the design, such as this one on a mirror in the Museum of Far Eastern Antiquities, Stockholm: 'The Imperial mirror of the *Shang-fang* (imperial workshop),' it runs, 'is truly without blemish; a skilled artisan has engraved it and achieved a decoration; to the left the Dragon and to the right the Tiger eliminate what is baleful; the Red Bird and Black Warrior conform to the *yin* and *yang* forces; may your sons and grandsons be complete in number and be in the centre; on it are Immortals such as are customary (on mirrors); may you long preserve your two parents; may your joy and wealth be splendid; may your longevity outstrip that of metal and stone; may you be like a prince or a king.'[1]

The TLV design was not simply an auspicious cosmological diagram; it was also the board for playing *liu-po*, a popular game in Han times which is represented on a number of Han reliefs and in clay models. The object of this game, which Professor Yang

[1] B. Karlgren, 'Early Chinese Mirror Inscriptions', *B.M.F.E.A.* 6 (1934), 49.

Lien-sheng has reconstructed from ancient texts, is to capture your opponent's men or drive them into the 'benders' (presumably the L's on the outer edge), in order to attain the centre, or, as Cammann has put it; 'to establish an axis for symbolic control of the Universe'. In Han mythology *liu-po* was a favourite game of Tung Wang Kung, and of ambitious human heroes who sought to pitch their skill against that of the gods and, by defeating them,

Immortals playing *liu-po*; rubbing from stone relief from tomb at Hsin-chin, Szechwan. Han Dynasty.

to acquire magic powers. To judge by the mirror designs, the game seems to have gone out of fashion towards the end of the Han Dynasty. The mirror-backs of Late Han and the Three Kingdoms often preserve the directional symbolism, but now become crowded with figures fully modelled in relief; for the most part these are Taoist fairies and immortals, but after A.D. 300 Buddhist themes begin to appear as well.

In jade carving the main technical advance at the end of the Chou Dynasty and the beginning of the Han was in the introduction of iron cutting tools. The iron drill made it possible to cut deep into the stone, while the rotary cutting disc enabled the lapidary to hollow out quite large pebbles into the form of toilet boxes and bowls such as the *yü-shang*, 'winged wine cup', a small oval bowl with flanges on the long sides made for offerings in the tombs. They have been found sometimes in sets standing on a tray, not only in jade but also in pottery, silver and lacquer. This new technical freedom made the lapidary more adventurous, inspiring him to carve, in three dimensions, figurines and animals — of which perhaps the most beautiful specimen is the famous horse in the Victoria and Albert Museum (Plate 19a). He no longer rejects the flawed stone, but begins to exploit the discolorations: the brown stain, for instance, becomes a dragon on a white cloud. Jade has by this time begun to lose its ritual significance; it now becomes instead the delight of the scholar and the gentleman, for whom its ancient associations and beauty of colour and texture will become a source of the profoundest intellectual and sensual pleasure. Henceforward he will be able to enjoy his pendants and garment-hooks, his seals and the other playthings on his desk, in the confident knowledge that in them aesthetic and moral beauty are united.

Under the Han Dynasty, the customs and amenities which in Shang and Chou had been confined to a minute privileged aristocracy in a small region now spread over a much wider area and a much larger segment of society. At the same time, Chinese handicrafts have been found far beyond her own frontiers — in Indochina and Siberia, Korea and Afghanistan. The ruins of a Chinese-style palace recently discovered in Southern Siberia contained Chinese bronze fittings, coins, tiles and pottery house models, the latter presumably made locally by Chinese potters. Chinese archaeologists have suggested that this might have been the palace of the daughter of Madame Wen-chi, who had been married to a chieftain of the Hsiung-nu in A.D. 195 but eventually was forced to return to China leaving her devoted husband and children behind.

Chinese textiles, too, reached the limits of the civilized world. The Greek word Seres, 'the Silk People,' was probably first used not of the Chinese themselves — of whom the Greeks had no direct knowledge — but of the Western Asiatic tribes who traded in this precious commodity. Direct intercourse with China came only after Chang Ch'ien's expedition, and the establishment of the 'Silk Road' across Central Asia. This great caravan route, leaving China at the Jade Gate in modern Kansu, crossed Central Asia to north or south of the Taklamakan Desert, reuniting in the region of Kashgar whence one branch led westwards across Persia to the Mediterranean world while the other struck south into Gandhāra and India. Chinese stuffs have been found in the Crimea, in Afghanistan, Palmyra and Egypt, while in Rome in the time of

Figured silk fabric from Noin-Ula, Siberia. Han Dynasty.
(Redrawn by the Author.)

Augustus there was a special market for imported Chinese silk in Vicus Tuscus. According to legend, it was the consort of the Yellow Emperor herself who first taught the Chinese people the cultivation of the mulberry on which the silk-worms feed, the spinning, dyeing and weaving of the threads, and so important has the industry been to China that, until the Revolution of 1911, the Empress sacrificed to her spirit every year in her own temple in Peking. Evidence of the art of weaving was found in the Neolithic village of Pan-p'o in Honan; the Shang people at Anyang had tailored clothing of silk and hemp, while a number of passages in the *Book of Songs* refer to coloured woven silk. Silk panels with painted designs have been found in Late Chou graves at Changsha; but the most remarkable finds of early Chinese textiles were made by Sir Aurel Stein in the desert sand of Loulan in Mongolia, and by the Kozlov expedition in waterlogged tumulus graves in the Noin-Ula region of Siberia. The Noin-Ula graves were as richly festooned with silk hangings as a modern Russian railway carriage. The techniques included moiré, damask, gauze, quilting and embroidery, and the designs were basically of three kinds: pictorial, generally representing fierce animal combats such as appear also on the Ordos bronzes; diapered, with geometrical motifs repeated over the whole surface; or, thirdly, composed of those endless rhythmic cloud-volutes which we have already encountered on the inlaid bronzes, set about with horsemen, deer, tigers and more fabulous creatures (Plate 19b.) The remarkable silk panel from Noin-Ula illustrated on facing page is a kind of 'Taoist' landscape composed of giant spirit-fungus (*ling-chih*) alternating with rocky crags topped by phoenixes and adorned with formalised trees, executed in a mixed Chinese-Western style which suggests that Chinese weavers were already designing for the export market.

Han ceramics vary enormously in quality, from unglazed and roughly modelled earthenware to a high-fired, glazed stoneware verging on porcelain. The character *tz'u*, which already in the Han dictionary *Shuo-wen* denoted earthenware, probably did not come to mean true porcelain until the T'ang period; during the Six Dynasties it referred to a hard fine stoneware, or 'proto-porcelain', which rang when struck. Most of the grave goods however were in coarse pottery generally covered with a lead glaze which easily oxidizes, producing that silvery-green iridescence which is so attractive a feature of this class of Han wares. The technique of lead glazing was known in the Mediterranean world before the Han, and if not discovered independently may have been introduced by way of Central Asia. The finest of these lead glazed wares are the jars (*hu*) for grain or wine, — one labelled 'for white wine' has recently been found in a tomb in Wen-teng-hsien, Shantung. Their shapes are simple and robust, the imitation of bronze being aided by very precise finish and the application of *t'ao-t'ieh* masks in relief, while incised lines or geometric motifs round the shoulder enhance the beauty of their form. Sometimes they are decorated with a frieze depicting, in relief under the glaze, a 'hunt among mountains', in which all manner of creatures real and imaginary chase each other round and round — as on those extraordinary full-scale models of Mount P'eng-lai which were made to appear at the hunting feasts of the Han Emperors. These reliefs, in which we often find towering ranges of hills, may well preserve the designs of Han scroll paintings on silk.

In Han times, many people believed that on quitting this world one who had the secret of immortality could take with him to

The hunt among the mountains. Relief on the shoulder of a pottery *hu* in the collection of H.M. the King of Sweden. (After Palmgren, *Selected Antiquities from the Collection of Gustav Adolf, Crown Prince of Sweden*.)

heaven his family, servants, personal possessions, domestic animals, and even his house. As these could not actually accompany him, models (*ming-ch'i*) were placed in the tomb, and the custom persisted long after belief in immortality died out. Thus we find in the Han tombs a retinue of servants and guards, farm hands, musicians and jugglers such as its occupant probably never enjoyed in his lifetime. There were barns with fowl modelled in relief on the top. There were tall watch-towers in several storeys, their wooden beams and transoms either indicated by incisions in the clay or painted in red. A celebrated three-storey house in the Nelson Gallery has its structural parts picked out in colour while the magical *fu-sang* tree with its crows, emblems of the sun and of the south, are painted in panels on its walls — possibly to counteract the effects of an inauspicious orientation of the tomb (Plate 20a). The houses and barns of the South China tombs are raised on stilts, like those in Southeast Asia today. Farm animals are modelled with uncanny realism; watchdogs from Szechwan graves are squat and menacing; those from Changsha, with heads erect and muzzles quivering, so alert one can almost hear them sniffing (Plate 21b). These figurines are a useful source of information on the daily life, beliefs and economy of Han China. They illustrate too the extent of China's foreign contacts at this time. The pottery stand for a bronze 'coin-tree' (Plate 20b) found in a grave in Szechwan, for example, is decorated with a frieze of elephants in relief, modelled with a lively naturalism that has no counterpart in other Han reliefs, but at once calls to mind the animals of the Four Quarters carved on the capital of the Aśokan column at Sarnath. Some of the Han figurines were individually modelled, but the majority of the smaller pieces were mass-produced in moulds: though the forms are reduced to essentials, none of their vitality and character is lost. At Changsha, where the clay was often poor and glazes apt to flake off, the *ming-ch'i* were generally made of painted wood, which, like the silk and lacquer found in the Changsha tombs, has miraculously survived the ravages of time.

Of quite a different kind was the fine quality felspathic stoneware, which was made in a number of centres in Chekiang. This ancestor of the Sung celadons has a hard body and thin glaze ranging in colour from grey through olive-green to brown. It is often called Yüeh ware because the type-site is at Chiu-yen near Shao-hsing, the old name of which is Yüeh-chou. Recent Chinese writers confine the term Yüeh ware to the porcellanous celadon made for the court of Wu-Yüeh in the tenth century, calling all earlier celadons simply *ch'ing tz'u*, 'green porcelain'. However, in translation this is misleading, as some of it can hardly be called green, and none of it is true porcelain. In this book, therefore, the term Yüeh ware is retained to cover the whole huge family of pre-Sung Chekiang celadons.[1]

[1] As fresh discoveries increase the number of known kilns,— only a very few of which are mentioned in this book,— the problem of nomenclature becomes more and more acute. But until Chinese ceramics experts produce a new definitive classification it would not be helpful to the reader to depart too far from accepted names for well-known wares. A full inventory of discoveries between 1950 and 1965 (in Chinese) will be found in *Wen Wu* 1965.9, pp. 46–54.

The Chiu-yen kilns were in operation at least from the first century A.D., those at Te-ch'ing, north of Hangchow, perhaps even earlier. Many of their products, found in dated tombs in the Nanking region, are imitations of bronze vessels, even to the loop-handles and *t'ao-t'ieh* masks that adorn them. Some are stamped with geometric or diaper designs under the glaze (Plate 21a), preserving an ancient tradition of Central and South China which spread not only northwards but also into the Nan-hai, the peninsula and islands of Southeast Asia. Gradually, however, true ceramic forms began to emerge, aided by a rich, luminous and even luscious glaze. The Chiu-yen kilns seem to have closed down in the sixth century, after which the Yüeh tradition was carried on in many parts of Chekiang, the chief factories being round the shores of Shang-lin Hu in Yü-yao-hsien, where the remains of more than twenty celadon kilns have so far been discovered.

CHAPTER SIX

The Six Dynasties

During the four hundred years between the fall of the Han Dynasty and the rise of the T'ang, China went through a period of political, social and intellectual ferment comparable to that of modern Europe. No less than thirty dynasties and lesser kingdoms passed across the scene before the Sui reunited the Empire in 581. At the fall of the Han Dynasty in A.D. 220 China was divided into the Three Kingdoms of Wu, Wei, and Shu; in 280 it was once more reunited under a Wei king who named his dynasty Chin. Beyond the northern frontiers, the Hsiung-nu and the Hsien-pi were watching with interest the incessant civil wars to which the now shrunken empire was victim. When, soon after A.D. 300, two rival princes rashly appealed to them for aid, they promptly advanced into China. In 311 the Hsiung-nu captured Loyang, massacred twenty thousand of its inhabitants and took the Emperor prisoner; they then moved on to Changan which they put to the sack, while the Chin court fled in panic to Nanking. The Hsiung-nu and Hsien-pi were not the only tribes to take advantage of China's weakness to invade the north; sixteen petty barbarian kingdoms were to rise and fall before the Toba Wei, a Turkish tribe, brought the whole of North China under their rule in 469. They established their capital near Ta-t'ung in Northern Shensi, abandoned their nomadic way of life and adopted Chinese dress, eventually becoming so sinicized that the use of the Toba language was forbidden altogether. At the same time, they energetically defended their northern borders against other and more barbarous tribes, and pushed their cavalry as far as Kucha in the Tarim Basin, thus reopening the great trade route into Central Asia.

The barbarian invasions had split China into two countries, with two cultures. Thousands of Chinese had migrated to the south. Nanking now became the cultural and political centre of 'free China', to which merchants and Buddhist missionaries came from Southeast Asia and India. Yet this region was in a perpetual state of turmoil and unrest, in which enormous quantities of art treasures were destroyed. Four more dynasties — the Liu Sung, Ch'i, Liang and Ch'en — ruled from Nanking before the split between north and south was healed. The Confucian order was undermined and the monasteries now grew to such vast proportions — particularly under Liang Wu Ti (502–50) — that they constituted a serious threat to the political and economic stability of the realm. With the eclipse of the Confucian bureaucracy it was often the great families who exerted the most influence on politics and the arts, outliving the dynasties themselves.

The intellectuals in the South, meanwhile, were seeking escape from the chaos of the times in Taoism, music, calligraphy, and the delights of pure talk (ching-t'an). Taoism came into its own in the third and fourth centuries, for it seemed to answer the yearnings of men of feeling and imagination for a vision of the eternal in which they could forget the chaos of the present. This conglomeration of folklore, nature-worship, and metaphysics was rooted in the native soil of China. It had first become a cult in the Late Han when Chang Tao-ling, a mystic and magician from Szechwan who called himself the T'ien-shih, 'Heavenly Master,' gathered round him a group of followers with whom he roamed the countryside in search of the elixir. Sometimes he would take them to the top of the Cloud Terrace Mountain (Yün-t'ai-shan) and there invent ordeals to test their magic powers. By the Chin Dynasty the movement that had originated as a private revolt against the established order had grown into a fully-fledged 'church', with a canon of scriptures, a hierarchy, temples, and all the trappings of a formal religion copied from the Buddhists.

On a higher level, however, the Taoists were the intellectual avant-garde. The reaction against Confucianism had produced a 'thaw' in the rigidly traditional view of art and literature, and now the imagination took flight once more in poetry more inspired than any since the elegies of Ch'u. Typical of the age is the poet T'ao Yüan-ming (365–427) who, though forced several times to take office to support his family, retired whenever he could to his country cottage where he grew his own vegetables, drank excessively and read books, though he said he did not mind if he failed to understand them completely. This was not merely escape from political and social chaos; it was escape also into the world of the imagination. For it was in these turbulent years that the Chinese painter and poet first discovered himself. Lu Chi's *Wen-fu*, written in A.D. 300, is a penetrating, even passionate, rhapsody on that ordeal which T. S. Eliot called the 'intolerable wrestle with words and meanings', and on the mysterious sources of poetic inspiration. In the traditional Confucian view, art had served a primarily moral and didactic purpose in society. Now that position was abandoned, and new critical standards were evolved, culminating in Hsiao T'ung's preface of A.D. 530 to his anthology *Wen-hsüan*, in which he wrote that his selection had been guided not by moral considerations, but by aesthetic merit alone. This sophisticated position was not reached at once, however. Literary criticism in the third and fourth centuries had taken the form of *p'in-tsao* — a mere classification according to merits and faults, first applied to statesmen and other public figures, then to poets. The great painter Ku K'ai-chih used it in discussing artists of Wei and Chin (if indeed the surviving text is from his hand). It was employed more methodically by Hsieh Ho in his famous *Ku hua p'in lu* (Ancient Painters' Classified Record), written in the second quarter of the sixth century, in which the author grades forty-three painters of former times into six classes, a useful but undistinguished contribution to art history. What has made this brief work so significant for the whole history of Chinese painting is its preface, which sets out the Six Principles (*liu fa*) by which paintings, and painters, are to be judged.

Much — perhaps too much — has been written about the Six

Principles. But they cannot be passed over, for they have, with some variation or rearrangement, remained the pivot around which all subsequent art criticism in China has revolved. They are:

(1) *Ch'i yün sheng tung:* Spirit Harmony — Life's Motion (Arthur Waley); Animation through spirit consonance (Alexander Soper).

(2) *Ku fa yung pi:* bone-means use brush (Waley); structural method in the use of the brush (Soper).

(3) *Ying wu hsiang hsing:* fidelity to the object in portraying forms (Soper).

(4) *Sui lei fu ts'ai:* conformity to kind in applying colours (Soper).

(5) *Ching ying wei chih:* proper planning in placing [of elements] (Soper).

(6) *Ch'uan i mu hsieh:* that by copying, the ancient models should be perpetuated (Sakanishi).

The third, fourth, and fifth Laws are self-explanatory. The sixth involves on the one hand the need to train one's hand and acquire an extensive formal repertoire, and on the other a reverence for the tradition itself, of which every painter felt himself to be in a sense a custodian. Making exact copies of ancient, worn masterpieces was a way of preserving them; while, at a later date, working 'in the manner of' great painters of the past, while adding something of oneself, was a way of putting new life into the tradition.

The experience of the painter — what Cézanne called, in a celebrated phrase, 'une sensation forte devant la nature' — is enshrined in the phrase *ch'i-yün*, Soper's 'spirit consonance'. *Ch'i* is that cosmic spirit (literally breath or vapour) that vitalizes all things, that gives life and growth to the trees, movement to the water, energy to man, and is exhaled by the mountains as clouds and mist. It is the task of the artist to attune himself to this cosmic spirit and let it infuse him with energy so that in a moment of inspiration — and no word could be more appropriate — he may become the vehicle for its expression. William Acker once asked a famous calligrapher why he dug his ink-stained fingers so deep into the hairs of his huge brush when he was writing; the calligrapher replied that only thus could he feel the *ch'i* flow down his arm, through the brush and on to the paper. The *ch'i* is a cosmic energy that, as Acker puts it, 'flows about in ever-changing streams and eddies, here deep, there shallow, here concentrated, there dispersed.' It infuses all things, for there is no distinction between the animate and the inanimate. Seen in this light the third, fourth and fifth principles involve more than mere visual accuracy; for, as the living forms of nature are the visible manifestations of the workings of the *ch'i*, only by representing them faithfully can the artist express his awareness of this cosmic principle in action.

The quality in a painting through which awareness of the inner vital spirit is expressed is the second of Hsieh Ho's principles, *ku*, the 'bone', the structural strength of the brushstroke itself, whether in painting or calligraphy. The sudden flowering of calligraphy at the end of the Han Dynasty as an art form in its own right was partly due to the development of the 'draft character' (*ts'ao-shu*), the cursive script which freed the scholar from the formal angularity of the typical Han *li-shu*, 'clerical hand', and enabled him to express himself in a style more personal, more charged with energy and grace, than any other writing that man has devised.[1] It is no accident that many of the greatest calligraphers of this period, including Wang Hsi-chih and his son Hsien-chih, were ardent Taoists. Both the techniques and the aesthetic of this subtle art had a considerable influence upon the development of Chinese painting during the three centuries following the fall of the Han.

The Taoist ideal in action is illustrated in the life and work of Tsung Ping, a distinguished Buddhist scholar and painter of the early fifth century, who spent his life wandering amid the beautiful hills of the south with his equally romantic wife and

[1] These and other styles are illustrated on pp. 210–11.

who, when he was too old to wander any more, recreated the landscapes that he loved on the walls of his studio. A short *Preface on Landscape Painting (Hua shan-shui hsü)*, one of the earliest surviving writings on this new art form, is attributed to him. In it he maintains that landscape painting is a high art because land-scapes 'both have material existence, and reach out into the realm of the spirit'. He declares that he would like to be a Taoist mystic, meditating upon the void. He has tried it and is ashamed to confess that he failed; but, he asks, is not the art of the land-scape painter, who can reproduce the very forms and colours that inspire the Taoist adept, even more wonderful? He is innocently amazed at the power of the artist to bring down a vast panorama of mountains within the compass of a few inches of silk. Visual accuracy he holds to be essential, for if the landscape is well and convincingly executed, if the forms and colours in the picture correspond to those in nature, then 'that correspondence will stir the spirit, and when the spirit soars, truth will be attained. . . . What more', he asks, 'could be added to this?'

Another brief essay, attributed to Wang Wei, a scholar, musician and man of letters who died in 443 at the age of twenty-eight, starts by pointing out that paintings must correspond to the *pa kua*, the 'eight trigrams', meaning that just as the *pa kua* is a symbolic diagram of the workings of the universe, so must landscape painting be a symbolic language through which the painter may express not a relative, particularized aspect of nature seen at a given moment from a given viewpoint, but a general truth, beyond time and place. Though he too is full of wonder at the artist's mysterious power of pictorial compression he insists that painting is more than the exercise of skill: 'the spirit must also exercise control over it; for this is the essence of painting.' The landscapes of Wang Wei, Tsung Ping and their contem-poraries have all been lost centuries ago, but the ideals that are enshrined in these and other writings of this critical formative period have been the inspiration of Chinese painters up to the present day.

The life and work of Ku K'ai-chih, more perhaps than that of any other creative personality of this time, seem to embody the forces that inspired men in these turbulent years. Himself wildly unconventional and yet a friend of the great at court, a calligrapher and painter of Taoist landscapes who yet was seldom far from the hurly-burly of intrigue in the capital, he moved unharmed among the rival politicians and warlords, protecting himself by that aura of idiocy which the Taoists held to be the only true wisdom. His biography tells us that he was famous for his portraits, in which he captured not merely the appearance but the very spirit of his subject.[1] A fascinating essay attributed to him describes how he would go about painting the Cloud Terrace Mountain and the ordeal to which Chang Tao-ling subjected one of his disciples on the top of a precipice. The text shows that he conceived of the mountain in strictly Taoist terms, bracketed east and west by the green dragon and the white tiger, its central peak ringed with clouds and surmounted by the strutting phoenix, symbol of the south. We do not know whether he ever painted this picture or not, though he probably did. Only three paintings associated with his name have survived. One, of which there are Sung versions in the Freer Gallery and in the Palace Museum, Peking, illustrates the closing moments in the *fu* of the Fairy of the Lo River by Ts'ao Chih. Both these copies preserve the archaic style of his time, particularly in the primitive treatment of the landscape which provides the setting for the scene where the fairy bids farewell to the young scholar who had fallen in love with her, and sails away in her magic boat.

The Lo-shen scroll makes use of the technique of continuous narration, in which the same characters appear several times, whenever the story requires. This device seems to have come from

[1] There are a number of delightful stories about him in his official biography and in that fascinating collection of gossip *Shih-shuo hsin-yü*. See Arthur Waley's account of him in his *Introduction to the Study of Chinese Painting*, and Ch'en Shih-hsiang's translation of the official life, No. 2 in the University of California's Chinese Dynastic Histories translations (Berkeley, 1953).

India with the introduction of Buddhism, for there is no evidence for it in Han art. Probably the Han scrolls most often used the convention which is employed in the two other surviving works connected with Ku K'ai-chih, the *Lieh-nü t'u*, illustrating four groups of famous women of antiquity, with their parents,[1] and the Admonitions of the Instructress to the Court Ladies. Here the text, a poem by Tso Ssu, alternates with the illustrations. The Admonitions scroll is not included among recorded works of Ku in T'ang texts, and is first attributed to him in the catalogue of the collection of the Sung Emperor Hui-tsung; there are indeed details in the landscape treatment which indicate that it is unlikely to be earlier than the tenth century. Yet it clearly derives from a painting by a Six Dynasties master, whether or not it is from the hand of Ku K'ai-chih himself. The scroll is much damaged and restored, and the first two scenes are missing together with the text of the third which tells of the heroism of Lady Feng, concubine of a Former Han Emperor, who threw herself between her lord and a bear, happily without fatal results except for the very small bear, who was promptly killed by attendants. The fourth scene illustrates Lady P'an refusing to distract the emperor from the affairs of state by going out with him in his litter. To show the interior of the litter, the artist has used the technique that the Han artist employed, pulling the front round till it is almost parallel with the nearest side, in such a way that instead of diminishing in width with distance it seems to get wider. The same primitive device is used with more skill and subtlety in the delightful bedroom scene, illustrating the homily, 'if the words that you utter are good, all men for a thousand *li* around will make response. But if you depart from this principle, even your bed-fellow will distrust you.' We see the Emperor sitting on the edge of his consort's bed with a somewhat plausible

---

[1] A splendid late Sung version of the *Lieh-nü t'u* in Peking is illustrated in *Wen-wu ts'an-k'ao tzu-liao* 1958, 6, 22–24. The copyist has made effective use of the shading technique for drapery (visible also in the bed-hangings of the Admonitions scroll) which seems to have been a peculiarity of Ku's style, and suggests possible foreign influence.

smile on his face, while from within the curtains she looks at him with sharp suspicion (Plate 22).

When Liang Yüan Ti abdicated in 555, he deliberately consigned to the flames over two hundred thousand books and pictures in his private collection, so it is not surprising that nothing has survived of the works of the other leading masters of the Southern Dynasties who were active in Nanking. The *Li-tai ming-hua-chi*, however, records the titles of a number of paintings of this period, from which we know what kinds of subjects were popular. There were the stock Confucian and Buddhist themes, great panoramas illustrating the descriptive *fu* and other shorter poems, landscapes depicting famous mountains and gardens; there were scenes of city, village and tribal life, fantastic Taoist landscapes and pictures of the figures symbolizing the constellations, illustrations of historical events and legends such as the story of Hsi Wang Mu. Most must have had landscape settings, while several were pure landscapes, and at least three paintings of bamboo are recorded. The great majority were presumably either standing screens or long handscrolls, for the vertical banner was an innovation that came in with Buddhism.

We can obtain some notion of the style of the time from the paintings that line the walls of tombs in North Korea, notably the 'Tomb of the Dancing Figures' and the 'Tomb of the Wrestling Scene' at T'ung-kou on the Yalu River. Although painted as late as the sixth century, these lively scenes of feasting and hunting amid mountains are in the tradition of the Han tomb paintings at Liao-yang. But to see the most advanced treatment of landscape in this indigenous style we must look not at the provincial tomb decorations, but at the engraved slabs from North China, of which the most beautiful examples are the sides of a stone coffin now in the Nelson Gallery, Kansas City, adorned with incidents in the lives of six famous filial sons of antiquity. The figures seem hardly more than the excuse for magnificent landscape panoramas, so richly conceived and so beautifully drawn that they must surely have been copied from a handscroll or, as Sickman suggests, a wall-painting, by an accomplished artist. Each incident is set off from its neighbours by hills with overlapping tops called *ch'üeh* which have powerful Taoist associations; half a dozen kinds of tree are distinguishable, tossed by a great wind that sweeps through their branches, while above the distant hills the clouds streak across the sky (Plate 23). The scene is astonishing in its animation, and only in his failure to lead the eye back through a convincing middle distance to the horizon does the artist reveal the limitations of his time. Though its subject is respectably Confucian, its treatment exudes a wild and exultant joy in the face of living nature that is purely Taoist. It serves also to remind us that in spite of the ever-growing demands of Buddhism for art of an entirely different kind, there already existed at this time a purely native landscape tradition allied to calligraphy and based on the language of the brush.

Buddhist communities were already established in North China before the end of the Han Dynasty. Now, however, political and social chaos, loss of faith in the traditional Confucian order and the desire to escape from the troubles of the times all contributed to a wave of remarkable religious enthusiasm, and the new doctrine spread to every corner of the empire. Its acceptance, except among the lowest strata of society, was not due to blind and innocent faith — for that is not a sentiment to which the educated Chinese are prone — but perhaps to the same motives as have led to the triumph of communism today: the times are out of joint, people seemed to say, our old gods and traditional ways have failed us; let us see what Buddhism can do. The new faith must have proved an effective consolation, if we are to judge by the vast sums spent on the building of monasteries and temples and their adornment during these troubled years.

We must pause in our narrative for a moment to consider the life and teachings of the Buddha, which form the subject-matter of Buddhist art. Gautama Śākyamuni, called the Buddha, or the Enlightened One, was born about 567 B.C., the son of a prince of the Śākya clan ruling on the border of Nepal. He grew up surrounded by the luxuries of the palace, married, and had a son Rāhula. His father deliberately shielded him from all contact with the miseries of life beyond the palace gates, but in spite of the care with which his excursions were planned for him, Śākyamuni was finally confronted with the reality of old age, sickness, and death, and he saw a vision of an ascetic, pointing his future path. Deeply disturbed by his experience, he resolved to renounce the world and search for the cause of so much suffering. One night he stole out from the palace, cut off his hair, bade farewell to his horse and groom, and embarked upon his quest. For many years he wandered, seeking, first with one teacher and then with another, the answer to the mystery of existence, and as way of release from the intolerable cycle of endless rebirths to which all living things are subject according to *karma*, the inexorable law of cause and effect. Then one day at Bodhgayā he entered into a trance seated under a pippala tree. For three days and nights he remained motionless. The demon Māra sent his host to assault him and his three lovely daughters to dance seductively before him, but without moving from where he sat, the Lord rendered the former powerless while the latter he transformed into withered hags. Finally, in the moment of enlightenment, the answer came to him. In his first great sermon in the Deer Park at Benares, he gave his message to the world in the form of the Four Noble Truths:

> 'All existence is suffering (*dukkha*).
> 'The cause of suffering is craving, lust, desire — even desire for existence itself.
> 'There is an end to suffering, for this craving can be suppressed.
> 'There is a way of suppression, through the Noble Eightfold Path.'

The Buddha also taught that there is no such thing as a soul, but that all life is transitory, all in a perpetual state of becoming. By following the Eightfold Path, which involves right conduct, right belief, and right meditation, the devotee can break the cycle of rebirths which binds us eternally to the wheel of existence, and so secure his release and his final merging in eternity, as a cup of water poured into the sea. Śākyamuni achieved enlightenment in his lifetime, although he continued to walk the earth, gathering disciples, performing miracles, and spreading his teaching, until his final departure, the *mahāparinirvāna*, at the age of eighty. His teaching was austere, and moreover only for the chosen few who were prepared to renounce the world and face the rigours of life as a mendicant or, later, the regimen of the monastery. Its appeal lay partly in its simplicity — a welcome relief from the complexities of Hindu theology and metaphysics — and partly in the hope it offered of release from a destiny from which Hindu doctrine saw no escape.

The new faith grew slowly, and it was not until it was embraced by King Aśoka (272?–232 B.C.) that it became a truly national religion. That monarch devoted himself with such tremendous energy to its propagation that legend has it that he erected 84,000 *stūpas* (relic mounds) in a single day, while his monastic and temple foundations were on a scale which every pious Buddhist ruler has since tried to emulate. His missionary activities brought the faith to Ceylon and to Gandhāra in Northwest India, where it came in contact with the religious ideas and artistic forms of the provincial Graeco-Roman world. It was probably in Gandhāra that, under these influences and encouraged by the great conference organized by King Kanishka (second century A.D.) of the Kushans, the first great development in Buddhist doctrine took place. The core of the dogma remained unaltered, but the new schools — who called themselves Mahāyāna (greater vehicle), referring derogatively to the more conservative sects as the Hīnayāna (lesser vehicle) — taught that salvation was open to all men, through faith and works. Now the Buddha ceased to be an earthly teacher, but was conceived of as pure abstraction, as the universal principle, the Godhead, from whom Truth, in the form of the Buddhist *dharma* (law), radiates with a blinding light across the universe. By this elevation to a status parallel to that of the Hindu Brahmā, the

Buddha receded far beyond the reach of mortal man. *Bhakti*, the adoration of a personal god, expressed in Hinduism in the love of Krishna, demanded a more approachable deity. So there came into existence the *bodhisattva*, 'one destined for enlightenment,' who has postponed his own end that he might bring help and comfort to suffering mankind. Of the bodhisattvas the most popular was Avalokiteśvara, 'the Lord who looks down (in mercy)', who on his translation to China as Kuan-yin became identified both with his female reflex Tārā and with the ancient Chinese mother-goddess, and thus imperceptibly changed his sex — a transformation that was complete by the end of the tenth century. Almost as important, were Mañjuśrī (Chinese Wen-shu) the God of Wisdom, and Maitreya, the deity who, though now still a bodhisattva, will in the next cycle descend to earth as the Buddha; to the Chinese he has become Mi-lo-fu, the pot-bellied 'god of wealth' who sits grinning at the entrance to every temple. In time the pantheon grew to extraordinary proportions, the vast array of Buddhas and bodhisattvas being attempts to express the infinite aspects and powers of God. These developments were however for the theologians and metaphysicians. The common man needed only the comfort of Avalokiteśvara, or the secure knowledge that, merely by speaking once the name of the Buddha Amitābha, he would on quitting this world be reborn in his Western Paradise beyond the sunset.

It was probably in Gandhāra, and under western influence, that the Buddha was first represented in sculpture. The style of Gandhāra is a curious mixture of the classical realism of Graeco-Roman provincial art with the Indian genius, fostered at the Southern Kushan capital of Mathurā, for giving concrete, plastic expression to an abstract, metaphysical concept. From Gandhāra Buddhism, and with it this new synthetic art, spread northwards across the Hindu Kush to Central Asia, there to run like a powder trail along the string of oases to north and south of the Tarim Basin.

Buddhist sculpture preceded Buddhist architecture into China, for it was the images — brought in the luggage of returning pilgrims, who were no doubt prepared to swear that what they carried was an exact replica of some famous icon in India or Central Asia — which were most deeply venerated. They were set up in shrines built in the traditional Chinese style, which grew until the monastery or temple became a kind of palace, with endless courtyards, pavilions, galleries and gardens. No attempt was made in these timber buildings to imitate the Indian temple. But the *stūpa* presented a different kind of challenge. The monk Sung Yün, returning from Gandhāra early in the sixth century, had described (as doubtless many before him) the gigantic *stūpa*

Types of Pagodas. 1–3 derived from the Han timber *lou*: 1. Yün-kang (N. Wei); 2. Sian (T'ang); 3. Canton (Ming); 4 and 5 derived from the Indian *stūpa*: 4. Sung-shan (*c.* 520, plate 26a); 5. Sian (T'ang).

erected by King Kanishka, one of the wonders of the western world. Built in timber, it was no less than seven hundred feet high, in thirteen storeys, capped by a mast with thirteen golden discs. The Chinese already possessed, in the towers called *lou* and *ch'üeh*, multi-storey timber buildings which could be adapted to this new purpose (see page 99). The Chinese examples of this period have all perished, but the pagodas at Hōryūji and Yakushiji near Nara in Japan still stand as monuments to this simple, graceful style. The earliest surviving dateable pagoda on Chinese soil, however, is the twelve-sided stone tower on Mount Sung in Honan, erected in 520 (Plate 26a). It has no Chinese antecedents.

Its profile echoes the curve of the Indian *śikhara* tower; the arched recesses on the main faces recall the niches on the great *stūpa* at Bodhgayā, and, as Soper has observed, many of the details are Indian, or based on Southeast Asian modifications of the Indian style found in the Kingdom of Champa, with which China was now in contact. But gradually the Indian elements were absorbed, and the later stone and brick pagodas will imitate, in their surface treatment, the posts, brackets and projecting roofs of their Chinese timber prototypes.

At Bāmiyān in Afghanistan a high cliff more than a mile in length had been hollowed out into cave shrines decorated with frescoes, and bracketed at either end by colossal standing Buddha figures carved out of the rock, plastered and painted. This fashion for decorated cave shrines, which had originated in India, spread to Khotan, Kucha and other Central Asian city-states, where the already syncretic Graeco-Indian tradition of painting and sculpture became mixed with the flat, heraldic, decorative style of Parthia and Sasanian Persia. The routes that skirted the Taklamakan desert joined at Tunhuang, the gateway to China. There in A.D. 366 pilgrims had hewn from the soft rock the first of what were to develop during the next thousand years into a range of more than four hundred shrines, set about with plaster sculpture and adorned with frescoes. Further stages on the pilgrim route into China were marked by cave shrines at P'ing-ling-ssu, about fifty miles southwest of Lanchow, and Mai-chi-shan, twenty-eight miles southeast of T'ien-shui. The former was only rediscovered in 1951, while restoration of the latter, which had always been known to the people of the T'ien-shui district, did not begin till 1953. In their spectacular sites and the quality and richness of their sculpture these shrines surpass Tunhuang, whose glory lies chiefly in its paintings.

In 386 the Toba Turks established their ascendancy over North China as the Wei Dynasty, with their capital at Ta-t'ung. Their rulers had embraced Buddhism with enthusiasm for, like the Kushans in India, they were excluded from the traditional social

Map showing the spread of Buddhism from its birthplace in the Ganges Valley into Central and East Asia and religious system of those they had conquered.[1] At the urging of the overseer of monks, T'an-yao, they began in 460 to hew out of the cliffs at Yünkang a series of shrines and colossal figures, possibly in emulation of the 'thousand foot' Maitreya at Darel, which were to be a monument not only to Buddhism but also to the splendour of the royal house itself. By the time the capital was moved south to Loyang in 494, twenty large caves and some minor ones had been excavated, while work was resumed between 500 and 535, and again between 916 and 1125, when Ta-t'ung became the western capital of the Liao Dynasty. The earliest caves — those numbered XVI to XX — are cut into the living rock to expose colossal seated Buddhas carved almost in the round, and originally protected by a timber roof which in some of the cave shrines was to develop into an elaborate façade in several storeys. The colossus in Cave XX, forty-five feet high, sits in an attitude of meditation (Plate 26b); his shoulders and chest are massive and yet finely proportioned, his face is clear-cut with something of the mask-like quality often found in Gandhāra, while the drapery is suggested by flat strap-like bands which disappear into points as they pass round the countour of arm or shoulder. Perhaps, as Sickman has suggested, this curious convention is the result of the sculptor's following, and not properly understanding, a line-drawing of some western prototype, for great pains were taken to copy the style of the more venerated images as closely as possible.

By the end of the fifth century the native predilection for abstract expression in terms of rhythmic line had begun to modify this all-too-solid and somewhat ungainly imported style. The carvings in Cave VII, one of the most richly decorated of all, bear witness to this transformation. Every inch of the walls and great central core is decorated with vigorous reliefs which were once

---

[1] This motive was frankly admitted in an edict of one of the barbarian rulers of Later Chao (about 335): 'We were born out of the marches,' he declared, 'and though We are unworthy, We have complied with our appointed destiny and govern the Chinese as their prince. . . . Buddha being a barbarian god is the very one we should worship.' See Arthur Wright, 'Fo-t'u-teng, a Biography', *Harvard Journal of Asiatic Studies* II (1948), 356.

painted in bright colours, and testify to the gratitude, to the generosity, and perhaps also to the anxiety about their future destiny of a multitude of donors. In long panels the life of the Buddha is told in a series of vivid reliefs, while above is the heavenly host — Buddhas, seated or standing, bodhisattvas, flying *apsarases*, musicians and other celestial beings (Plate 24a). The decoration of this cave reminds us, in its wealth of detail, its contrast between the realism of the earthly figures and the serenity of the heavenly ones, of the beatific visions of the Italian primitives.

The Loyang region was closer to the centre of the purely Chinese tradition of pictorial expression in linear, as opposed to plastic, terms; and so it was inevitable that this tendency, already becoming apparent in the later caves at Yünkang, should have found its fulfilment after the move to the south in 494. At Lungmen, only ten miles from the new capital, sculptors found a fine grey limestone which permitted of greater refinement of expression and finish than the coarse sandstone of Yünkang. The new style reached its culmination in the cave known as Pin-yang-tung, probably completed in 523. Against each of the interior walls is a large seated figure of the Buddha, attended by standing bodhisats or the favourite disciples Ānanda and Kāśyapa. On either side of the entrance the walls were decorated with godlings in relief, *Jātaka* tales, scenes of the celebrated debate between Vimalakīrti and Manjuśrī and two magnificent panels showing the Emperor and Empress coming in procession to the shrine attended by their retinue. The Empress panel, badly damaged in removal many years ago, has been restored and now forms part of the important Chinese collection in Kansas City (Plate 24b). Executed in flat relief, its sweeping linear rhythms and wonderful sense of forward movement suggest the translation into stone of the style of wall-painting which must have been current at the Wei court, and is further proof that beside the imported, hieratic forms reserved for the deities themselves there existed another and more purely Chinese style, to which painters and sculptors instinctively turned in representing secular themes.

Because of the great scarcity of Buddhist sculpture from the southern kingdoms, we are apt to think that the stylistic revolution which reached its culmination at Lungmen must have originated in the north and gradually spread southwards. But recent discoveries and research suggest that the opposite was the case, and that it was the art of the southern courts centred in Nanking which was the dominating factor in the development of Buddhist sculpture in the Six Dynasties. One of the earliest innovators had been Tai K'uei, a contemporary of Ku K'ai-chih at the Chin court in Nanking. His work, in which he is said to have raised the art of sculpture to a new level, very probably reflected the style of contemporary painting, — the flat, slender body, sweeping robes and trailing scarves that we see in copies of the Ku K'ai-chih scrolls. This concept of figure and drapery does not appear in the sculpture of the North until a century later, when we first encounter it in the later stages at Yünkang and the earliest caves at Lungmen, and there is much evidence to show that it was introduced by artists and sculptors from the South.

The arrangement of the Pin-yang cave at Lungmen was probably intended to suggest the interior of a temple, whose equipment would also have included free-standing images in stone, stone votive steles and gilded bronze images. The steles were carved and set up in the temple as an act of piety or gratitude by one or more subscribers, whose names they often bear. They consisted either of a flat slab shaped like a pippala-leaf against which one, or more often a group of three figures, stands out almost in the round; or of a rectangular slab decorated, often on all four sides, with Buddhas, bodhisats and lesser deities, illustrations to favourite texts such as the *Lotus Sūtra* (*Saddharmapundarīka Sūtra*), and scenes from the life of the Buddha carved in relief. Their peculiar interest and value lies in the fact that they concentrate in little space the essentials of the style and iconography of the period, and that they are frequently dated.

In Cave 133 at Mai-chi-shan a group of eighteen of these steles still stand in their original position against the walls where they were set up by pious devotees. Three of these are splendid examples of the mid-sixth century style. The upper central panel of stele No. 11 (Plate 25) is devoted to the incident in the *Lotus Sūtra* in which Śākyamuni by the power of his preaching causes Prabhūtaratna, a Buddha of the distant past, to appear beside him. In the centre and below are Buddhas flanked by bodhisats — a simple presentation of the Paradise theme. The side panels show, on the left: Śākyamuni descending from the Tuṣita Heaven where he had preached to his deceased mother; Śākyamuni as a young prince; the Renunciation, and the First Preaching in the Deer Park. On the right: a bodhisattva meditating under a tree; the Mahāparinirvāna; Samantabhadra on his elephant; the Temptations of Māra; and the theological disputation between Manjuśrī and Vimalakīrti (holding the fan).

Very few of the great bronze images of this period have survived. They were nearly all destroyed or melted down in the persecutions which intermittently scarred the history of Buddhism in China. To see the largest, if not the finest, example of an altarpiece in the Wei linear style we must journey to Japan where, in the Kondō (Golden Hall) of the Monastery of Hōryūji at Nara, is a magnificent Buddha trinity which, though executed by a Japanese sculptor in 623, is a late survival of the style of mid-sixth-century China. Some of the smaller gilded bronze images, made most probably for domestic chapels, escaped destruction. Because of the precision of their modelling and the beauty of their material, these bronzes — ranging from simple seated Buddhas to elaborate altar groups complete with stand, flame mandorla and attendant deities — are among the supreme examples of Chinese Buddhist art. The earliest surviving dated specimen, cast in 338, has all the squat clumsy charm of an archaic piece. One of the most perfect examples of the mature Wei style is the exquisite Maitreya in the University of Pennsylvania Museum in Philadelphia, dated 536 (Plate 27a). The form is expressively attenuated; the eyes slant, the mouth wears a sweet, withdrawn smile, while the body seems about to disappear altogether under a cascade of drapery that no longer defines the figure beneath but, like the drapery of the Romanesque sculpture of Moissac or Vézelay, in its expression of a state of spiritual ecstasy seems to deny the body's very existence. Here, the influence on sculpture of the sweeping rhythms of the painter's brush is very apparent.

After the middle of the sixth century a further, equally momentous change came over the style of Chinese Buddhist sculpture. Now the body began to expand once more, filling the robes which, instead of fluttering free with a life of their own, began to mould themselves to the cylindrical form, subtly accentuating its mass. Against these now smooth surfaces the jewellery of the bodhisattvas provides a contrasting ornament. The

The development of the Buddha image. 1. Yünkang (*c.* 460–490); 2. Lungmen (*c.* 490–550); 3. Ch'i-chou (*c.* 550–580); 4. Sui (*c.* 580–620); 5. T'ang (*c.* 620–750). (After S. Mizuno, *Chinese Stone Sculpture.*)

head becomes rounded and massive, the expression austere rather than spiritual. In the stone sculpture of Northern Ch'i (Plate 28a) Chinese craftsmen produced a style in which precision of carving and richness of detail are subordinated to a total effect of grave and majestic dignity. While the change was stimulated by a renewal of Indian influence on Chinese Buddhist art, this time it came not across Central Asia, where contact with the West was now broken by fresh barbarian incursions into the Tarim Basin, but up from the Indianised kingdoms of Southeast Asia, with which the court at Nanking had close diplomatic and cultural relations. There are abundant records of Buddhist images being sent to Nanking from Indochina in the sixth century, though none of these have yet been identified. However in 1953 there was found in the ruins of a temple at Chengtu in Szechwan a buried hoard of about two hundred pieces of Buddhist sculpture, much of it of superb quality. Some of these pieces show the indirect influence of Gupta art (Plate 28b), others have stylistic affinities with the sculpture of the Dvāravatī kingdom of Thailand, and with figures and reliefs excavated at Dong-duong and other sites in the ancient kingdom of Champa (Vietnam). Nothing comparable to the Chengtu find has yet been unearthed at Nanking itself, where the destruction of early Buddhist monuments was almost complete; but there is no doubt that Chengtu was strongly influenced by artistic developments at the southern capital.

As with sculpture, so did the introduction of Buddhism give birth to a new school of painting of which both the content and the forms were largely foreign. A Sung writer tells of a certain K'ang Seng-hui, a Sogdian, who in A.D. 247 came to the Wu Kingdom (Nanking) by way of Indochina, 'to instal icons and practise ritual circumambulation. It so happened that Ts'ao Pu-hsing saw his iconographic cartoons for Buddhas (in the style of) the Western Regions, and copied them; whence it came about that the Ts'ao (style) has been popular through the generations all over the world.' (Before the end of the sixth century, however, nothing survived of Ts'ao's work 'except the head of one dragon in the Privy Pavilion'.) The new style culminated in the work of Chang Seng-yu, the greatest of the painters working for the Liang Emperors at Nanking. His work was remarkable — according to contemporary accounts — for its realism: he painted dragons on the wall of An-lo-ssu, and when, in spite of his warning, he was persuaded to paint in their eyes, they flew away amid thunder and lightning. He decorated many Buddhist and Taoist temples in Nanking with frescoes; he was a portraitist, and also executed long scrolls illustrating such homelier themes as Han Wu Ti Shooting the Dragon, the Drunken Monk, and Children Dancing at a Farmhouse; but all were lost centuries ago, and none of the later pictures claiming to be copies of his work, such as the 'Five Planets and Twenty-four Constellations' in the Abe Collection in

Osaka, give more than a hint of his style. Nevertheless we may be sure that one feature of this imported manner was the Indian technique of arbitrary shading, found in the wall-paintings at Ajantā, which was used to give an effect of roundness and solidity unlike anything that China had seen before.

Fortunately the wall-paintings at Tunhuang, Mai-chi-shan and P'ing-ling-ssu have survived — though for the most part they are but a faint echo of the grand manner of metropolitan China. The first chapel at Tunhuang had been dedicated in 366. Today paintings of the Northern and Western Wei can be seen in thirty-two of the caves, and there were probably many more before dilapidation and later repainting took their toll. Of these the finest are in Caves 257 (P. 110) and 249 (P. 101).[1] The vigorous rendering of the preaching Buddha in Cave 249 (Plate 27b) is a good example of the mixture of styles that we find everywhere at Tunhuang. The stiff heraldic pose of the Buddha shows how the 'painterly' Chinese manner which we have already seen influencing the sculpture of the period (Plate 27a) has been frozen into a flat decorative pattern, indicating perhaps the hand of some itinerant painter from Central Asia, who has also attempted, not very successfully, to suggest an Indian fulness in the modelling of his attendant bodhisats and apsarases. The subjects of these early frescoes are generally Buddhist trinities, scenes from the Life, and endless *Jātaka* tales which, under the guise of recounting incidents in the Buddha's previous incarnations, draw upon a rich storehouse

[1] The caves were first published by Sir Aurel Stein, who visited them in 1907 and brought away with him a rich collection of manuscripts and paintings from a sealed library. In the following year the great French sinologue Paul Pelliot systematically photographed and numbered the caves. His numbers, totalling nearly 300, are familiar to western readers, and appear in my text in brackets preceded by the letter P. A second system of numbering was used by the noted painter Chang Ta-ch'ien who with his assistants copied some of the frescoes during the Second World War. A third system was adopted by the National Art Research Institute of Tunhuang which since 1943 has been actively engaged in preserving, restoring and copying the paintings under the directorship of Ch'ang Shu-hung. This organization has now identified 486 caves and niches, and I have used their system in this book.

of Indian legend and folklore. It is these delightful scenes, and not the hieratic Buddhas and bodhisats crudely copying some western model, that reveal the Chinese journeyman artist at his most spontaneous: indeed, it is not unlikely that while some of the main figures were executed by artists from Central Asia and beyond, donors were content to leave these accessory scenes to local talent.

A famous panel in Cave 257 tells the story of the Buddha's incarnation as a golden gazelle (Plate 28c). The simple humped hills slant back diagonally in rows like the seated figures in the Han banqueting scenes. Between them the participants are painted almost in silhouette on a flower-strewn ground. The sense of open space is Chinese, as is the emphasis on linear movement; but the decorative flatness of the figures, the dappled deer and flower-sprinkled ground, have a Near Eastern origin. Most striking are the *Jātaka* scenes in Cave 428 (P. 135) dated 538-9, whose decorative scheme gives the impression of a long landscape scroll cut into three sections pasted one above the other on the wall. The scenes are divided, like those on the sarcophagus in Kansas City, into 'space cells' set off by ranges of mountains, trees, and buildings which reach back diagonally to the upper border, while the sense of depth is aided by the groups of horsemen who appear from behind a hill, a convention already used in Han art and later to become very popular in landscape painting.

Although this was the heyday of Buddhism in China, the Confucian rites and ceremonies were not altogether neglected, and the Imperial burials — particularly in the south — were as spectacular as ever. Although a pious Buddhist, Liang Wu Ti was buried outside Nanking in the most splendid fashion in a tomb whose 'spirit way' was lined on either side with heraldic lions carved in the native tradition, like the magnificent winged beast illustrated in Plate 30a. These creatures have about them a dynamic linear movement which also found expression in miniature in the beautiful gilt bronze lions, tigers and dragons of which there are many examples in Western museums. But, on the whole, there seem to have been fewer elaborate tombs than before, and indeed until the last few years so few had been reliably excavated that experts were very reluctant to ascribe any grave goods to this period at all.

It is only recently that we have begun to get a clear picture of the pottery of the Six Dynasties. There was in North China a deterioration in the quality and variety of the *ming-ch'i*. Much rarer now are the farms and pig-sties that give so delightful a picture of Han rural economy; but to compensate, the best of the grave figurines have an almost fairy-like elegance which reminds us of the ladies in the Ku K'ai-chih scrolls; while the horses are no longer the tough, stocky, deep-chested creatures of Han art; they seem rather in their heraldic grace of form and the richness of their trappings to evoke the atmosphere of a bygone age of chivalry. Most of these figures are unglazed, but some are attractively painted with colours which have mellowed to soft reds and blues through long burial.

This was not, in general, a period of great advance in ceramics, an industry which flourishes best in settled conditions, but the ground was being laid for the great achievements of the T'ang. Typical is a primitive 'northern celadon' (see page 197), and a white slipped porcellanous ware with an ivory crackled glaze, found in Sui tombs at Anyang, which is but a step from the pure white porcelain of the T'ang Dynasty.

The position in the lower Yangtse valley is quite different. Kilns have been located in ten counties in Chekiang alone, while many of their products have been unearthed from dated tombs of the third and fourth centuries in the Nanking region. Of these pottery centres the most important were those in Shang-yü-hsien and around the shores of Shang-lin-hu in Yü-yao-hsien, active into the T'ang and Five Dynasties. In addition to celadon, the kilns at Te-ch'ing, north of Hangchow, also produced a ware with a rich black glaze. Some jars and vases show the influence of Near Eastern art, introduced with Buddhism: the strapwork, hanging tassels, rosettes and acanthus scrolls on the famous vase in Kansas

City (Plate 29) are all derived from Sasanian ornament. But in general the early Chekiang celadons show, in the growing strength and purity of their shapes, the final emancipation of the Chinese potter from his earlier bondage to the aesthetic of the metal-worker.

Indeed, freedom in the arts seems to be the keynote of this period, — not only in technique and design, but also in the attitude of the privileged classes to the arts. For this was the age of the first critics and aestheticians, the age of the first gentlemen painters and calligraphers, the age of the first great private art collections and of the birth of such cultivated pursuits as garden designing and conversation as a fine art. Just as the sixth-century anthologist Hsiao T'ung selected the poems for his *Wen-hsüan* on grounds of literary merit alone, so it seems did patrons in the Six Dynasties come for the first time to value their possessions — whether paintings or calligraphy, bronzes, jade or pottery — simply because they were beautiful.

CHAPTER SEVEN

Sui and T'ang

The Six Dynasties had been a period when new forms, new ideas and values were first, and often tentatively, tried out — ideas which could not find their fullest expression in those restless centuries, but needed an era of stability and prosperity to bring them to fruition. The founder of the Sui Dynasty was an able general and administrator, who not only united China after four hundred years of fragmentation, but also carried the prestige of her arms out into Central Asia. But his son Yang Ti squandered the resources of the empire on palaces and gardens built on the scale of Versailles, and on vast public works. These included a long section of the Grand Canal, constructed to link his northern and southern capitals, for the building of which over five million men, women and children were recruited into forced labour. These vast projects, as a Ming historian put it, 'shortened the life of his dynasty by a number of years, but benefited posterity unto ten thousand generations.' Combined with four disastrous wars against Korea, they were too much for his long-suffering subjects, who rose in revolt. Soon a ducal family of the name of Li joined the insurrection, and the Sui Dynasty collapsed. In 617 Li Yüan captured Changan, and in the following year was placed on the throne as first emperor of the T'ang Dynasty by his able and energetic son Li Shih-min. In 626 Li Yüan abdicated in favour of Shih-min, who then at the age of twenty-five ascended the throne as T'ang T'ai-tsung, thereby inaugurating an era of peace and prosperity which lasted for well over a century.

T'ang culture was to that of the Six Dynasties as was Han to the

Warring States or, to stretch the parallel a little, Rome to ancient Greece. It was a time of consolidation, of practical achievement, of immense assurance. We will not find in T'ang art the wild and fanciful taste of the fifth century, which saw fairies and immortals on every peak. Nor does it carry us, as does Sung art, into those silent realms where man and nature are one. There is metaphysical speculation certainly, but it is that of the difficult schools of Mahāyāna idealism which interested a small minority, and is expressed moreover in forms and symbols which touch neither the imagination nor the heart. For the rest, T'ang art has incomparable vigour, realism, dignity; it is the art of a people thoroughly at home in a world which they knew to be secure. There is an optimism, an energy, a frank acceptance of tangible reality which gives the same character to all T'ang art, whether it be the most splendid fresco from the hand of a master or the humblest tomb figurine made by the village potter.

By the time of his death in 649, T'ai-tsung had established Chinese control over the flourishing central Asian kingdoms of Kucha and Khotan, the conquest of Korea had been begun, Tibet linked to the royal house by marriage, and relations established with Japan and the Southeast Asian kingdoms of Funan and Champa. Changan, laid out by the Sui, now became a city of a size and splendour rivalling, if it did not surpass, Byzantium. It was planned on a grid six miles by five. In the northern sector lay the government buildings and the royal palace, Ta-ming Kung, which has been located and partially excavated. In its streets one might have encountered priests from India and Southeast Asia, merchants from Central Asia and Arabia, Turks, Mongols and Japanese, many of whom are humorously caricatured in the pottery figurines from T'ang graves. Moreover they brought their own faiths with them — which flourished in an atmosphere of rare religious tolerance and curiosity. T'ai-tsung himself, though personally inclined towards Taoism, at the same time for reasons of state supported the Confucians and strengthened the administrative system. This astonishing man also treated the Buddhists with respect — notably that great traveller and theologian Hsüan-tsang, who had left China in defiance of an imperial order in 629 and after incredible hardships and delays reached India, where he acquired a great reputation as a scholar and metaphysician. In 645 he returned to Changan bringing with him the texts of the idealistic Vijñānavādin School of the Mahāyāna. The Emperor came out to meet him, and his entry into the capital was a public triumph. Never before had Buddhism stood so high in Chinese history; but it was not the only foreign religion on Chinese soil. There were also Zoroastrian temples, Manichaean and Nestorian Christian churches in the capital and, from the mid-eighth century onwards, Moslem mosques; and the art of this period is as full of imported motifs as were the streets of Changan with foreigners.

That China enjoyed a hundred years of peace and prosperity at home and enormous prestige abroad was due not only to the achievement of Li Shih-min but also to two outstanding personalities who succeeded him. His former concubine Wu Tse-t'ien was Empress only from 683 to 705, but throughout the reign of Kao-tsung (649–83), she was the able and unscrupulous *éminence grise* behind the throne. A woman capable of the most bestial cruelty and the profoundest Buddhist piety, she ruled China with a rod of iron until she was forced to abdicate at the age of eighty-two. Seven years later the throne passed to the man who as Hsüan-tsung (Ming Huang, 713–56), was to preside over the most brilliant court in Chinese history, a period comparable to the Gupta in the reign of King Harsha or Florence under Lorenzo dei Medici. Like T'ai-tsung he cherished and upheld the Confucian order, and in 754 founded the Imperial Academy of Letters (*Han-lin Yüan*) which, as Joseph Needham has observed, is older than any existing European academy by nearly a millennium. All the talent and wealth of the country which was not given to the construction and adornment of Buddhist temples seemed to be concentrated on his court, his palaces, his favourite scholars, poets and painters, his schools of drama and music, his orchestras (two of which came from Central Asia), and — finally — on his mistress, the lovely Yang Kuei-fei. Through her influence An Lu-shan, a general of Mongol or Tungus origin, had become a favourite with Ming Huang. Suddenly in 755 he revolted, and the Emperor and his court fled in panic from Changan. To appease his escort Ming Huang, now over seventy, was forced to hand his favourite over to the soldiers, who promptly strangled her. A few years later the empire was restored by the efforts of his son Su-tsung; but its power was broken, its glory past.

In 751 Chinese armies in Central Asia had been heavily defeated by Moslems advancing from the west, and Chinese Turkestan came permanently under Moslem influence. The Arab conquest of Central Asia began the destruction of that chain of prosperous, civilized kingdoms which had provided the overland link between China and the west in the seventh century, a process which was in due course to be completed by the ferocity of the Mongols. However, contact with the western world was maintained by way of the southern ports. The bustling quays of Canton were thronged with Chinese and foreigners who lived in peace and considerable prosperity with each other until Huang Ch'ao massacred the latter in 879, while at Ch'üan-chou in Fukien (Marco Polo's Zayton) recent excavations have revealed that as late as the thirteenth century Hindus, Arabs, Manichaeans and Jews were settled in that great trading port, whose cosmopolitanism is symbolized by the 'twin pagodas' of the K'ai-yüan temple, built in the twelfth century by Chinese and Indians working side by side.

As so often happens in history, China became less tolerant as her power declined, and the foreign religions suffered accordingly. The Taoists were jealous of the political power of the Buddhists and succeeded in poisoning the mind of the Emperor against them, while the Confucians had come more to look upon Buddhist practices (particularly celibacy) as 'un-Chinese'. The government also viewed with increasing alarm the vast sums spent on the monasteries and their unproductive inmates, who now numbered several hundred thousand. In 845 all foreign religions were proscribed, and all Buddhist temples confiscated by imperial edict. The ban on Buddhism was later relaxed, but in the meantime so thorough had been the destruction and looting that today very little survives of the great Buddhist architecture, sculpture and painting of the seventh and eighth centuries. Again we must look to Japan, and it is the monasteries at Nara, itself a replica of Changan, that preserve some of the finest of T'ang art. Tōdaiji was not an exact copy of a T'ang monastery, but in its grandeur of scale and conception it was designed to rival the great Chinese foundations. It was built on a north-south axis with pagodas

Main hall of Fu-kuang-ssu, Wu-t'ai-shan (ninth century).

flanking the main approach. A huge gateway leads into a courtyard dominated by the great Buddha Hall (Daibutsuden) 290 feet long by 170 feet deep by 156 feet high housing a gigantic seated Buddha in bronze, consecrated in 752. Much restored and altered, this is today the largest wooden building in the world, though in its time the Chien-yüan-tien at Loyang, long since destroyed, was even larger.

The earliest known T'ang wooden temple building is the small main hall of Nan-ch'an-ssu in Wu-t'ai-hsien, Shansi, built in 782; the largest is the main hall of Fu-kuang-ssu on Wu-t'ai-shan, built in the mid-ninth century. Its roof-line is still practically straight in silhouette, though the eaves and corners are beginning to show that graceful lift which from the tenth century onwards will impart such lightness and grace to Chinese architecture. Much has been written about this curve; it has even been seriously suggested that it was an attempt to imitate the sagging lines of the tents used by the Chinese in some long-forgotten nomadic stage. It is more likely that it was influenced by the architecture of China's neighbours in Southeast Asia with whom she was now coming into close contact for the first time.

The sketch on this page shows a conjectural restoration of one

Conjectural Reconstruction of the Lin-te-tien of the Ta-ming Kung, Ch'ang-an. T'ang Dynasty. (Drawn by T. A. Greeves.)

of the palaces of the Ta-ming Kung. It is interesting to compare this with the three great halls of the Forbidden City in Peking (page 207). While the latter is far larger in scale, the grouping of the buildings is much less interesting. The interlocking of masses on ascending levels buttressed at the sides by wings and towers, which gives such strength to the T'ang complex, was not attempted in Peking. T'ang (and indeed Sung) palaces seem to have been not only more enterprising architecturally but also more liveable than the vast, isolated and coldly ceremonial structures of the Ch'ing Dynasty, and suggest a more human concept of the rôle of the Emperor. By the T'ang Dynasty the heavy bracketing system (which, with the column it is poised upon, constitutes the nearest Chinese architecture comes to an 'order' in the Western sense), is becoming a little more complex; the brackets extend outwards and upwards to support two slanting cantilever arms called *ang*, the inner ends of which are anchored to a cross beam. In Sung and Yüan construction, the *ang* ride freely balanced on the bracketing system, creating a dynamic and meaningful play of forces that reminds us of Gothic vaulting. During the Ming and Ch'ing,

The development and decline of the bracket order. 1. T'ang (857); 2. Sung (1100); 3. Yüan (1357); 4. Ming; 5. Ch'ing (1734).

however, as the details become increasingly fussy and elaborate, the true function of *ang* and bracket is lost, and the whole degenerates into an intricate but structurally meaningless assemblage of carpentry, a mere decorative frieze running under the eaves.

A few T'ang stone and brick pagodas have survived. Some — the pagoda of Hsüan-tsang's temple at Sian, for example (page 132, 2) — are straightforward translations of a form of construction derived from the Han timber tower (*lou*). The Chien-fu-ssu at Sian (page 132, 5), on the other hand, derives ultimately from the Indian *śikhara* tower of stone, which we have already encountered in its purest form in the pagoda on Mount Sung (Plate 23a, and page 132, 4). Imitation of Indian forms is carried still further in the

Treasure Pagoda of the Fu-kuang temple on Wu-t'ai-shan, which originally had a dome, copied perhaps from a sketch or souvenir brought back by a returning pilgrim. Under the influence of the mystical Mahāyāna sects, an attempt was even made to incorporate the dome of a stūpa into a timber pagoda; none survive in China, but the twelfth-century Tahōtō of Ishiyamadera is a Japanese example of this odd misalliance.

Until the dissolution of the monasteries in 845, their insatiable demands for icons, banners and wall-paintings absorbed the energies of the great majority of painters and sculptors. Some of the sculptors' names are recorded: we read in Chang Yen-yüan's history, for example, of Yang Hui-chih, a painter in the time of Wu Tao-tzu, who 'finding that he made no progress, took to sculpture, which he thought was an easier craft'. Chang also mentions other pupils and colleagues of Wu's who became noted for their work in clay and stone; indeed, as we shall see, T'ang sculpture in its extraordinary linear fluidity seems often to have been formed by the brush rather than the chisel. Very little secular sculpture was carried out, if we except the guardian figures and winged horses and tigers, which lined the 'spirit way' leading to the imperial tombs. The earliest and most famous example of T'ang funerary sculpture is the set of panels depicting in relief the six favourite chargers of T'ang T'ai-tsung, executed, according to tradition, after designs by the great court painter Yen Li-pen; the style is plain and vigorous, the modelling so flat that the origin of these monumental silhouettes in line-drawings seems not at all improbable (Plate 30b).

The great Buddhist bronzes of the seventh and eighth centuries have all disappeared, melted down in the persecution of 845 or lost through subsequent neglect, and the style can best be seen in the temples at Nara in Japan. Only in the cave shrines has stone and clay sculpture survived in any quantity. At Lung-men, in 672 the Emperor Kao-tsung ordered the carving of a colossal figure of the Buddha Vairoćana flanked by the disciples Ananda and Kāśyapa, with attendant bodhisattvas. Obviously intended to rival in size and magnificence the great Buddha of Yünkang, this figure of the Buddha of Boundless Light far surpasses it in power of modelling, refinement of proportion and subtlety of feeling. Even though badly damaged, the Vairoćana well expresses the ideal of the Mahāyāna which saw the Buddha not as a great teacher but as a universal principle radiating out in all directions for all time. More directly modelled on an Indian prototype — perhaps on a version of the celebrated sandalwood image reputedly made by King Udayana in the Buddha's lifetime, a copy of which was brought back by Hsüan-tsang in 645, — is the thoroughly Gupta torso in marble from Ch'ü-yang-hsien, Hopei, in the Victoria and Albert Museum (Plate 31a). This tendency to treat stone as though it were clay reached its climax in the cave shrines carved out at T'ien-lung-shan during the reigns of Wu Tse-t'ien and Ming Huang (Plate 33). Here the figures are carved fully in the round with the exquisite grace and richly sensuous appeal that we find in Greek sculpture of the fourth century B.C. The modelling has an all-too-Indian suavity and voluptuousness; the drapery seems as though poured over the fleshy body, the face is over-full, the mouth small and pouting. But, to compensate, there is in these figures a new mobility of movement. In these figures the Indian feeling for solid swelling form and the Chinese genius for expression in terms of linear rhythm are at last successfully fused, to produce a style which was to become the basis of all later Buddhist sculpture in China.

The Buddhist painting of this period must have contained as rich a mixture of native and foreign elements as did sculpture. During the seventh century the most popular subjects were those that illustrated the teachings of the T'ien-t'ai sect based on the *Lotus Sūtra*, an encyclopaedic text which in its combination of theology and metaphysics, ethics, magic and simple human appeal seemed to satisfy all human needs; we have already encountered some of its themes on the sculptured steles of the Northern Wei. Even more popular were the teachings of the *Ching-t'u* (Pure Land) school, which had cut its way through the growing forest of metaphysical abstractions of the later Mahāyāna with the doctrine that through simple faith one might be reborn in one of the Buddhist Paradises and so find release and eternal bliss. By the mid-seventh century, however, new concepts were coming into Buddhism which were eventually to bring about its decline. The later Mahāyāna in India had become deeply coloured by a highly abstract and idealistic metaphysics on the one hand, and by the practices of the Tantric sects of revived Hinduism on the other. Tantrism held that by sheer concentration of will-power, aided by magic spells (*mantra*) and diagrams (*mandala*) a deity could be invoked and desirable changes in the order of things thus brought about. This school also believed in the Hindu concept of the *Śakti*, a female emanation, or reflex, of a deity who would be doubly efficacious if represented clasping her in ecstatic union. At its finest this new art has a formidable power that is overwhelming, but it too easily degenerated into the soulless repetition of magical formulae.[1] It found its true home in the bleak wastes of Tibet, whence it reached out to paralyse the art of Tunhuang during the Tibetan occupation from about 750 to 848. In course of time, the revolt of the Chinese spirit against the sentimental, the over-intellectual and the diabolical aspects of these sects found expression in the Ch'an (Zen) school of contemplative mysticism, but as this doctrine did not greatly affect painting until the Sung Dynasty we will defer discussion of it to the next chapter.

Chang Yen-yüan's catalogue in the *Ming-hua-chi* of frescoes in the temples of Loyang and Changan is as full of the names of great painters and their works as Baedeker's guide to Florence; but the

---

[1] It was probably the demands of Mahāyāna Buddhism for the endless multiplication of icons, diagrams, spells and texts that brought about the rapid development of block printing in the T'ang Dynasty. The earliest printed text yet discovered is a Buddhist charm dated equivalent to A.D. 770, found at Tunhuang by Sir Aurel Stein. It is likely, however, that the Chinese and Tibetans had been experimenting with block printing since the middle of the sixth century, while the use of seals in Shang China and the practice of taking rubbings of inscriptions engraved on stone (made possible by the Han invention of paper) point to the existence of printing of a sort at a far earlier date.

persecution of 845, coupled with wars and rebellions, fire and sheer neglect, have destroyed them all. According to contemporary accounts the work of the foreign painters aroused much interest and had considerable influence on local artists. During the Northern Ch'i there had been Ts'ao Chung-ta, whose figures 'were clad in garments which clung to the body; they looked as if they had been drenched in water', — an apt description also of the sculpture at T'ien-lung-shan. The Khotanese painter Yü-ch'ih (or Wei-ch'ih) Po-chih-na had come to Changan in the Sui Dynasty; he specialized not only in Buddhist subjects but also in strange objects from foreign lands, and flowers which he painted with great realism. His son (?) I-seng was honoured by T'ai-tsung with a ducal title. 'His paintings,' says the *T'ang-ch'ao ming-hua-lu*, 'whether votive images, human figures, or flowers and birds, were always foreign-looking and not like Chinese things,' while Chang Yen-yüan said of his brushwork that it was 'tight and strong like bending iron or coiling wire'. A Yüan critic wrote of him that 'he used deep colours which he piled up in raised layers on the silk'. His work is of course long since lost, but a painting of Śākyamuni standing under a flowering tree which bears the inscription 'Ch'en Yung-chih (an eleventh-century painter) respectfully copied', now in the Museum of Fine Arts, Boston, has all the characteristics of the Yü-ch'ih style — flowers painted in relief, fine wire-like brush-lines and strong colour — and may well be a copy of one of I-seng's paintings. It seems that his 'relief style' of flower painting was not a subtle use of shading to give an effect of solid volume as is often supposed on the basis of descriptions in early texts, but a much cruder technique wherein the pigment was piled up in a heavy impasto till the flowers actually *did* stand out from the wall.

While some T'ang painters were no doubt seduced by such devices into thoroughly un-Chinese experiments, Wu Tao-tzu, the greatest of them all, seems from contemporary accounts to have subordinated them into a truly Chinese style, which in its grandeur of conception and fiery energy of execution makes him one with Michelangelo. Born about 700, he is said before he died to have painted three hundred frescoes (using the term in the general sense) in the temples of Loyang and Changan. None of his pictures have survived; indeed by the eleventh century the poet Su Tung-p'o could say that he had seen but two genuine ones, his friend Mi Fei three or four. But we can obtain a vivid idea of the vigour, the solidity and realism of his work from descriptions written by those who had seen it — more vivid certainly than is provided by the third-hand copies, odd rubbings and sketches on which our estimates are generally based. The twelfth-century writer Tung Yu said of him, 'Wu Tao-tzu's figures remind me of sculpture. One can see them sideways and all round. His line-work consists of minute curves like rolled copper wire' — (another writer says this was more characteristic of his early work: it suggests the influence of Yü-ch'ih I-seng) — 'however thickly his red or white paint is laid on, the structure of the forms and modelling of the flesh are never obscured.' Earlier Tung Yu had remarked that 'when he paints a face, the cheek-bones project, the nose is fleshy, the eyes hollow, the cheeks dimpled. But these effects are not got by heavy ink shading. The shape of the features seems to have come spontaneously, yet inevitably'. All spoke of the whirlwind energy of his brush, so remarkable that crowds would gather to watch him as he worked.

No major works survive in China itself to demonstrate that fusion of Indian metaphysical and formal ideals with the traditional Chinese language of the brush, which took place in the T'ang Dynasty. But such a fusion did take place — probably it was that very fusion which made Wu Tao-tzu the focus and begetter of a whole school of religious painting — and was in turn passed on to Japan. Early in the eighth century, the walls of the Kondō (Golden Hall) of Hōryūji Monastery at Nara were decorated by an unknown master with four large square panels depicting the Paradises of the Buddhas of the four directions, and eight vertical panels with bodhisattvas. These paintings, after miraculously surviving for twelve hundred years, were almost totally destroyed by fire in 1949, a disaster to the art of the world as great as if the frescoes in the Sistine Chapel or those in the cave temples of Ajantā had been consumed. A part of the most popular paradise — that of Amitābha — is illustrated in Plate 32a. The composition is a simple and serene arrangement of deities, the bodhisattvas Mahāsthāmaprāpta and Avalokiteśvara standing on either side of Amitābha, who sits turning the wheel of the law on his lotus throne beneath a bejewelled canopy. The figures are drawn with a sweeping brush-line of extraordinary delicacy and precision which evokes a feeling of the solid form, from which the Indian tactile sensuality has been abstracted away. Indeed, except for the iconography and the contours themselves there is little that is Indian here. Arbitrary shading is used with great restraint to amplify the roundness of an arm or chin, but much more is accomplished by the almost imperceptible modulations of the brush-line itself, while the folds of the drapery are emphasized by a kind of shading which — if the Admonitions scroll is a faithful copy of the style of Ku K'ai-chih — goes back to the fifth century. Only in the jewellery is there a hint of that rich impasto with which the Yü-ch'ih had astonished Changan. Apart from these details, the forms, as Tung Yu said of Wu Tao-tzu, 'seem to have come spontaneously, yet inevitably'.

Long after the cult of Amitābha had declined in metropolitan China it lived on in the hearts of the pilgrims and country folk at Tunhuang, who must have gazed with awe and wonder at the huge heavenly visions which filled the walls of the seventh- and eighth-century caves. In a walled-up library at Tunhuang Sir Aurel Stein found a great hoard of manuscripts and silk banners. Many were craftsman's work, but, taken as a whole, they represent the only considerable group of undoubtedly genuine Chinese silk paintings from the T'ang Dynasty that have survived. The most remarkable is a banner on which are very carefully drawn a series of Buddha figures almost certainly copied from sketches of well-known Indian images made on the spot.[1] One represents the Buddha of

[1] The paintings discussed in this paragraph are illustrated in L. Binyon, *The Thousand Buddhas* (London, 1921).

the Enlightenment at Bōdhgāya, two are faithful reproductions of Gandhāran models, another shows the Buddha preaching on the Vulture Peak, while Stein identified yet another as identical in style with two great stucco reliefs which he discovered in the ruins of a monastery in Khotan. The banners also include a number of paradises, and single deities (especially the increasingly popular Kuanyin), painted in warm colours, with a wealth of detail and floral ornament. The most appealing and lively parts of these banners are the little panels at the sides which, like the predella of a quattrocento altarpiece, tell in miniature the story of the Buddha's life on earth, generally in a landscape setting. It seems that until Tibetan esoteric Buddhism laid its cold hand on Tunhuang, the Chinese painters there used a landscape setting wherever they could. Sometimes, indeed, it dominates the theme in a thoroughly un-Indian fashion. In Caves 103 (P. 54) and 217 (P. 70), for example, the old subdivision into superimposed horizontal scrolls has been replaced by a panoramic landscape of towering peaks which fills the whole wall. There is still a tendency to break it up into smaller connected 'space cells', and the transition through the middle distance to the horizon is hardly better managed than on the stone sarcophagus in Kansas City. But other paintings at Tunhuang, notably the landscape vignettes in Cave 323, show that this problem was successfully solved in the eighth century.

We must return from the rustic pleasures of Tunhuang naturalism to the splendour of the T'ang court. A famous scroll in Boston bearing portraits of thirteen emperors from Han to Sui has traditionally been attributed to Yen Li-pen, the son and brother of two famous artists, who had been a court painter in attendance (*tai-chao*) to T'ai-tsung and rose to the high office of Minister of the Right under his successor. This great handscroll — or part of it, for more than half is a copy of the Sung Dynasty — is the very epitome of the Confucian ideal, now restored to its proper place as the pivot of Chinese society (Plate 32b). While each group makes a monumental composition by itself, together they form a royal pageant of incomparable dignity. The figures are full, the robes ample, the brush-line fluent and of even thickness. Arbitrary shading is used with great restraint to give volume to the faces, more generously in the folds of the robes, as on the Amitābha in the Kondō at Hōryūji.

The wealth, ease and security of T'ang court life is further revealed in the paintings attributed to Chou Fang and to Chang Hsüan, a court painter under Ming Huang who was chiefly celebrated for his paintings of 'young nobles, saddle horses and women of rank'. So far as is known none of his works survive in the original, but the Sung Emperor, painter and connoisseur Hui-tsung copied his 'Court Ladies preparing Silk' (Plate 34). We see a lady, about to pound the silk strands, rolling up her sleeves; another draws out the thread, a third is sewing, while in the centre a servant fans the charcoal brazier. On the left, a little girl critically inspects the ironing process from below. The colour is rich and glowing, the detail of jewel-like precision. There is neither ground nor background, but the picture has depth, and there is a wonderful and uniquely Chinese sense of almost tangible space between the figures.

Court painters such as Chou Fang and Chang Hsüan were kept busy by the Emperor, as were the poets, in celebrating the more memorable social and cultural events of court life, and in portrait painting. This included portraits not only of the Emperor's favourite concubines and virtuous ministers, but also of strangers from the west whose exaggerated features have been a never-failing source of delight to the Chinese. In more serious vein were portraits of Buddhist priests, such as the series of the patriarchs of the *Chen-yen* (Shingon) sect, painted by Li Chen, a contemporary of Chou Fang. Long forgotten in China, the work of this artist has been cherished in Japan for its austere and noble evocation of the spirit of mystical Buddhism.

Court artists were not always treated with the respect they felt was due to them. Chang Yen-yüan noted the indignity to which the great Yen Li-pen was once subjected, when he was peremptorily summoned, sweating and panting, to sketch an unusual bird that had alighted on the lake in front of T'ai-tsung, after which he advised his son never to become a court painter. Ming Huang was passionately fond of horses, particularly the tough, stocky ponies from the western regions, and is said to have had over forty thousand in his stables. The striking painting of one of his favourites, Light of the Night, has long been attributed to the noted horse-specialist Han Kan (Plate 35a). Tethered to a post, he rears up with eyes dilated as though suddenly startled. All but the head, neck and forequarters are the work of a later restorer (who also forgot the tail), but enough remains to suggest a dynamic energy of movement and solidity of modelling such as we find also in the best of the T'ang pottery figurines.

During these prosperous years, when painters were busily occupied with Buddhist frescoes, portrait painting and other socially useful activities, their hearts, if not their feet, were roaming the hills and valleys far from the glitter of the capital. The tradition of landscape painting which was later to rise to such supreme heights had been born in the Six Dynasties, but it had advanced little — partly because of the ever-increasing demands for Buddhist icons, partly because artists were then still struggling with the most elementary problems of space and depth. But during the T'ang Dynasty these difficulties were mastered.

According to later Chinese critics and historians, two schools of landscape painting came into being in the T'ang Dynasty. One, created by the court painter Li Ssu-hsün and his son Li Chao-tao, painted in a precise line technique, adding decorative mineral colours; the other, founded by the poet-painter Wang Wei, developed landscape painting in monochrome ink; the former, later called the 'northern school', became in course of time the special province of court painters and professionals, while the latter, the so-called 'southern school', was the natural mode of expression for scholars and amateurs. As we shall see when we come to a discussion of Ming painting, this doctrine of the northern and southern schools, and of the founding rôle of Wang

Wei, was invented by a group of late Ming scholar-critics to bolster up their belief in the superiority of their own kind of painting over that of the professionals and court painters of the day. In fact, the line between the two kinds of painting was not so sharply drawn in the T'ang Dynasty. Wang Wei is known to have painted in colour, and there were other far more original painters than he active in the eighth and ninth centuries. His elevation to this pinnacle in the history of Chinese painting was an expression of the belief, shared by all scholar painters from the Sung Dynasty onwards, that a man's painting, like his handwriting, should be the expression, not of his skill, but of his quality as a man. Because Wang Wei was the ideal type of man, it was argued, he must also have been the ideal type of painter.

A gifted musician, scholar and poet, Wang Wei (699–759) joined the brilliant group of painters and intellectuals round Ming Huang's brother, Prince Ch'i. He got into political difficulties at the time of the An Lu-shan rebellion, but was extricated by his brother and restored to imperial favour. When his wife died in 630 he became a devout Buddhist, though whether this influenced his painting is not known. He was famous in his lifetime for his snow landscapes, but the work for which he is best remembered by later painters was the long panoramic handscroll depicting his country estate, Wang-ch'uan, outside Changan. This picture disappeared long ago, and although the general composition has been preserved in many later copies, these give little idea of the style, still less of the technique. Perhaps the nearest we shall ever get to him is the beautiful little Riverside under Snow, formerly in the Manchu Household Collection (Plate 35b), which, to judge from reproductions, could be a late T'ang or tenth century painting. The landscape conventions are archaic, the technique simple, yet no early Chinese landscape painting evokes more movingly the atmosphere of a river bank in the depths of winter, when the snow covers the ground, the roofs, and the bare branches, and men hurry home to their cottages at dusk.

A brilliant example of the so-called northern tradition of Li

Ssu-hsün (651–716) and Li Chao-tao (died about 735) is the small hanging scroll called Ming Huang's Journey to Shu, in the Palace Museum collection in Taiwan (Plate 36). This jewel of a picture is believed to illustrate the flight of the emperor from An Lu-shan in 756, though the tragic event is here represented as a happy excursion through the mountains on a summer day. The tripartite divison of the composition, the exaggerated peaks and slab-like *ch'üeh*, and the carefully-drawn trees lining the edges of the contours, are all archaic features; the brush drawing is fine and precise, and a richly decorative effect is achieved by the use of malachite green and azurite blue — the so-called *ch'ing-lü* (blue and green) style. It is not known precisely when this picture was painted. In all essentials it preserves the T'ang courtly style of landscape painting, but may possibly be a Sung copy of a T'ang original. This tradition was further developed in the Sung Dynasty by such painters as Chao Po-chü, and in later centuries by a host of academicians and professionals, of whom the most accomplished were T'ang Yin and Ch'iu Ying (Plate 57b).

The objects, apart from paintings and sculpture, with which our western collections illustrate the achievements of T'ang culture are, for the most part, grave goods. These, though they have an appealing vigour and simplicity of form and decoration, bear little relation to the finest of T'ang decorative arts. Some objects of fine quality have been found in tombs, and others have been handed down in private collections, but if all of it were put together it would not give the overwhelming impression of the splendour and refinement of T'ang decorative art that we get from one single collection in Japan. In 756 the Empress Kōken dedicated to the great Buddha of Tōdaiji at Nara the treasures which her deceased husband Shōmu had collected in his lifetime. These and other objects were put in a treasury, called the Shōsōin, in which they have survived virtually intact until this day. This remarkable collection contains furniture, musical instruments and gaming boards painted, lacquered, or inlaid with magnificent floral and animal designs in mother-of-pearl, tortoise-shell, gold and silver;

there are glass vessels from the Arab world,[1] silver platters, jugs and ewers, mirrors, silk brocades, weapons, pottery, maps, paintings and calligraphy. What is astonishing about this collection is the extent of the foreign influence present. This is particularly true of the art of the goldsmith and silversmith which came into their own in the T'ang Dynasty. Hitherto silverwork had been largely dominated by bronze design, but under Near Eastern influence it is emancipated. Some silver vessels, such as the two huge bowls in the Shōsōin, were cast, but precious metals were scarce, and a massive appearance was often gained with little material by soldering thin sheets together to form the outer and inner surface. Many of the shapes such as the stem-cup (Plate 38b), foliated bowl and flat platter with animal designs in repoussé were of Persian origin; the decoration, applied with a typically T'ang combination of lavishness and delicacy, includes animals and figures, hunting scenes, flowers, birds and floral scrolls, generally chased or engraved, and set off against a background of rows of tiny punched circles, a technique borrowed from Sasanian metalwork.

The extravagant taste of the T'ang Dynasty also demanded that mirror-backs be gilded or silvered. The old abstract and magical designs have now been replaced by a profusion of ornament whose significance is auspicious in a more general way. Symbols of conjugal felicity, entwined dragons, phoenixes, birds and flowers in relief or inlaid in silver or mother-of-pearl account for most of the designs. Two beautiful mirrors in the Shōsōin retain something of the ancient symbolism of the TLV design by bearing landscapes of foam-washed peaks ringed with clouds and set about with fairies, immortals and other fabulous creatures; while the influence of Manichean symbolism may be seen, as Cammann

[1] Glass seems to have reached China from the Near East in the eighth or seventh century B.C. Glass beads have been unearthed in Chou tombs, while in a tomb of the Western Han period discovered in Changsha in 1956 were found a cap to a sword hilt engraved with dragons and a beautifully-shaped spearhead, both made of glass (K'ao-ku hsüeh-pao 1957, 4; p. 56 and Plate 9).

believes, in the so-called sea-horse and grape design which was extremely popular for a short time (Plate 38a): its sudden disappearance may have coincided with the suppression of foreign religions in 843–5. T'ang ceramics too made much use of foreign shapes and motifs. The metal ewer was copied in stoneware, often with appliqué designs in relief under a mottled green and brown glaze; the rhyton was reproduced from an old Persian shape; the circular pilgrim bottle, which appears in the blue-glazed pottery

a   *b*

Bird-headed ewers; *a*: T'ang glazed earthenware; *b*: Sasanian parcel-gilt from Kharkov, U.S.S.R. (After Willetts.)

of Parthian Persia and Syria, reappears in China, decorated rather roughly in relief with vintaging boys, dancers, musicians, and hunting scenes. The Hellenistic amphora in Chinese stoneware loses its static symmetry; the playful dragon handles, the lift and buoyance of its silhouette, the almost casual way in which the glaze is splashed on, all bespeak the touch of the Chinese craftsman, who brings the clay to life under his hands.

The T'ang Dynasty is notable in the history of Chinese ceramics for the dynamic beauty of its shapes, for the first use of coloured glazes, and for the perfecting of porcelain. Now no longer are potters limited to the simple green and brown-tinted glazes of the Han; the fine white earthenware of the T'ang Dynasty is often clothed in a polychrome glaze, made by mixing copper, iron or cobalt with a colourless lead silicate to produce a rich range of colours from blue and green to yellow and brown; this glaze is applied more thinly than before, often over a white slip, is generally very finely crackled and stops short of the base in an uneven line (Plate 39a). Dishes are stamped with elaborate foliate or lotus patterns and decorated with coloured glazes, which are confined by the incised lines of the central design, whereas elsewhere the colours tend to run together. The T'ang love of rich effects is seen also in the marbled wares, made by mixing two different clays together and covering the vessel with a transparent glaze. The more robust T'ang wares were exported to the Near East where they were widely imitated in the poor-quality clays of Persia and Mesopotamia.

These coloured earthenwares were produced chiefly in North China, though they were imitated elsewhere. One of the Honan kiln sites was discovered in 1957 in Kung-hsien, thirty miles east of Loyang. Koyama, who has made an extensive study of this period, believes that the polychrome wares began to decline after the middle of the eighth century, although they persisted in grave figurines in Szechwan and in the ceramic sculpture of North China well into the Sung Dynasty. In the meantime however, Yüeh ware had reached a high pitch of perfection at the Shang-lin-hu kilns near Hangchow. The body is porcellanous; bowls and vases (the most common shapes) are decorated with moulded or incised decoration under an olive-green glaze. The soft-bodied North China wares have a flat or slightly concave base, but the Yüeh wares have a fairly high and often slightly splayed foot.

It was probably in the late seventh or early eighth century that the Chinese potters perfected true porcelain, by which is meant a hard, translucent ware fused at high temperature with the aid of a high proportion of felspar, causing it to ring when struck. In 851 a work entitled 'The Story of China and India' by an unknown author appeared at Basra; it contained information about the Cantonese supplied by a certain merchant named Sulaiman, who writes of them, 'they have pottery of excellent quality, of which bowls are made as fine as glass drinking cups: the sparkle of water can be seen through it, although it is pottery.'[1] Indeed this white ware was already in demand far beyond China's shores, for fragments both of green Yüeh ware and white porcelain were found in the ruins of the Abbasid city of Samarra which was the summer residence of the Caliphs from 836 to 883. Although the site was occupied after that date, the greater part of the huge quantity of shards belongs to the years of its heyday and bears witness to a flourishing export trade in Chinese ceramics. What was this white ware? An *Essay on Tea*, the *Ch'a-ching*, written it is believed by the poet Lu Yü in the latter half of the ninth century, says that for drinking tea one should use Yüeh bowls which give it the colouring of ice or jade, or the ware of Hsing-chou which was as white as snow or silver. A number of pieces have been identified as possibly Hsing-yao on account of their hardness, their creamy-whiteness and their typically T'ang shapes, but the kilns have not yet been discovered and its identification remains uncertain.[2] In these white wares the most characteristic shapes are bowls, often with a slightly everted and foliated lip, globular jars and ewers (Plate 39b) of generous contour, and stemcups imitating silver vessels.

The white porcelain soon became popular and was widely imitated, notably in the white-slipped stonewares of Hunan and Szechwan. At the same time the number of kilns making the finer wares begins to multiply. In the latter half of the dynasty white porcellanous wares were made — if a single reference in a poem of Tu Fu is acceptable evidence — at Ta-yi in Szechwan; while a

---

[1] *Abbar as-sin wa l-hind.* Translated and edited by Jean Sauvaget (1948), 16, Section 34.

[2] The Ting ware kilns at Chien-tz'u-ts'un in Hopei were already producing a fine white porcelain, which may have been the elusive Hsing-yao.

pale bluish-white ware, the predecessor of the lovely Sung *ch'ing-pai* (*ying-ch'ing*), was already being produced in the Shih-hu-wan kilns near Ching-te-chen, and at Chi-chou, both in Kiangsi. Yüeh-type celadons were being manufactured near Changsha in Hunan, and in Hsiang-yin-hsien north of the city, where some of the earliest experiments in underglaze and enamel painting in China were undertaken. One final group consists of a hard grey stoneware made in North China in full, massive shapes and covered with a rich brown or black felspathic glaze often made even more striking by bluish-white phosphatic splashes. This, the ancestor of the famous splashed Chün wares of the Sung Dynasty, was made in kilns in Chia-hsien, not far from Chün-chou.

The fact that most of the T'ang wares that we enjoy today were made, not for the collector's pleasure, not even for domestic use, but simply as cheap grave goods probably accounts for their unsophisticated charm and vigour. These qualities are most apparent in the great numbers of figurines placed in the tombs, which give a vivid picture of daily life in T'ang times. They vary in size from animals and toys a few inches high to gigantic horses, Bactrian camels, armed men and fantastic squatting guardian creatures popularly called *ch'i-t'ou* or *pi-hsieh*. They include a fascinating array of officials, servants, dancing girls and musicians; indeed, among them women predominate. Women rode horseback with the men, and even played polo. A passage in the 'Treatise on Carriages and Dress' in the *Chiu T'ang-shu* (*Old T'ang History*) records that 'At the beginning of the K'ai-yüan period (713–42) the palace ladies who rode behind the carriages all wore Central Asian hats, exposing the face, without a veil. Suddenly their hair also was exposed when they broke into a gallop. Some were wearing men's dress and boots.'[1]

Something of the gaiety of this courtly life is recaptured in these pottery figurines. The fairy-like slenderness of the Six Dynasties women has now given way to an almost Victorian rotundity — Yang Kuei-fei herself was said to have been plump.

[1] See *Chinese Tomb Pottery Figurines* (Hongkong, 1953), p. 9.

But these women make up in character for what they lack in elegance, while Chinese potters derived much amusement from caricaturing the extraordinary clothes, the beards and great jutting noses of the foreigners from Central and Western Asia. The human figurines were almost always made in moulds, the front and back being cast separately, while the larger figures and animals were made in several pieces, generally with the base, or underside of the belly, left open. Though sometimes left in the slip and painted, they are most often lavishly decorated with three-colour glazes, which in time acquired a minute crackle very difficult for the forger to imitate.

CHAPTER EIGHT

The Five Dynasties and Sung

T'ang China never fully recovered from the An Lu-shan rebellion, and gradually what had been a great empire shrank, both in body and spirit. The loss of Central Asia to Islam, the Tibetan invasion, rebellions by local war-lords and the consequent breakdown in the irrigation system on which prosperity and good order depended, all made the downfall of the dynasty inevitable. In 907 China finally disintegrated into the state of political chaos dignified with the name of the Five Dynasties. The title is an arbitrary one, chosen to cover those royal houses which had their capitals in the northeast; set up mostly by military adventurers, they had such grandiloquent names as Later T'ang, Later Han and Later Chou. Between 907 and 923 Later Liang had four rulers belonging to three different families. Although the south and west were divided among the Ten (lesser) Kingdoms, in fact those regions were far more peaceful and prosperous. Szechwan, as before when the country was disunited, was, until the destruction of 'Former Shu' by Later T'ang in 925, a flourishing kingdom, distinguished for its scholars, poets and artists who had come as refugees from the T'ang court, bringing with them something of the imperial splendours of Changan and Loyang. The tomb of the first Shu Emperor Wang Chien (907–18), excavated in 1942–43, was found to contain jades, wall-painting, silverwork and sculpture of a high order, and purely in the T'ang tradition.

Meantime, as before, the northern barbarians watched with patient interest the disintegration of their old enemy. In 936 the first ruler of Later Chin made the fatal gesture of ceding to the

Khitans the area between Peking and the sea south of the Great Wall, with the result that for the first time the northern nomads had a footing on the edge of the North China plain. Ten years later they established the kingdom of Liao over a wide area of North China, which was not to be finally restored to Chinese hands for over four hundred years.

In 959 the last emperor of the Later Chou died and in the following year the regent, General Chao K'uang-yin, was persuaded to ascend the throne as the first emperor of a new dynasty. At first it seemed that the Sung would be just one more in a succession of

North China in the Eleventh Century

short-lived houses. But Chao was an able man; in sixteen years of vigorous campaigning he had practically united China, though, as Goodrich observed, his armies never succeeded in breaking the iron ring that had been forged round the imperial boundaries by the Khitan (until 1125), the Jurchen Tungus (until 1234) and the Mongols in the north; by the Tangut, a Tibetan people (c. 990–1227), and the Mongols in the northwest; and by Annam and Nan Chao in the southwest. In 1125 the dynasty suffered a disaster from which it barely recovered, when the Jurchen raided the capital at Kaifeng and captured the whole court including the Emperor Hui-tsung, famous throughout history as a painter, collector and connoisseur. In 1127 a young prince and the remaining officials fled south beyond the barrier of the Yangtse, where the court wandered from place to place for ten years before they set up what they hoped was to be their temporary capital at Hangchow. The Jurchen, who named their dynasty Chin, were now in control of all China north of the Yangtse. Like the Liao, they were only prevented from further incursions into Sung territory by the enormous tribute which China paid every year, chiefly in coin and rolls of silk, until Genghis Khan with his savage hordes descended from the north, obliterating friend and foe alike.

Hemmed about by hostile powers, the Sung looked inward upon herself. Han China had lived in a fabulous world whose boundaries were mythical K'un-lun and P'eng-lai far beyond the horizon; T'ang China flung out her arms to embrace Central Asia and welcome all that the west had to offer. Sung China, at peace with itself and buying peace with its neighbours, proceeded to examine the world with a new curiosity, a deeper reverence. She rediscovered the world of feeling and imagination which had been revealed to her in the Six Dynasties, but had been lost again under the strong light of T'ang positivism. It was this depth of philosophical insight, combined with a perfect balance of creative energy and technical refinement, that made the tenth and eleventh centuries one of the great epochs in the history of Chinese art.

During this time, China was ruled by a succession of emperors more truly cultivated than any before or since. Under them the intellectuals who ran the government were a privileged élite, permitted to remain seated in the imperial presence, and to debate rival policies with complete freedom. Their prestige was perhaps partly due to the rapid spread of printing, for which Chengtu, the capital of Shu, was already the chief centre in the ninth century. There the first paper money had been printed, the first edition of the Classics was issued in 130 volumes between 932 and 953, the Buddhist *Tripitaka* in over 5000 volumes and the Taoist canon before the end of the century. With the aid of this new craft it became possible to synthesize knowledge as never before, and there began the unending compilation of dictionaries, encyclopaedias and anthologies which was to become ever more characteristic of Chinese intellectual activity until the Revolution. It was this desire for intellectual synthesis which led to the founding by Chou Tun-i and Chu Hsi of the doctrine of Neo-Confucianism, in which Confucian morality (*li*) became identified with the Taoist first cause (*t'ai-chi*) seen as a moral force, and at the same time was enriched by a theory of knowledge and a way of self-cultivation derived partly from Buddhism. To the Neo-Confucianists *li* became the governing principle which gives to each form its inherent nature. By 'investigating things' — that is, by a process of study, part scientific, part intuitive, and leading outwards from the near and familiar — the cultivated man could deepen his knowledge of the world and of the workings of *li*. The trend in Sung painting (particularly in bird-and-flower and bamboo painting), towards the intimate 'close-up' bears witness to the profound and subtle examination of the visible world which the Neo-Confucian doctrine inspired.

An important by-product of the Confucian revival, or parallel manifestation of the same backward-looking impulses perhaps, was the new interest taken in ancient arts and crafts, creating a demand for reproductions of archaic ritual vessels and implements, in bronze and jade, which was to grow with the centuries. Some Sung copies are hard to distinguish from Shang and Chou pieces with any certainty. They are of superb craftsmanship (even the patina was imitated), less vigorous in form than their ancient models, but much closer to them than the fanciful archaisms of the Ch'ien-lung period. Illustrated catalogues of the Sung imperial collections were compiled, but they only survive in late, unreliable editions, and are of little help in separating Sung reproductions from the genuine archaic bronzes and jades which enthusiastic antiquarians were beginning to unearth.

It is also in character with the 'intellectualizing' trend of the period that the first great manual on architectural practice, the *Ying-tsao fa-shih* (presented to the emperor in 1100), should have been written in the Sung Dynasty. The author, Li Chiai, a practising architect in the service of the state, combines historical scholarship with a considerable amount of straightforward technical information on materials and construction, which in his time was becoming increasingly complex and refined — if not so grand in scale as in the T'ang Dynasty. The *ang*, for example, is now no longer a simple cantilevered beam jutting out to hold up the eaves; it is cut loose from supports at either end and poised on the top of an intricate bracketing system, held in balance by a complex play of stresses and strains. In time this intricacy for its own sake will lead to degeneration, but in Sung timber construction it combines structural boldness with refinement of detail. Sung taste also preferred the delicate to the robust, the tall and slender to the gigantic and solid, and Kaifeng was a city of spires. Temples had roofs of yellow tiles and were floored with yellow and green. Timber and stone pagodas now acquired little projecting roofs at each storey, curving up at the point where two faces met. On the subject of curved roofs, Soper quotes a remark made by the master builder Yü Hao who had come up to the capital from the south early in the dynasty: 'They certainly were capable enough in those days,' he is reported to have said on looking at a T'ang gate tower, 'The only thing is, they didn't understand how to curve up their eaves' — at the corners. We have seen that the curving eaves and sweeping roof line began in the south, probably under the influence of China's Southeast Asian and island neighbours; they were used on some Five Dynasties pagodas in the Yangtse region and, perhaps, were brought to Kaifeng by Yü Hao himself. Temples were further embellished with elaborate timber cupolas over the images, while libraries had model pavilions surmounting each bay, and huge revolving bookcases for the *sūtras*, such as that which still survives in the eleventh-century Lung-hsing-ssu at Cheng-ting-hsien in Hopei. Slightly later but more splendid in total effect is the Buddha Hall of Upper Hua-yen monastery at Tatung in Shansi, dedicated in 1140 (Plate 40a). Here, architect, sculptor and fresco-painter have combined their arts in the service of theology to create a fabulous Buddha-world by which the worshipper, on entering the hall, is surrounded and enveloped. Buddhas, bodhisats, guardians and arhats take their apportioned place in a gigantic three-dimensional *mandala*, the total effect of which is to saturate the eye, and the mind, of the believer with the manifold and all-embracing powers of God.

As the Toba Wei had fostered Buddhism because they themselves were aliens on Chinese soil, so did the Liao and Chin support it, and under their patronage the old faith was vigorously revived. The largest surviving bronze image in China, a many-armed Kuanyin consecrated in 971, can still be seen in its temple at Cheng-ting-hsien in Liao territory, but it is a wretched effort. Rather more successful and interesting are the colossal Buddhas and bodhisattvas carved at Yünkang, in so close an imitation of the Sui work nearby that their Liao date has only recently been established by Japanese scholars. Perhaps the most impressive — and deceptive — of Liao-Chin sculpture is the set of pottery figures of *lohan* (*arhats*) which were found some years ago in a cave at I-chou near Peking. One is in the British Museum, five others in western collections. The vigorous modelling, the dignity and realism, and above all the three-colour glaze, all suggested a T'ang date at a time when the possibility of art of any quality being produced under the Liao and Chin was not seriously considered. But it is now known that North China at this time was the centre of a flourishing culture in which the traditions of T'ang art were preserved, with subtle differences, not only in sculpture but also in ceramics, and there is no disgrace in assigning them to the Liao or Chin. These figures, and others executed in dry-lacquer, are not so much portraits of individual monks, as expressions of a variety of spiritual states. In the face of the young Arhat in the Nelson Gallery is portrayed all the inward struggle, the will to triumph, the intensity of concentration of the meditative sects of which Zen was the chief. When we turn to the figure in the Metropolitan Museum (Plate 40b), we see in the bony skull, lined features and deep-set eyes of an old man, the outcome of that struggle; it has taken its toll of the flesh, but the spirit has emerged serene and triumphant.

But not all sculpture of this period was an archaistic revival, or a prolongation of the T'ang tradition. The figures in wood and plaster, of which a number still stand in the temples of North China, represent an evolution beyond the T'ang style. The Buddhas and bodhisattvas are still fully modelled — even to the extent of a fleshiness that can be displeasing, but what they have lost in dynamic energy they gain in a new splendour of effect. They stand against walls covered with huge frescoes painted in the same ample and spectacular manner — such as can still be seen today in the upper hall of Hua-yen-ssu at Tatung (Plate 40a). In fact, so closely does the style of the one echo that of the other that Sickman's vivid description of the sculpture could apply equally to the painting: 'An almost uncanny impression of movement, as though the gods were stepping forward with an easy, stately pace, or had just taken their seats on the lotus throne, is produced by the great agitation and restless movement of the garments and encircling scarves. These latter accessories are especially important in creating an almost spiral movement in three dimensions as the long, broad ribbons trail over the arms, loop across the body and curve around the back. In the actual carving the folds are deep, with sharp edges, so that the maximum contrast is obtained between highlight and shadow. Frequently the ends of garments and scarves are caught up in whorls and spirals obviously derived from the calligraphic flourishes of painting.'[1] This suave and restless splendour was clearly designed, like that of the Baroque art with which it has so much in common, to capture the attention of the worshipper through its emotional appeal. It is no accident that it finds its most splendid expression in the figures of Kuanyin, the comforter, the giver of children, the preserver from peril of all those who call upon her name (Plate 41). She looks down upon suffering humanity with calm detachment; yet she is not indifferent, and her regard is full of sweetness without being

[1] *The Art and Architecture of China*, 97–98.

sentimental. In this beautiful figure a potential extravagance of effect is held delicately in check by the refinement of Sung taste.

Buddhism as a popular religion never fully recovered from the suppression of 845. During the later T'ang the speculative and tantric sects decayed, partly because they had no roots on Chinese soil. But for the Ch'an sect (known in Japan as Zen) the position was different. It emphasized quietism, self-cultivation, the freeing of the mind from all intellectual and material dross so as to leave it open and receptive to those flashes of blinding illumination when suddenly, for a moment, the Truth is revealed. To create the right atmosphere for meditation, the Ch'an monks built their temples in beautiful secluded places where the only sound was the wind in the trees and the rain falling on the stones of the temple courtyard. Their aims, and the very techniques by which they were to be realized, were almost identical with those of the Taoists. So it was that after Buddhism had been on Chinese soil for nearly a thousand years, it finally came to terms with Chinese ideals.

In seeking a technique with which to express the intensity and immediacy of his intuition, the Ch'an painter turned to the brush and monochrome ink, and with the fierce concentration of the calligrapher proceeded to record his own moments of truth in the outward forms of Buddhas and arhats. Already in the last century of the T'ang Dynasty there were artists practising techniques as wildly eccentric as those of any modern western 'action painter'. None of their work survives, but contemporary descriptions of it suggest that these individualists were either Zen adepts or were fired by the same impulse towards irrationality and spontaneity as that which inspired the Zen painters. Only slightly later was Kuan-hsiu who, after a lifetime of painting Buddhist subjects in the lower Yangtse region, came, full of years and honour, to the court of Wang Chien at Chengtu, where he died in 912. His arhats were drawn with that exaggeration bordering on perversity which is typically Zen; with their bony skulls, huge eyebrows and pronounced Indian features they have the ugliness of caricatures, as if only by deliberate distortion can the sudden, electrifying experience of the Ch'an mystic be suggested. For the experience itself is incommunicable: all the artist can do is to give the viewer a shock which may jolt him into awareness. The few surviving copies of Kuan-hsiu's work are treasured in Japan, where Zen long outlasted its popularity in China. When Kuan-hsiu died his mantle fell upon Shih K'o (Plate 42a), a wild and eccentric individual who, according to an eleventh century historian, 'liked to shock and insult people and compose satirical rhymes about them.' By this time writers were fond of classifying painters into three grades: *neng* (capable), *miao* (wonderful) and *shen* (divine, super-human); but for Shih K'o and his like even *shen* was not enough, for it still implied obedience to the rules. For them they coined the term *i*, meaning 'completely unrestrained by rules'. 'Painting in the *i* style,' said another author, 'is most difficult; those who follow it . . . despise refinement and rich colouring and draw the forms quite sketchily, but they grasp the natural (*tzu-jan*) spontaneously.'

In the meantime quite another tradition was flourishing at Nanking, whose painters must have raised their hands in horror at the antics of the *fauves* up in Chengtu. There Li Hou-chu, the 'emperor' of Southern T'ang, had recreated in miniature the luxury and refinement of the T'ang court under Ming Huang. One recent writer describes the art produced under his patronage as the twilight of the T'ang, another as 'premature Sung'; all we can say is that it provides an important link between the two great epochs. Under his patronage the spirit of Chou Fang and Chang Hsüan was reborn in Chou Wen-chü and Ku Hung-chung. The painting of which a detail is reproduced in Plate 42b is probably a very close copy, dating from about the twelfth century, of a scroll by Ku Hung-chung depicting the nocturnal revels of the vice-president Han Hsi-tsai, rumours of whose thoroughly un-Confucian behaviour with singing and dancing girls, of whom he had at least a hundred, had reached the ears of the emperor. Li Hou-chu sent a painter in attendance (*tai-chao*) to observe and record what was going on, and then confronted Han Hsi-tsai with the evidence of his dissipation. The scene looks respectable enough; but the casual attitudes of Han, his friends and his singing girls, the meaningful glances, the figures half hidden behind bed-curtains, are all highly suggestive; indeed not the least intriguing thing about this picture is the way in which licentiousness is suggested in a formal language of such exquisite refinement and dignity. The painting, which the fourteenth-century writer T'ang Hou considered 'not a pure and fitting object for a high-class collection', is also extremely revealing as a document on tenth-century costume, furniture and porcelain, and shows also how lavishly paintings, including monochrome landscapes, were used in interior decoration, forming panels on the beds as well as tall free-standing screens. It would seem that the hanging scroll has not yet become fashionable.

The last great exponent of the T'ang figure-painting tradition was Li Kung-lin (1040-1106), better known as Li Lung-mien from the name of his country estate of which he, in emulation of Wang Wei, painted a long panoramic handscroll. Several versions of it exist. Li Lung-mien moved in an intellectual circle at court that included the poet Su Tung-p'o and the historian Ou-yang Hsiu, while it is recorded that even the great statesman Wang An-shih, who was 'careful in choosing his friends', condescended to visit him. In early life he was a famous painter of horses — until, so the story goes, a Taoist told him that if he continued much longer in this vein he would become like a horse himself, whereupon he switched to other themes. He was thoroughly eclectic, spending years in copying the old masters, and though his own technique was restricted largely to ink-line (pai-miao) his subject-matter included everything from horses and genre scenes to Taoist fairy landscapes, Buddhist figures and paintings of Kuanyin amid rocks, of which he created an ideal conventional type.

The reverence for the past revealed in Li Lung-mien's sedulous copying of the old masters is from now on to loom large in Chinese connoisseurship, and to present the most formidable problems to the expert. In the case of a master we may assume that his motives were the honourable ones of training his hand and of transmitting the ancient models in the spirit of the sixth principle of Hsieh Ho. To paint in the manner of Wu Tao-tzu, therefore, was no less 'original' than for a pianist to play the works of Bach and Beethoven; for what the artist sought was not originality but a sense of identity, both with nature and with the tradition itself. The western artist particularizes, and is at liberty to pursue his researches in any chosen direction. The Chinese painter seeks always to express a total experience in terms of a general statement, and any work which explored one aspect of appearance at the expense of the whole would be considered immature. To achieve this he must, like the pianist, have the language of expression at his fingertips so that no technical impediment, no struggle with form or brushwork, should come between the experience and its realization. An important part of his training is the study of the old masters. He might perhaps make an exact reproduction by tracing (*mu*), he might copy the picture with the original before him (*lin*), or he could freely interpret the manner of the master (*fang*). Paintings in either of the first two categories which passed into the hands of unscrupulous (or even well-intentioned but ignorant) collectors would often acquire false signatures and seals, and the new attribution would then be attested by further colophons. In many cases, such are the vicissitudes through which the painting has passed that the truth can never be known, and the most that can be said is that a given work is in the style of a certain master or period and *looks* old enough, and good enough, to be genuine. Sometimes a painting is exposed as a copy by the subsequent appearance of a still finer version. In this most difficult branch of connoisseurship there is not an expert who has not been deceived, and the recent tendency in the West has been perhaps towards an excessive caution not shared by Chinese and Japanese connoisseurs.

This uncertainty applies particularly to the few great landscape paintings of the Five Dynasties and Early Sung which are generally attributed to such masters as Ching Hao, Li Ch'eng, Tung Yüan and Chü-jan, all of whom were working in the tenth century, and Fan K'uan, Hsü Tao-ning and Yen Wen-kuei who were active into the eleventh. In the hundred years between 950 and 1050 a host of great names succeed each other in what must be looked upon as perhaps the supreme moment in classical Chinese landscape painting. Ching Hao, who was active from about 900 to 960, spent much of his life in retirement amid the mountains of eastern Shansi. An essay attributed to him, the *Pi-fa chi* (*Record of Brush Methods*) or *Hua shan-shui lu* (*Essay on Landscape Painting*), puts his thoughts on the art into the mouth of an old man whom he pretends he met when wandering in the mountains, and who gave him a lecture on principles and technique. The old man tells him of the six essentials in painting: the first is spirit, the second rhythm, the third thought, the fourth scenery, the fifth brush, the sixth ink; a more logical system than that of Hsieh Ho, for it proceeds from the concept to its expression, and thence to the composition, truth to nature (scenery), and finally technique. The sage further distinguishes between resemblance, which reproduces the outward, formal aspect of objects, and truth, which involves a perfect integration of form and content. He seeks a just correspondence of the type of brush-stroke with the object depicted. He insists that flowers and trees should be those appropriate to the season, and that men be not larger than trees — not simply for the sake of objective realism, but because only by faithfully reproducing the visible forms of nature can the artist hope to express, through them, their deeper significance. To default in this, therefore, is a sign that the artist has not fully attuned himself. This view is elaborated in a well-known essay by the eleventh-century master Kuo Hsi, who combined in his spectacular landscapes the strong drawing and jagged silhouette, which we associate with Li Ch'eng, with a modelling of relief in ink wash which was probably derived from the Late T'ang individualists. Kuo Hsi was to Sung landscape what Wu Tao-tzu had been to T'ang Buddhist art — a painter of enormous energy and output, who loved to cover large walls and standing screens with monumental compositions. In his *Advice on Landscape Painting* (*Shan-shui hsün*), he insists again and again on the necessity, amounting to an ethical obligation, for the artist to study nature in every aspect, to mark the procession of the seasons, the way the same scene may look at morning and evening; to note and express the particular, unique character of every changing moment; to select with care; to impart movement to water and cloud, for, as he says, 'water-courses are the arteries of a mountain; grass and trees its hair; mist and haze its complexion.' Indeed, as the painter knows the very mountains to be alive, so must he transmit that life (*ch'i*) into the mountains that he paints.

How was it then, one might ask, that the Chinese painter, who insisted on truth to natural appearance, should have been so ignorant of even the elementary laws of perspective as the West understands it? The answer is that he deliberately avoided it, for the same reason that he avoided the use of shadows. Scientific perspective involves a view from a determined position, and includes only what can be seen from that single point. While this satisfies the logical western mind, it is not enough for the Chinese painter: for why, he asks, should we so restrict ourselves? Why, if we have the means to depict what we know to be there, paint only what we can see from one viewpoint? In the Sung Dynasty Shen Kua criticized Li Ch'eng for 'painting the eaves from below' and thereby putting an arbitrary restriction on his power to 'view the part from the angle of totality'. 'When Li Ch'eng paints mountains, pavilions and buildings,' he writes in his *Meng-ch'i pi-t'an*, 'he paints the eaves from below. He believes that looking up one perceives the eaves of a pagoda as a person on the level ground and is able to see the beams and rafters of its structure. This is absurd. All landscapes have to be viewed from "the angle of totality to behold the part", much in the manner in which we look at an artificial rockery in our gardens. If we apply Li's method to the painting of real mountains, we are unable to see more than one layer of the mountain at a time. Could that be called art? Li Ch'eng surely does not understand the principle of viewing the part from the angle of totality. His measurement of height and distance certainly is a fine thing. But should one attach paramount importance to the angles and corners of buildings?'[1]

The composition of a Chinese painting is not defined by the four walls of its mount as is a European painting within its frame. Indeed, the Chinese artist hardly thinks of it as a 'composition' at all. Those formal considerations to which the western painter devotes so much attention he takes very largely for granted. Rather is his picture, as Shen Kua suggests, a fragment — chosen as it were at random, yet profoundly significant — of eternity. What the Chinese artist records is not a single visual confrontation, but an accumulation of experience touched off perhaps by one moment's exaltation before the beauty of nature. The experience is transmitted in forms that are not merely generalized, but also richly symbolic. This kind of generalization is quite different from that of Claude and Poussin, in whose idyllic landscapes the evocation of a Golden Age is deliberate. The Chinese artist may paint a view of Mount Lu, but the actual shape of Mount Lu is of little interest to him in itself; the mountain is significant only if in contemplating it, wandering through it, painting it, he is made aware of those things which for him make Mount Lu, for the moment, the very embodiment of 'mountainness'. Likewise, the bird on a branch painted by some Sung academician is not a thing in itself, defined by its frame, but seems poised in limitless space, a symbol chosen by the artist to express what we might call the 'bird-on-bough' aspect of eternity. We are often told that the Chinese painter leaves large areas of the picture space empty so that we may 'complete it in our imagination'. But that is not so.

[1] Slightly adapted from Tsung Pai-hua, 'Space-consciousness in Chinese painting', *Sino-Austrian Cultural Association Journal* I (1949), p. 27 (tr. Ernst J. Schwartz). Chinese theorists distinguish three kinds of perspective in Chinese painting: *kao yüan*, or 'high distance', depicts the mountains as they would be seen by someone looking upwards from below (Plate 44); *shen yüan* ('deep distance'), presents a bird's-eye view over successive ranges to a high and distant horizon, while *p'ing yüan*, or 'level distance', involves a continuous recession to a rather low horizon such as we most often encounter in European landscape painting (plate 37).

The very concept of completion is utterly alien to the Chinese way of thinking. The Chinese painter deliberately avoids a complete statement because he knows that we can never know everything, that what we can describe, or 'complete', cannot be true in the larger sense. All he can do is to liberate the imagination and set it wandering over the limitless spaces of the universe. His landscape is not a final statement, but a starting point; not an end, but the opening of a door. For this reason, Rembrandt's drawings, and the work of the modern abstract expressionists, are much closer to the spirit of Chinese art than are the idealized, classical compositions of the great European landscape painters of the seventeenth century.

In the passage I have quoted above, Shen Kua clearly explains the attitude behind what we might call the 'shifting perspective' of Chinese painting, which invites us to explore nature, to wander through the mountains and valleys, discovering fresh beauty at every step. We cannot take in so great a panorama at a glance; indeed, the artist intends that we should not. We would need perhaps days or weeks to walk the length of the stretch of country-side he presents in his scroll; but by revealing it to us little by little as we proceed, he combines the element of time with that of space, in a four-dimensional synthesis such as western art has never achieved. The nearest parallel is to be found not in European art, but in music, in which the theme unfolds and develops in time. As we unroll as much of the great panorama as we can comfortably pass from right hand to left (never opening it out fully as is often done in museums), we find ourselves drawn unwittingly into the scene spread out before us. The artist invites us to follow him down the winding paths, to wait at the river-bank for the ferry boat, to walk through the village — disappearing from view for a few moments, perhaps, as we pass behind a hill — to re-emerge and find ourselves standing on the bridge gazing at a waterfall; and then perhaps to saunter up the valley to where the monastery roof can just be seen above the tree-tops, there to rest, fan ourselves after our exertions, and drink a bowl of tea with the monks.

Only by a shifting perspective, which opens out a fresh view at every turn of the path, is such a journey possible. Indeed we can only truly appreciate a great Chinese landscape painting if it does have this power to send our spirits wandering. At the end of the scroll the artist will leave us standing at the lake shore, gazing out across the water to where distant peaks rise through the haze, while an infinity of space stretches above them, carrying us with it beyond the horizon. Or he may close the scroll with a rocky tree-clad spur in the foreground, and thus bring us back to earth once more.

This power in a great Chinese landscape painting to 'take us out of ourselves' was widely recognized as a source of spiritual solace and refreshment. Kuo Hsi opens his essay by declaring that it is especially the virtuous man who delights in landscapes. Why the virtuous man particularly? Because, being virtuous (in other words, a good Confucian), he accepts his responsibilities to society and the state, which tie him down to the urban life of an official. He cannot 'seclude himself and shun the world', he cannot wander for years among the mountains, but he *can* nourish his spirit by taking imaginary journeys through a landscape painting into which the artist has compressed the beauty, the grandeur and the silence of nature, and return to his desk refreshed.

The great masters of the tenth and eleventh centuries are sometimes called 'classical' because they established an ideal in monumental landscape painting to which later painters returned again and again for inspiration. In nearly every case the attributions to such masters as Ching Hao, Li Ch'eng, Kuan T'ung and Kuo Chung-shu are merely traditional. But by a miracle there has survived one masterpiece bearing the hidden signature of the great early Sung painter Fan K'uan which is almost certainly an original from his hand. Born about the middle of the tenth century, and still living in 1026, Fan K'uan was a shy, austere man who shunned the world. At first, like his contemporary Hsü Tao-ning, he modelled himself on Li Ch'eng, but then it came to him that nature herself was the only true teacher, and he spent the rest of his life as a recluse in the rugged Ch'ien-t'ang Mountains of Shansi, often spending a whole day gazing at a configuration of rocks, or going out on a winter's night to study with great concentration the effect of moonlight upon the snow. If we were to select one single painting to illustrate the achievement of the Northern Sung landscape painters we could not do better than to choose his 'Travelling amid Mountains and Gorges' (Plate 44), in which we see a train of pack horses hurrying out of a wood at the base of a huge precipice. The composition is still in some respects archaic; the dominating central massif goes back to the T'ang Dynasty, the foliage retains several early conventions while the texture-strokes (ts'un) are still almost mechanically repeated and narrow in range; their full expressive possibilities are not to be realized for another two hundred years. This painting is overwhelming in its grandeur of conception, its dramatic contrasts of light and dark in the mist, rocks and trees, and above all in a concentrated energy in the brushwork so intense that the very mountains seem to be alive, and the roar of the waterfall fills the air around you as you gaze upon it. It perfectly fulfils the ideal of the Northern Sung that a landscape painting should be of such compelling realism that the viewer will feel that he has been actually transported to the place depicted.

These painters were all men of North China, nurtured in a hard, bleak countryside whose mood is well conveyed in the austerity of their style. The painters of the south lived in a kinder environment. The hills of the lower Yangtse Valley are softer in outline, the sunlight is diffused by mist, and winter's grip less hard. In the works of Tung Yüan and Chü-jan, both active in Nanking in the latter half of the tenth century, there is a roundness of contour and a looseness and freedom in the brushwork that is in marked contrast to the angular rocks and crabbed branches of Li Ch'eng and Fan K'uan. Shen Kua said that Tung Yüan 'was skilled in painting the mists of autumn and far open views,' and that 'his pictures were meant to be seen at a distance, because their brushwork was very rough.' Tung also, rather surprisingly, worked in a coloured style like that of Li Ssu-hsün. The revolutionary impressionism which Tung Yüan and his pupil Chü-jan achieved by means of broken ink washes and the elimination of the outline is well illustrated by his scroll depicting scenery along the Hsiao and Hsiang rivers in Hunan, sections of which are now in the museums in Peking and Shanghai (Plate 37). In this evocation of the atmosphere of a summer evening, the contours of the hills are soft and rounded, the mist is beginning to form among the trees, the diminutive figures of fishermen and travellers, picked out in white, catch the last rays of the setting sun. Over the scene hangs a peace so profound that we can almost hear their voices as they call to each other across the water. Here an element of pure lyricism appears in Chinese landscape painting for the first time.

The high point of Northern Sung realism, shown in a remarkable documentary scroll depicting life in the capital on the eve of the Ch'ing-ming festival, was reached shortly before the débacle of 1125. The painter, Chang Tse-tuan, a member of the official class, shows not only acute powers of observation (Plate 43) but also mastery of shading and foreshortening, techniques which were to be almost completely abandoned after the fall of Northern Sung. For even while this climax was approaching, elsewhere the subtle change which first showed itself in the work of some of the T'ang scholar painters was coming out into the open, and the tradition of the painting of the literati, the *wen-jen hua*, was being firmly established. By the eleventh century, and indeed long before, the scholars had come to look on the kind of painting they did as being different in kind from that produced by professional artists. To the literati, painting was, like poetry and calligraphy, primarily a means of self-expression. They painted not so much to evoke in the viewer the same kind of feelings that he would have before a real scene, as to convey to others of their class something of themselves. Of the panorama of the Hsiao and Hsiang rivers the scholar painters might say, not 'From this you can see what the scenery of Hsiao and Hsiang is like,' but 'From this, you can tell what kind of a man Tung Yüan was.'

In the landscapes of the scholar painters, the passion of a Fan K'uan for the hills and streams gave way to a more urbane, detached attitude. They avoided becoming too deeply involved, either in nature or in material things. They spoke of merely 'borrowing' the forms of rocks, trees or bamboo as something in which, for the moment, to find 'lodging' for their feelings. Above all, they were amateurs. They affected to be merely playing with ink, even pretended to be clumsy, because mere skill was an attribute of professionals and court painters. By choice they painted, as the poets and calligraphers wrote, in ink on paper, deliberately avoiding the visual seductions of colour and silk. It is not surprising that of all the streams of Chinese painting, the *wen-jen hua* is the hardest to appreciate, even for the Chinese themselves. Like a rare, dry wine, it is often a little rough on the palate at first, but deepening familiarity brings its rich rewards.

The Sung *wen-jen hua* crystallised round a group of remarkable personalities in the eleventh century that included the poet Su Tung-p'o (1036–1101) and his teacher in bamboo painting Wen T'ung (d. 1079), Mi Fei (or Mi Fu, 1051–1107), and the great calligrapher Huang T'ing-chien (1045–1105). No certain painting from the hand of Mi Fei or Su Tung-p'o has survived, and the short handscroll illustrated in Plate 45 was first attributed to the latter in the thirteenth century. But it is typical of the taste and technique of the eleventh-century scholar painters in its choice of medium, its dry, sensitive brushwork, its avoidance of obvious visual appeal, and in the sense that this is a spontaneous statement as revealing of the man himself as of what he depicts.

The work of the early scholar painters was always original, not because they strove for originality for itself, but because their art was the sincere and spontaneous expression of an original personality. One of the most remarkable of these men was Mi Fei, critic, connoisseur, and eccentric, who would spend long evenings with his friend Su Tung-p'o, surrounded by piles of paper and jugs of wine, writing away at top speed till the paper and wine gave out, and the small boys grinding the ink were ready to drop with fatigue. In painting landscapes, Mi Fei, it is said, abandoned the drawn line altogether, forming his mountains of rows of blobs of ink laid on to the paper with the flat of the brush. This striking 'Mi-dot' technique, as it came to be called, had its dangers, however; in the hands of the master or of his son Mi Yu-jen (1086–1165) it achieved marvels of breadth and luminosity with the simplest of means, but it was fatally easy to imitate.

So radical was this technique of Mi Fei's that the emperor Hui-tsung, himself an accomplished painter and connoisseur, would have none of his work in the imperial collection, nor would he permit the style to be practised at Court. It is not known whether an official painting academy ever existed before the Southern Sung. Painters at the T'ang court had been given a wide variety of civil and military ranks, most of which were sinecures. Wang Chien, ruler of Former Shu, seems to have been the first to give his painters appointments in his own Hanlin Academy of Letters, and this practice was followed by the Southern T'ang emperor Li Hou-chu at Nanking, and by the first emperors of the Sung. Contemporary writers often speak of distinguished painters as being in attendance (*tai-chao*) in the Yü-hua-yüan (Imperial Academy of Painting); yet no such institution is ever mentioned in the Northern Sung history, and if such a body did in fact exist, it was presumably a subdivision of the Hanlin Academy.

The tradition of direct imperial patronage culminated in Hui-tsung (1101–1125), the last emperor of Northern Sung, whose passion for pictures and antiquities blinded him to the perils into which his country was drifting. In 1104 he set up an official School of Painting (*Hüa-hsüeh*) in the palace, but in 1110 this was abolished and painting was once more put under the Hanlin Academy. Hui-tsung kept tight control over the painters at Court. He handed out the subjects to be painted and set examinations as though the painters were candidates for administrative posts. The theme was generally a line from a poem, and distinction went to the most ingenious and allusive 'answer'. When, for example, he chose the theme 'A Tavern in a Bamboo Grove by a Bridge', the winner did not put in the tavern at all, but simply suggested it by a sign-board set among the bamboos. Thus what Hui-tsung required of these artists was not mere academic realism, so much as the kind of intellectual agility, the avoidance of the obvious, the play upon ideas that was expected also of literary scholars. But the Emperor, himself a painter of great ability, tolerated no indiscipline in the ranks. He imposed a dictatorship of form and taste upon his academicians as rigid as that of le Brun over the artists working for Louis XIV, who were in much the same position. The penalty for independence was dismissal. For all his talent and enthusiasm, his influence cannot have been beneficial. The imposition of a rigid orthodoxy laid the foundation for a decorative, painstaking 'palace style' which was to govern court taste until modern times, while his insatiable and somewhat unscrupulous demands as a collector — demands which no owner could refuse — helped to ensure the destruction, in the disastrous events of 1125-7, of most of the still-surviving masterpieces of ancient art.

Whenever Hui-tsung produced a masterpiece, the painters in the 'Academy' vied with each other in copying it and, if they were lucky, succeeded in having their versions stamped with the Emperor's own seal. So closely indeed did they model their work on his that it is now almost impossible to disentangle the one from the other, though some attempts have been made to do so. It would even be wrong to assume that the better the painting the more likely it is to be from the Imperial hand. The pictures associated with his name are for the most part quiet, careful studies of birds on branches — 'A Dove on a Peach Tree,' 'Sparrows on Bamboo,' and so on, painted with exquisite precision, delicate colour, and faultless placing. Often their beauty is enhanced by the Emperor's highly elegant calligraphy which, we may be sure, was not infrequently applied also as a mark of approval to paintings executed by members of the Academy. A typical product of this sophisticated circle is the famous Five-colour Parakeet, illustrated in Plate 46, which bears a poem and signature penned by the Imperial brush. This exquisitely balanced picture reveals a certain stiffness (much clearer in the original than in the photograph), an anxiety to be correct at all costs — just the qualities we might expect to find in Hui-tsung himself.[1]

The art of flower painting which Hui-tsung and his academicians practised was not, in origin, wholly Chinese. It had been brought from India as a part of the decorative panoply of Buddhist banner painting towards the end of the Six Dynasties, when its greatest exponent was Chang Seng-yu. Speaking of some of Chang's paintings in a temple at Nanking, a T'ang author had written, 'All over the gate of the temple "flowers-in-relief" are painted. . . . Such flowers are done in a technique brought here from India. They are painted in vermilion, malachite greens and azurite blues. Looking at them from a distance, one has the illusion that they are (carved) in relief, but close at hand they are seen to be flat.'[2] T'ang Buddhist art is rich in this decorative style of flower painting, but by the tenth century it had become an art in its own right. Later painters loved to animate their flower studies with birds, and thus 'birds and flowers' (*hua-niao*) became recognized as an independent category in the repertoire.

The tenth-century master Huang Ch'üan is said to have invented a revolutionary technique of flower painting at the court of Wang Chien in Chengtu; he would apply his colours directly in light washes without a drawn outline — a style that came to be known as *mo-ku hua* ('boneless painting'). The technique of his contemporary and great rival at Nanking, Hsü Hsi, was precisely the opposite: he drew his flowers and leaves swiftly in ink, adding only a little colour; later this became formalised as the *kou-le tien-ts'ai*, 'outline filled with colour', style. Huang Ch'üan's

---

[1] The paintings in monochrome ink attributed to him — they include a long handscroll of birds and water-plants and a very beautiful landscape, both in the former Palace Museum collection— are all problem pieces. They are discussed by Benjamin Rowland in his article, 'The Problem of Hui Tsung', in *Archives of the Chinese Art Society of America* 5 (1951), 5–22.

[2] Slightly adapted from Naitō Tōichirō, *The Wall-Paintings of Hōryūji*. Tr. William Acker and Benjamin Rowland Jr. (Baltimore, 1943), 205–6.

manner was considered the more skilful and decorative, and eventually became more popular with professionals and court painters, while Hsü Hsi's, because it was based on the calligraphic brushstroke, found favour among the literati. Huang Ch'üan's son Huang Chü-ts'ai, and some other bird and flower painters, successfully combined elements of both styles. No original from the hand of Huang Ch'üan or Hsü Hsi has survived, but the former's 'boneless' manner is preserved in Ch'ien Hsüan's Sparrow (Plate 56a), while something of Hsü Hsi's firm outline style can be detected in Hui-tsung's Parakeet (Plate 46).

A comment by the critic Shen Kua on the work of Huang and his son on the one hand and Hsü on the other throws an interesting light on the standards by which this kind of painting was judged in the Sung Dynasty. 'The two Huangs' flower paintings are marvellous (miao),' he writes, 'in their handling of colours. Their brushwork is extremely fresh and finely detailed. The ink lines are almost invisible, and are supplemented only by washes of light colours. Their sort of painting you might call sketching from life. Hsü Hsi would use his ink and brush to draw in a very broad way, add a summary colouring, and that would be all. With him the spiritual quality is pre-eminent, and one has a special sense of animation. Ch'üan disliked his technique, called his work coarse and ugly, and rejected it as being without style.'

When, after the disaster of 1125, the Sung shored up the ruins of their house amid the delights of their 'temporary' capital at Hangchow, they set out to recapture the dignity and splendour of the old life at Kaifeng. At Wu-lin outside the city a formal Academy of Painting, Hua-yüan, was set up, for the first and only time in Chinese history. Venerable masters from the North were assembled there to re-establish the tradition of court painting, and no national catastrophe it seemed, provided that it was ignored, could disturb the even tenor of their life and art. Or was it that, with the northern barbarians in occupation of half of China, who could tell when the final and complete disaster might not come? Chao Po-chü, who excelled in panoramic landscapes with figures in the green-and-blue style which originated with Li Ssu-hsün, became a special favourite of Kao-tsung (1127–62). The grandeur of the tradition of Fan K'uan and Kuan T'ung was transmitted by Li T'ang, now in his seventies. It seems that his early work at Kaifeng had also been in the decorative green-and-blue style. Just before the débâcle he executed his only dated landscape which has survived, a towering crag rising out of thick woods with rocks and a waterfall, painted with a hard gloomy brilliance that is almost frightening (Plate 48). Much of the effect is derived from the 'big axe' texture strokes (*ta fu-pi ts'un*) with which he hacks out the angular forms of the rocks. This single picture is enough to establish Li T'ang not only as the greatest landscape painter of his day, but also as an important link between the remote grandeur of Northern Sung and the brilliant romanticism of Southern Sung painters such as Ma Yüan and Hsia Kuei.

For some reason not fully explained, the work of the 'Ma-Hsia school', as it is called, has come in western eyes to represent the very quintessence of Chinese landscape painting; and not only in the west, for this style was to have a profound influence too on the development of landscape painting in Japan. Its language of expression was nothing new. We have found its spectacular contrasts in the landscapes of Fan K'uan, its claw-like trees and roots in the art of Li Ch'eng, its pointed rocks in Hsü Tao-ning, its axe-strokes in Li T'ang, its breadth of vision in Tung Yüan. But in the art of Ma Yüan and Hsia Kuei these elements all appear together, united by a consummate mastery of the brush which would border on mannerism if it were not so deeply infused with poetry. Without this depth of feeling, the style in itself is decorative and easily imitated in its outward aspects — qualities which were to be eagerly seized upon by the painters of the Kanō school in Japan.

Ma Yüan became a *tai-chao* at the end of the twelfth century, Hsia Kuei early in the thirteenth. It is not always easy to disentangle the style of one from the other. If we say, looking at the 'Four Old Recluses' (Cincinnati) attributed to Ma Yüan, that his brushwork is bold and fiery, we will find the same qualities even more brilliantly displayed in Hsia Kuei's magnificent landscape scroll formerly in the Palace Museum, of which a section is shown in Plate 47. It is hard to believe that the painter of this almost violently expressionistic work was a senior member of the Imperial Academy. Both he and Ma Yüan used Li T'ang's axe-stroke *ts'un* with telling effect, both exploited brilliantly the contrast of black ink against a luminous expanse of mist; all we can say is that of the two Ma Yüan generally seems the calmer, the more disciplined and precise, Hsia Kuei the expressionist, who may in a fit of excitement seem to stab and hack the silk with his brush. The brilliant virtuosity of his style appealed strongly to the Ming painters of the Che school, and there is little doubt that the great majority of paintings generally attributed to Hsia Kuei — including the celebrated handscroll 'Ten Thousand *Li* of the Yangtse River', which aroused such enthusiasm at Burlington House[1] — are in fact pastiches by Tai Chin and his followers. For there is in the real Hsia Kuei a noble austerity of conception, a terseness of statement, a brilliant counterpoint of wet and dry brush, a sparing and telling use of *ts'un*, which his imitators failed altogether to capture.

The art of Hsia Kuei is not far removed, in the explosive energy of its brushwork, from that of the Ch'an Buddhist masters, who at this time were living not far from the capital in point of distance — their monasteries bordered the West Lake near Hangchow — but who were in their lives and art far removed from the court and all it stood for. Of these, the chief were Liang K'ai, who after rising to be *tai-chao* under Ning-tsung (1195–1224), retired to a temple, taking with him the brilliant brush style of Hsia Kuei, and Mu-ch'i, who from his monastery, the Liu-t'ung-ssu, dominated the painting of the Hangchow region throughout the first half of the thirteenth century. There was hardly a subject that Mu-ch'i did not touch. Landscapes, birds, tigers, monkeys, bodhisattvas — all were the same to him. In all

[1] Reproduced in Cohn, *Chinese Painting*, Plates 94–96.

he sought out and expressed an essential nature that was not a matter of form — for his forms may break up or dissolve in mists — but of inner life, which he found because it was in the painter himself. His 'Six Persimmons' has been too often published to need reproducing again. Instead I have chosen a detail of his Shrike on a Pine-trunk, in the Matsudaira Collection (Plate 49a). Here Mu-ch'i achieved a dramatic contrast in texture between the tree-trunk, sketched in jagged swirls of a dry stubby brush, and the shrike plucking at its feathers, which he draws powerfully in rich dark ink. The vital brushwork expresses both the life of nature and Mu-ch'i's excitement in the act of painting; the surrounding emptiness speaks of eternity. In Mu-ch'i and his fellow monk Ying Yü-chien, the power of brush and ink painting to convey mystical experience reached its limit; beyond lay the pure abstractions of calligraphy.

The influence of the academic attitude to art in the Sung Dynasty is revealed in a growing tendency to categorize. The catalogue of the Emperor Hui-tsung's collection, *Hsüan-ho hua-p'u*, for instance, was arranged under ten headings: Taoist and Buddhist themes (which, though less popular than before, still preserved a prestige conferred by hallowed tradition); figure paintings (including portraits and *genre*); palaces and buildings (particularly those in the ruled *chieh-hua* style); foreign tribes; dragons and fishes; landscapes; domestic animals and wild beasts (there was a whole school of painters specializing in water-buffaloes); flowers and birds; ink bamboo; and vegetables and fruit. The last category requires no special mention; and bamboo we will leave to the next chapter. But before leaving the subject of Sung painting we must say a word on the subject of dragons. To the 'man in the street' the dragon was a benevolent and generally auspicious creature, bringer of rain and emblem of the Emperor. To the Ch'an Buddhists he was far more than that. When Mu-ch'i painted a dragon suddenly appearing from the clouds, he was depicting a cosmic manifestation and at the same time symbolizing the momentary, elusive vision of Truth which comes to the Ch'an adept. To the Taoists, the dragon was the *Tao* itself, an all-pervading force which momentarily reveals itself to us only to vanish again and leave us wondering if we had actually seen it at all. 'Hidden in the caverns of inaccessible mountains,' wrote Okakura Kakuzo, 'or coiled in the unfathomable depths of the sea, he awaits the time when he slowly rouses himself to activity. He unfolds himself in the storm clouds; he washes his mane in the blackness of the seething whirlpools. His claws are in the forks of the lightning, his scales begin to glisten in the bark of rain-swept pine trees. His voice is heard in the hurricane which, scattering the withered leaves of the forest, quickens the new spring. The dragon reveals himself only to vanish.'[1] Ts'ao Pu-hsing in the third century had been the first prominent painter to specialize in dragons, but the greatest of all was Ch'en Jung, who combined a successful career as an administrator during the first half of the thirteenth century with a somewhat unorthodox technique as a dragon painter. His contemporary T'ang Hou tells us that when he was drunk he would give a great shout, seize his cap, soak it with ink and smear on the design with it, afterwards finishing the details with a brush. His celebrated 'Nine Dragons', painted in 1244, could well have been executed thus, the dragons with his brush, the clouds with his cap; indeed, on the original the imprint of some textile in the clouds can be seen quite clearly. This, the finest dragon painting in existence, and unquestionably authentic, is now one of the treasures of the Boston Museum of Fine Arts (Plate 49b).

The art of the Sung Dynasty which we admire today was produced by, and for, a social and intellectual élite more cultivated than at any other period in Chinese history. The pottery and porcelain made for their use is a natural reflection of their taste. Some T'ang wares may be more robust, Ch'ing wares more refined, but the Sung have a classical purity of form and glaze which holds a perfect balance between the vigour of the earlier wares and the refinement of the later. Although some of the

[1] *The Awakening of Japan* (1905), 77.

porcelain for the Northern Sung court came from kilns as far away as Chekiang and Kiangsi, the most famous of the Northern Sung *kuan* (official) wares was manufactured in the kilns at Ch'ien-tz'u-ts'un, near Ting-chou in Hopei, where a white porcelain with a greenish tint where it runs thick was already being made in the late T'ang Dynasty. The classic Ting ware is a finely-potted, high-fired white porcelain, with a creamy white glaze which has a brownish tinge where it runs into the 'tear-marks' described in early texts; the more elaborately decorated pieces have designs impressed from a mould before biscuit firing, the more beautiful ones have plants, flowers and birds freely incised in the paste with a stylus (Plate 50a). As the vessel was fired upside down, the rim was left unglazed and often had to be bound with bronze or silver. Chinese connoisseurs recognise, in addition to the true *pai* (white) Ting, a fine grained *fen* (flour) Ting, a *tzu* (purple — actually soya-sauce brown) Ting, and a coarse yellowish *t'u* (earth) Ting. Varieties of Ting and near-Ting, however, are not always easy to distinguish. The extensive surveys and excavations of the past fifteen years have made it apparent that not only was one type of ware often made in a number of different kilns, with the inevitable local variations in character and quality, but also that one kiln centre might turn out a wide range of products. To take two examples, Fujio Koyama and more recent Chinese investigators discovered in the ruins of the Ting kilns white, black, and persimmon-red glazed porcelain, unglazed porcelain, pottery with white slip, with patterns in iron oxide, with carved designs, with black, and with buckwheat brown glaze. The Sung kilns at Hao-pi-chi, T'ang-yin-hsien, Honan, first investigated in 1955, while turning out chiefly plain white wares, also produced coloured wares, white wares with coloured decoration, cups glazed black outside and white inside, a high-quality, Chün-type stone-ware, and black glazed vases with vertical yellowish ribs in relief, such as the lovely vessel in the collection of Mrs Alfred Clark (Plate 51a). The value and beauty of the Ting wares lies not merely in their glaze and decoration but also in the exquisite purity of their shapes, many of which were copied not only in other Sung kilns but also in the Korean wares of the Koryŏ period. After the fall of Kaifeng in 1127, wares of Ting type were made at Chi-chou in Central Kiangsi, very probably by refugee potters who had fled to the south. Before leaving the white wares, we must also mention the beautiful white stoneware jars and vases found in the ruins of the town of Chü-lu-hsien, between Ting-chou and Tz'u-chou, which was inundated and destroyed when the Yellow River changed its course in 1108. Long immersion in the river mud has given them a dull surface and large uneven crackle, and has stained them with subtle hues of pink and old ivory which by no means mar their beauty.

Since the Sung Dynasty, Chinese connoisseurs have classed Ting-yao as a 'classic' ware of Northern Sung, together with Ju-yao, Chün-yao, and the now legendary Ch'ia-yao, which had a glaze 'blue like the sky after rain'. When the too-fastidious Emperor Hui-tsung decided that, presumably because of its 'tear-drops' and metal rim, Ting-yao was no longer good enough for palace use, kilns were set up to make a new *kuan* ware, both at Ju-chou and within the confines of the capital itself. The latter kilns have long since been buried or swept away in the floods that periodically inundate the Yellow River Valley, and it is not known for certain what kind of porcelain they produced, although the Palace Museum authorities in Taiwan have recently published a number of fine pieces, close both to Ju and to Hangchow *kuan*, as products of the Kaifeng imperial kilns. Ju-yao, one of the rarest of all Sung porcelains, has been more positively identified. It has a buff or pinkish-yellow body, covered with a bluish-grey glaze with a lavender tint, netted over with a fine crackle like mica. The shapes, chiefly bowls, brushwashers and bottles, are of an exquisite simplicity matching the quality of the glaze. Ju-chou was also one of several centres in addition to the large factory in T'ung-ch'uan-hsien, north of Sian, which produced 'northern celadon' — an apt name for a stoneware often richly decorated with carved or moulded floral designs under a dull green glaze. A kind of celadon had been made at Yao-yao in T'ung-ch'uan-hsien as early as the Six Dynasties, but when the Sung expanded to absorb Chekiang, production and quality in the Yao-yao kilns seem to have been influenced by the Yüeh potters, some of whom may have been sent to North China.

Much more closely related to Ju, however, is the well-known Chün ware, made not only at Chün-chou and Ju-chou, but also at other centres in the neighbourhood of Hao-pi, Anyang, and Tz'u-chou. The finest Chün was of palace quality, and so is sometimes called *kuan* Chün by Chinese collectors. The potting is much heavier than that of Ju-yao, however, and myriads of tiny bubbles, which burst on the surface of the thick lavender-blue glaze, give it a seductive softness and warmth. It was the Chün potters who discovered that spots of copper oxidised in the glaze during firing produced crimson and purple splashes, a technique which they used with exquisite restraint. On later varieties of Chün ware, however, such as the numbered sets of flower pots and bulb bowls made in the Ming Dynasty at Te-hua and Canton, these 'flambé' effects are often used with tasteless extravagance.

The Tz'u-chou wares represent perhaps the most striking example of the extent to which the discoveries of the last fifteen years have altered the ceramic picture. Tz'u-chou is a convenient name for a large family of North China stonewares decorated chiefly by painting under the glaze or by carving or incising through a coloured slip. The technique of under-glaze painting may have been imported from the Near East, where it had long been known, but the magnificently buoyant shapes and the motifs used in the decoration are purely Chinese (Plate 52a). The unaffected grace and confidence of the brush drawing gives the Tz'u-chou wares an immediate appeal, although until very recently they have been considered too close to a peasant art to command the respect of educated people in China itself.

The kilns at Tz'u-chou are well known, and still active today, but recent Chinese excavation and research have revealed that the north China decorated stoneware, as perhaps it ought to be called, was made across the breadth of the country, from Shantung to Szechwan. Of the known kilns, the most important so far excavated, in addition to Tz'u-chou itself, are Hao-pi, already mentioned, the stratified kilnsite at Kuan-t'ai on the Honan-Hopei border, among whose products were black-glazed vessels like the superb vase in the collection of Mrs Alfred Clark illustrated on Plate 51a, and the kilns at Hsiu-wu (or Chiao-tso) on the Shansi-Honan border, which turned out striking vases with floral designs reserved on black or boldly carved through a black glaze.

Before the end of the Sung Dynasty, North China potters, at P'a-ts'un in Honan, at Pa-i in Shansi, and at Te-chou in Shantung, had developed the revolutionary technique of overglaze painting. Their delightful bowls and dishes decorated with birds and flowers swiftly sketched in tomato-red, green and yellow over a creamy glaze are the earliest examples of the enamelling technique which was to become so popular in the Ming Dynasty.

At the fall of the T'ang, the Northeast was lost to a Khitan tribe who called their dynasty Liao (907–1124). We have already noted how a 'T'ang revival' school of Buddhist art was flourishing at Yünkang and elsewhere under their patronage, and have assigned the famous ceramic Lohans to this period. Liao sites in Manchuria have yielded fragments of Chün, Ting and Tz'u-chou type wares, but Japanese scholars and collectors and, more recently, Chinese archaeologists have also recovered large quantities of a distinct local ware which combines something of the *sgraffiato* floral decoration of Tz'u-chou with the three-colour glazes and the robust — though now provincial and often ungainly — shapes of the T'ang Dynasty, such as the chicken ewer, pilgrim flask and trumpet-mouthed vase. The finest Liao wares are the equal of Sung porcelains in elegance, and even the rough grave wares such as the imitation of a leather water-flask carried at the saddle (Plate 51c) have the same spontaneous, unsophisticated charm that we admire in mediaeval European pottery.

Among the most striking of the northern wares are those with a black glaze, which used to be called 'Honan *temmoku*'. This name forms a link with South China, for it was in the south that tea-drinking had first become popular during the T'ang Dynasty and it was discovered that a black glaze effectively set off the pea-green colour of the tea. *Temmoku* is the Japanese equivalent of T'ien-mu, a mountain near Hangchow, whence certain of these southern wares were shipped to Japan. The true 'temmoku', made at Chien-an in Fukien as early as the tenth century, consisted almost exclusively of the type of tea-bowls which proved so popular in Japan. They have a dark stoneware body decorated with a thick, oily iron glaze running to big drops at the foot (Plate 52b).

The colour is basically a very dark brown verging on black, often streaked with blue or a steel grey, producing marks known as hare's fur, or bluish 'oil spots', caused by the coagulation of grey crystals. These were imitated in a rather coarse lustreless ware made at Chi-chou in Kiangsi, often confusingly called 'Kian ware' in older books, and at other kilns in Fukien such as Kuang-che, Fu-ch'ing, and Ch'uan-chou.

When, after a few years at Hangchow, the Southern Sung court began to realize that this was to be more than a temporary halting place, steps were taken to enlarge the palace and government offices, and to set up factories to manufacture utensils for court use which would duplicate as closely as possible those of the old northern capital. The Supervisor of Parks, Shao Ch'eng-chang, who was in charge of this work, established a kiln near his own office (Hsiu-nei Ssu) on Phoenix Hill just to the west of the palace, which lay at the southern end of the city. There, according to a Sung text, Shao's potters made 'a celadon which was called *Nei-yao* (palace ware). Its pure body of exceptional fineness and delicacy, its clear and lustrous glaze, have been prized ever since.' The Phoenix Hill area has been repeatedly built over and the kilns have not been discovered, nor is it known how long they were in operation. But before long another imperial factory was set up a mile to the southwest below the suburban Altar of Heaven (Chiao-t'an). This has become a place of pilgrimage to ceramics enthusiasts, who over the years have picked up quantities of shards of the beautiful 'southern *kuan*' which graces many Western collections. Its dark body is often thinner than the glaze, which is opaque, vitrified, and sometimes irregularly crackled, and ranges in colour from a pale bluish-green through blue to dove-grey. The ware has an air of courtly elegance combined with quietness and restraint that made it a fitting adornment for the Southern Sung court.

We should not try to draw too sharp a line between Hangchow *kuan* ware and the best of the celadons made at Lung-ch'üan in Southern Chekiang. The imperial kilns at Hangchow made a light-bodied ware in addition to the dark, while Lung-ch'üan turned out a small quantity of dark-bodied ware as well as the characteristic light grey. It seems certain that the finest Lung-ch'üan celadons were supplied to the court, and could hence be classed as *kuan*.

Probably of all Sung porcelains the celadons are the most widely appreciated — outside China, at least. The name is believed to have been taken from that of Céladon, a shepherd dressed in green who appeared in a pastoral play, *l'Astrée*, first produced in Paris in 1610. These beautiful wares, known to the Chinese as *ch'ing tz'u* (blue-green porcelain), were made in a number of kilns, but those of Lung-ch'üan were the finest, as well as the most abundant, and were, indirectly, the heirs of the Yüeh wares. The light grey body of Lung-ch'üan ware burns yellowish on exposure in the kiln, and wears an unctuous iron glaze ranging in colour from leaf-green to a cold bluish-green, which is sometimes though by no means always crackled. Crackle, originally an accidental result of the glaze shrinking more than the body in firing, was often exploited for its decorative effect, as in the 'ko' type celadons, in which a closer secondary crackle was also developed. To the finest Lung-ch'üan celadons, which have a lovely cloudy blue-green colour, the Japanese gave the name *kinuta* (mallet), perhaps after the shape of a particularly famous vase (Plate 51b). Almost every shape appears in the Lung-ch'üan repertoire: many are purely ceramic, but we also encounter adaptations of archaic bronze forms, notably incense-burners in the form of the three- and four-legged *ting* — a mark of that antiquarianism which was now beginning to develop in Chinese court art, and was to have an ever-increasing influence on cultivated taste. For the most part celadon relies for its beauty on the perfection of its form and glaze, but the bowls may be subtly decorated with lotus leaves on the outside, baluster vases and jars with flowers moulded in relief under the glaze; while in the fourteenth century spectacular effects were attained by leaving the decorative motifs in raised biscuit relief. We can trace the development of the Chekiang celadons ware through dated pieces well into the Ming Dynasty, when the potting become heavier, the glaze greener and more glassy, and the scale more ambitious. From Southern Sung onwards they formed a large proportion of China's export trade. Thousands of shards of Lung-ch'üan ware, for instance, have been picked up on the beaches at Kamakura near Tokyo. Until the Ming Dynasty, celadons, including much coarser imitations made in other kilns in Kiangsi and Fukien, formed the bulk of China's exports to Indo-China, Borneo, the Philippines, Malaya and Indonesia, while, as every amateur knows, the ware was much in demand among the potentates of the Arab world because they believed that it would crack or change colour if it came into contact with poison.

Also exported in large quantities (although it was originally a purely domestic ware), was a beautiful translucent porcelain with a granular sugary body and pale bluish glaze. Some doubt as to its respectability in Chinese ceramic history was long caused by the fact that the name for it used in the West is *ying-ch'ing*, a recent term which was invented by Chinese dealers to describe its shadowy blue tint, and for which scholars had searched in vain in Chinese works. In fact its original name *ch'ing-pai* (bluish-white) occurs frequently in texts going back to the Sung Dynasty. Because of its high felspar content, the hard clay could be potted in shapes of wonderful thinness and delicacy (Plate 50b). The tradition, which began humbly in the T'ang kilns at Shih-hu-wan some miles to the west of Ching-te-chen, achieved a perfect balance between living form and refinement of decoration in the Sung wares, whose shapes included teapots, vases, stemcups and bowls often with foliate rim and dragons, flowers and birds moulded or incised with incredible lightness of touch in the thin paste under the glaze. Already in the Sung Dynasty *ch'ing-pai* wares were being imitated in many kilns in South China, and a good proportion of their output was exported to Southeast Asia and the Indonesian archipelago, where the presence of *ch'ing-pai* or celadon in an archaeological site often provides the most reliable means of dating it. It may seem strange that a ware so fine should have been widely exported among the backward peoples of the *Nan-hai* ('South Seas') as the Chinese called it. But is it after all so surprising that the very delicacy which so satisfied Sung taste should also have evoked in the island peoples — and especially the women — the same response? It is perhaps significant that the most popular *ch'ing-pai* pieces found in the Nan-hai are the little round boxes, put up in sets of three within a larger box. They were originally intended for cosmetics, but in the Nan-hai they were often used to hold the paraphernalia for chewing betel.

CHAPTER NINE

The Yüan and Ming Dynasties

During the twelfth century China had come to uneasy terms with her northern neighbours and, after her custom, civilized them. But beyond them across the deserts of Central Asia there roamed a horde which Fitzgerald called 'the most savage and pitiless race known to history' — the Mongols. In 1210 their leader, the great Genghis Khan, attacked the buffer state of Chin, and destroyed their capital at Peking. In 1227 he destroyed the Hsia, leaving only one hundredth of the population alive, a disaster by which the northwest was permanently laid waste. Three years later Genghis died, but still the Mongol hordes advanced, and in 1235 they turned southward into China. For forty years the Chinese armies resisted them, almost unsupported by their own government. But the outcome was inevitable, and when in 1279 the last Sung pretender was destroyed, the Mongols proclaimed their rule over China, calling themselves the Yüan. China was spared the worst of the atrocities which had been visited upon all their other victims for, as a Khitan adviser had pointed out, the Chinese were more useful alive, and taxable, than dead. But the wars and break-up of the administration left Kubilai master of a weak and impoverished empire, whose taxpayers had been reduced from a hundred million under the Sung to less than sixty. Although Kubilai was an able ruler and a deep admirer of Chinese culture, the Mongol administration was not only utterly out of touch but ruthless and corrupt to boot. Seven emperors succeeded one another in the forty years following the death of Kubilai in 1294. Chinese discontent against the harsh rule of the last Khan broke into open rebellion in 1348. For twenty years rival bandits and warlords fought over the prostrate country, which the Mongols had long since ceased to control effectively. Finally, in 1368, the last Khan fled northwards from Peking, the power of the Mongols was broken for ever, and the short, inglorious rule of the Yüan Dynasty was at an end. In conquering China they had realised the age-long dream of all the nomad tribes, but in less than a century the Chinese drained them of the savage vitality which had made that conquest possible, and threw them back into the desert, an empty husk.

Politically, the Yüan Dynasty may have been brief and in-glorious, but it is a period of special interest and importance in the history of Chinese art — a period when men, uncertain of the present, looked both backward and forward. Their backward looking is shown in the tendency, in painting as much as in the decorative arts, to revive ancient styles — particularly those of the T'ang Dynasty, which had been preserved in a semi-fossilized state in North China under the alien Liao and Chin dynasties. At the same time, the Yüan Dynasty was in several respects revolutionary, for not only were those revived traditions given a new interpreta-tion, but the divorce between the court and the intellectuals, brought about by the Mongol occupation, instilled in the scholar class the conviction of belonging to a self-contained élite that was not undermined until the mid-twentieth century, and was to have an enormous influence on painting. On the technological level, the brief Yüan period saw several major innovations, such as the introduction of ceramic decoration in underglaze red and blue, and the carving of lacquer, that were to be fully exploited in succeeding centuries.

The Mongols themselves dated their Chinese empire from the year 1263, when Kubilai mounted the throne and established his capital at Peking, which he called Khanbalig, the City of the Great Khan. About twelve years later Marco Polo, then in the emperor's service, wrote a vivid description of Cambaluc, as he called it, of its palaces, its hall that could dine 6,000 people, its park:

'Between the two walls of the enclosure which I have described, there are fine parks and beautiful trees bearing a variety of fruits. There are beasts also of sundry kinds, such as white stags and fallow deer, gazelles and roebucks and fine squirrels of various sorts, with numbers also of that animal that gives the musk, and all manner of other beautiful creatures, insomuch that the whole place is full of them . . . and the Great Kaan has caused this beautiful prospect to be formed for the comfort and solace and delectation of his heart.'[1]

The architecture and art that Marco Polo is describing are purely Chinese — a magnificent recreation of the styles of the Sung Dynasty by Chinese architects, painters and craftsmen who no doubt had in mind the glories of Hui-tsung's capital at Kaifeng. All that the Mongols contributed was a colossal scale. When in 1417 the Ming Emperor Yung-lo moved his capital back from Nanking to Peking, he had only to expand the city laid out by Kubilai. Some of the Yüan work still survives (notably the sculptured gateways) but the bulk of what we see today in the so-called 'Tartar City' was originally built under the Ming. Surrounded by a wall fifteen miles long, it comfortably holds the Imperial City with a perimeter of six and a half miles, in the heart of which lies the 'Purple Forbidden City' — the Imperial Palace. South lies the commercial quarter, called by the Manchus the 'Chinese City', which was given its own wall, fourteen miles long, at a later date. Within it lie the three-tiered marble Altar of Heaven and the circular Ch'i-nien-tien, Hall of Annual Prayers — the 'Temple of Heaven', whose blue-tiled roofs are familiar to every visitor to Peking (Plate 64a).

Ancient Chou ritual, to which the Ming and Ch'ing rulers rigidly conformed, had prescribed that the Son of Heaven should rule from 'three courts'. Accordingly, the heart of the Forbidden City is dominated by three great halls of state, the San Ta Tien, set on an axis one behind the other (Plate 64b). The first and largest is the T'ai-ho-tien (Hall of Supreme Harmony) used by the emperor for his grander audiences, raised on a huge platform

[1] *The Book of Ser Marco Polo*, tr. Sir H. Yule (1903).

and approached by marble staircases. Behind it lies the waiting hall, Chung-ho-tien (Hall of Middle Harmony), while beyond is the Pao-ho-tien (Hall of Protecting Harmony), used for state banquets. The private apartments, offices of state, palace workshops and gardens occupy the northern half of this vast enclosure. Not many of the palace buildings we see today are the original structures, however. The T'ai-miao (Grand Ancestral Shrine) is

The Three Great Halls, *San Ta Tien*, of the Imperial Palace, Peking, looking south. (Drawn by T. A. Greeves.)

indeed Ming, having been rebuilt in 1464 after a fire; but the history of the T'ai-ho-tien is more typical. First built by Yung-lo in 1627, it was largely rebuilt on the same plan in 1645, while a further reconstruction was started in 1669 and not finished till thirty years later. It was again rebuilt in 1765, since when it has been frequently restored and repainted, though so conservative were the Ch'ing architects that it is unlikely that they departed much from the Ming original — which was itself a cautious repetition of the style of the fourteenth century. Indeed, from

Yüan times onwards, Chinese architecture became less and less adventurous. Gone are the daring experiments in quadripartite gables, spiral canopies and dynamic bracketing that give such interest and vitality to Sung architecture. Now each building is a plain rectangle. The eaves have become so heavily loaded with unnecessary carpentry that the architect has to place an extra colonnade under their outer edge to support the weight, thus making superfluous the elaborate cantilevered system of brackets and *ang*, which now shrinks away to a decorative and meaningless frieze or is masked behind a band of scroll-work suspended from the eaves. The splendour of the Forbidden City lies not in its detail, but rather its rich colour, the magnificently simple sweep of its roofs, and the stupendous scale of its layout. These buildings were all of timber. A few barrel-vaulted stone or brick temple halls were built in the late sixteenth century, but, as before, the use of the vault and dome was largely confined to tombs, a magnificent example being the tomb of the Wan-li Emperor in the Western Hills, the excavation of which, completed in 1958, occupied a large team of Chinese archaeologists for two full years.

Like other invaders before them the Mongols supported the Buddhists as a matter of policy. They were particularly attracted to the esoteric and magical practices of the Tibetan Lamaists, who were encouraged to set up their temples in Peking. The Buddhist architecture, sculpture and painting produced by Chinese craftsmen under their patronage represents no real advance upon that of the Sung Dynasty, except perhaps in sheer scale and magnificence. The truly significant developments in the arts were the work of the literati who had retired from public life, and spent their enforced leisure in the writing of a new kind of fiction and drama, still popular today, which has permanently enriched Chinese literature. With few exceptions, the great painters of the age also put themselves beyond their conquerors' reach. It would be strange indeed if so splendid a court as that of Kubilai Khan had had in its service no painters of talent, and in Chao Meng-fu (1254–1322) the emperor found a man ideally suited to bridge the gulf that lay between his régime and the Chinese educated class. Chao was a descendant of the first Sung Emperor, and had already served the old dynasty in a minor post for several years when Kubilai appointed him. His first job was the writing of memorials and proclamations, but he soon rose to the rank of Cabinet Minister, confidential adviser to the emperor, and secretary to the Hanlin Academy. Though he often regretted his decision to collaborate, it was men of his kind who civilized the Mongols and thus, indirectly, encompassed their eventual downfall. Chao Meng-fu was also a great calligrapher, versed in all the styles from the archaic 'old seal' script, through the clerical (*li*) style, the standard (*k'ai*) style, to the running draft character.

I have said little in this book about the eloquent and exacting art of calligraphy, an art whose finer points can only be appreciated with long study and training. 'Affection for the written word,' wrote Chiang Yee, 'is instilled from childhood in the Chinese heart.' From the merchant who hoists up his newly-written shop-sign with ceremony and incense to the poet whose soul takes flight in the brilliant sword-dance of the brush, calligraphy is revered above all other arts. Not only is a man's writing a clue to his temperament, his moral worth and his learning, but the uniquely ideographic nature of the Chinese script has charged each individual character with a depth of content and association the full extent of which even the most scholarly can scarcely fathom. The illustration on pp. 210 and 211 shows how the art has developed from the crude pictographs of the oracle bones (*chia-ku-wen*) through the script of the early bronze inscriptions (*chin-wen*) to the official 'big-seal' (*ta-chuan*) script of the Chou Dynasty. Directly evolved from the *ta-chuan* is the *hsiao-chuan*, 'small seal,' a standardized form credited to Li Ssu, the great minister of Ch'in Shih-huang-ti. With the fall of Ch'in these traditional scripts were lost or went suddenly out of fashion, and the *li-shu* (clerical script) of the Han Dynasty represents an abrupt departure from the ancient forms. From the *li-shu*, of which we illustrate a particularly elegant example, are derived the standard *k'ai-shu*,

前不見古人後不見
来者念天地之悠
獨愴然而涕下

大功飞虏之尹勿
以舶喊法及国立

偷
元
前
二
百

7. 6. 5. 4.

The evolution of the Chinese script. 1. *Chia-ku-wen*; inscription on a tortoise-shell from Anyang (Shang Dynasty). 2. *Ta-chuan* (big seal); inscription on bronze *ting* of the Chou Dynasty. 3. *Hsiao-chuan* (small seal); from a bronze inscription of Ch'in Shih-huang-ti. 4. *Li-shu* (clerical script); from stone tablet (Han Dynasty). 5. Chang *ts'ao-shu* (draft script of the Han Dynasty). 6. *K'ai-shu* (official script); a slightly cursive form bordering on *hsing-shu* (running script), in the 'thin gold' style of the Sung emperor Hui-tsung. 7. *Ts'ao-shu* (draft script); after an inscription by the Sung poet and calligrapher Huang T'ing-chien. Specially written for this book by Chuang Shang-yen, Deputy Director of the National Palace Museum, Taiwan.

Above: seals used on official documents, books and paintings: (a) Intaglio seal (po-wen) of a Han military official; (b) Positive seal (yang-wen) of the seventeenth century collector Liang Ch'ing-piao; (c) Private seal of the Sung painter-poet Mi Fei in T'ang chiu-tieh ('ninefold') script; (d) Gourd-shaped seal of the early Ch'ing painter Kao Feng-han, bearing his personal name Chieh-t'ing. (After van Gulik and Contag-Wang.)

still today the orthodox form, the running script (*hsing-shu*), and finally the cursive draft or rough script, *ts'ao-shu*, which first became fashionable in company with the 'intellectual Taoism' of the third and fourth centuries A.D. All of these styles were practised by the *wen-jen* of the Yüan Dynasty and by their followers up to recent times.

Chao Meng-fu's popular fame rests not only on his calligraphy, however, but also on his almost legendary skill in the art of painting horses, so much so that any good example with a respectable claim to antiquity is attributed to him. As court painter to the Mongols it would be surprising if his oeuvre had *not* contained a number of pictures of the animal so dear to their hearts. But it is chiefly as a landscape painter that Chao Meng-fu must be remembered. He might, indeed, have said of himself, with Cézanne, 'I am the primitive of the way I have discovered.' He occupies a pivotal position in the history of Chinese landscape painting, for, living at a time when the Sung tradition had exhausted itself, or exploded into Zen gestures with the brush, he united a direct, spontaneous expression of feeling with a deep reverence for the antique. Looking back beyond the orthodox Sung styles, he rediscovered the poetry and the brushwork of the long-neglected 'Southern' manner of Tung Yüan and Chü-jan. In doing so, he opened the way not only for the next generation of Yüan amateur painters — notably the 'Four Masters' discussed below — but for almost all subsequent scholarly landscape painting up to the present day. In his most famous surviving landscape (Plate 54), painted for a friend to remind him of his homeland, Chao Meng-fu with dry scholarly wit combines references to the quaintly archaic landscape style of the T'ang Dynasty and to the broad, calm vision of Tung Yüan.

The movement of which Chao Meng-fu was the initiator found its fulfilment half a century later in Huang Kung-wang (1269–1354) a detail of whose greatest work, Living in the Fu-ch'un Mountains, is reproduced in Plate 55. Little is known about the life of Huang Kung-wang, doyen of the Four Great Masters, except that for a time he held a minor official post, and that he retired to a life of scholarship, teaching, painting and poetry in his native Chekiang. His masterwork was painted slowly, as the mood took him, over a period of three years, being finished in 1350. The treatment is magnificently broad, relaxed and unaffected, with not the least hint of the decorative silhouette, the 'one-corner composition', and other mannerisms of the Hangchow Academy. We feel that this is the painter himself speaking from the depths of his heart. Colophons by Shen Chou and Tung Ch'i-ch'ang both mention Tung Yüan and Chü-jan as having inspired him, but the spontaneity of his touch shows clearly that Huang Kung-wang has caught the spirit of antiquity without becoming its slave.

This noble simplicity of utterance was carried even further by Ni Tsan (1301–74) who spent much of his life drifting in a houseboat with his wife through the lakes and hills of south-eastern Kiangsu, where he found escape from the turmoil into which China was thrown by the anti-Mongol rebellions. The establishment of the Ming Dynasty in 1368 enabled him to return to his old home and spend the last few years of his life in peace. To the Ming *wen-jen* he was the ideal type of the untrammelled scholar painter. If Huang Kung-wang was austere, then what word can we use to describe Ni Tsan? A few bare trees on a rock, a few hills across the water, an empty pavilion; that is all (Plate 53). The forms are spare and simple. The ink is dry and of an even greyness, touched here and there by sparsely-applied *ts'un* set down, very black, with the side of the brush: it was said of Ni Tsan that 'he was as economical of ink as if it were gold'. No concessions are made to the viewer; no figures, no boats or clouds enliven the scene, and nothing moves. The silence that pervades the picture is that which falls between friends who understand each other perfectly. The innumerable imitations of his style produced by later artists show clearly how much strength is hidden in his apparent weakness, how much skill in his fumbling with the brush, what richness of content in his emptiness. Of quite a different type was Wang Meng, whose turbulent, congested landscapes seem to embody something of the violence of the times he lived in. He had held office under the Mongols, and for his sins died in prison in 1385. He was a master of a closeknit texture made up of tortuous, writhing lines and a rich variety of *ts'un*; but though he seems to leave nothing out, his touch is sensitive and his composition clear-cut. He is one of the few Chinese painters — Shih-ch'i is perhaps another — who, though using a brush technique of restless intensity, can achieve a final effect of repose.

A gratifying number of great paintings of the Yüan Dynasty have survived to testify to the remarkable revolution by which these and other gifted men broke free from the conventions of Southern Sung and set Chinese painting upon a new path. Moreover the divorce which occurred under the Mongols between the court and its patronage on the one hand and the scholar painters on the other was to remain a feature of the painting of the Ming and Ch'ing Dynasties. It is with the Yüan painters that the intensely intellectual and literary associations of landscape painting come to the fore. Now it becomes customary for the painter himself to write a poem or inscription on the painting; this may be joined by others written by friends and later admirers till the picture is almost obliterated under inscriptions and seals which, far from ruining it in Chinese eyes, may greatly enhance its value.[1] From now on, also, painters of the literary school much prefer to paint, like the calligraphers, on paper, which is more absorbent than silk and consequently responds more readily to the touch of the brush.

Other Yüan landscapists such as Kao K'o-kung and Wu Chen (the fourth of the 'Four Masters'), helped to lay the foundations of the literary painting of the next five centuries, but some were more conservative. Chao Meng-fu's teacher Ch'ien Hsüan (*c.* 1235–

[1] This scarcely applies to the inscriptions penned by the Ch'ien-lung emperor on paintings in his collection. He had added no less than fifty-four to a Wang Meng langscape in the Imperial collection before he could bring himself to write, 'Hereafter when this painting is unrolled for my pleasure, never again will I inscribe it.'

after 1300), for example, carried on, though with subtle changes the ideals and techniques of the Southern Sung Academy. He has long been considered the author of the famous handscroll 'Early Autumn' in Detroit, details of which have been reproduced in the first English edition of this book, and elsewhere. However, recent research suggests that this exquisite painting may be not the work of Ch'ien Hsüan, but of his Ming follower Sun Lung.[1] No paintings can be attributed to Ch'ien Hsüan with absolute confidence, but a good case has been made out for two subtly brilliant exercises in the 'boneless' technique — the 'Squirrel on a Peach Branch' in the Palace Museum, and the 'Sparrow on an Apple Branch' (Plate 56a), which has recently been acquired by Princeton University. Here is a rarefied simplicity of statement recalling that of the Sung album paintings of birds and insects; the little creature is realized with a trembling spontaneity of touch, and we are hardly aware of the brushwork at all, so perfectly is it subordinated to the total vision. Beside this picture the 'Early Autumn', for all its poignant beauty, seems a virtuoso performance.

It is not surprising that the difficult art of bamboo painting should have found special favour in the Yüan Dynasty, for it was a natural subject for the proud and independent *wen-jen*, who lived out their secluded lives far from the Mongol court. To them, indeed, the bamboo was itself a symbol of the true gentleman, pliant yet strong, who maintains his integrity unsullied no matter how low the adverse winds of circumstance may bend him. The lithe grace of its stalk and the dashing swordpoint of its leaves offered the perfect subject to his brush; but above all the painting of bamboo in monochrome ink brought the painter closest to that most difficult of arts, calligraphy. In painting bamboo, the form and place of every leaf and stalk must be clearly adumbrated; the awkward junctures cannot be hid in mist as in landscape painting; the gradations from black ink in the near leaves to pale in the distance must be precisely judged, the balance of stalks to leaves,

---

[1] The whole question of Ch'ien Hsüan's *oeuvre* is discussed by Wen Fong in 'The Problem of Ch'ien Hsüan', *Art Bulletin* XLII, 3 (September 1960), 173–89.

of plants to empty space, exactly struck. Having achieved this the painter must still know how the bamboo grows, and give to his own the springing movement of the living plant. A great bamboo painting is a virtuoso performance of a very high order.

The art had first become fashionable in the Six Dynasties,[1] when it was the custom, except when painting on a very small scale, to outline the stem and leaves in ink and fill them with body-colour. This painstaking technique was chiefly handed down by the academicians, though the Sung artist Ts'ui Po and the fourteenth-century master Wang Yüan also used it occasionally. Bamboo painting seems to have gone somewhat out of fashion during the T'ang Dynasty (Hui-tsung had no T'ang speciments in his collection), but had become widely popular by Northern Sung, when its greatest exponents were Wen T'ung and the poet and calligrapher Su Tung-p'o. In the Yüan Dynasty several of the great literati were accomplished painters of bamboo in monochrome ink, notably Ni Tsan and Chao Meng-fu, although in this most exacting art the latter had a rival in his wife Kuan Tao-sheng, one of China's greatest woman painters. Li K'an (c. 1260–1310), who took as his master Wen T'ung, devoted his whole life to bamboo, which he studied both as an amateur botanist and as a painter. His illustrated manual on the art of bamboo painting, *Chu-p'u hsiang-lu* became an essential tool in the hands of every practitioner, as well as providing the starting point for all later writers on the subject. A more natural and spontaneous rendering of the subject than Li K'an ever achieved is the little album-leaf by Wu Chen illustrated in Plate 56b, remarkable for its economy of statement, and subtle union of the twin arts of painting and calligraphy.

The ferment into which central China had sunk as the Mongols lost control of the country was finally resolved when in 1368 Chu Yüan-chang, in turn shepherd, monk, bandit, warlord and

[1] Chang Yen-yüan in the *Li-tai ming-hua-chi* mentions three bamboo paintings executed before A.D. 600, and bamboo can be seen in the murals in several of the Six Dynasties caves at Tunhuang.

emperor, sent his armies north to occupy Peking, from which the last Yüan ruler had fled. He proclaimed himself Emperor of the Ming Dynasty, set up his capital in Nanking, and within four years had not only recovered all the territories held by the T'ang at the height of their power, but had extended his control over the Trans-Baikal region and Manchuria as well. He built at Nanking a capital with a city wall twenty miles in circumference, the longest in the world, and under him and his successor central and south China enjoyed a new importance and prosperity. But in 1417 the third emperor, the usurper Yung-lo,[1] moved his capital back to Peking whence he had received his chief support in his struggle for power, and it was he who rebuilt it on the scale we see today. But Peking, on two counts, was a bad site: it was situated too far to the north of China's new centre of gravity, the Yangtse Valley; it was also highly vulnerable. For China's northern enemies — now the Manchus — had only to cross the Great Wall to be at the gates of the city. The troubles that beset the Ming Dynasty throughout its subsequent history were largely due on the one hand to the remoteness of the capital from the parts of China that mattered most — the centre and south — and on the other to the constant tension along the Great Wall which lay only forty miles from Peking. Yung-lo was aggressive and secured the frontier, but his successors were weak and corrupt, the victims of eunuchs at court and rebellions in the provinces, and before long the northern defences were left unguarded.

We have already drawn a parallel between the Warring States and Classical Greece on the one hand and Han China and ancient Rome on the other. It is said that history never repeats itself, but

---

[1] Yung-lo is not properly speaking the name of the Emperor, but an aus picious title which he gave to his reign-period as a whole, thus doing away with the old system of choosing a new era name every few years. The custom continued in the Ch'ing Dynasty. K'ang-hsi, for example, is the title of the reign-period of the Emperor Sheng-tsu, Ch'ien-lung that of Kao-tsung. But because these reign-titles have become so well known in the west, chiefly through their use as marks on Chinese porcelain, we will continue to use them in this book even though, strictly speaking, they are incorrect.

the similar relationship of Ming China to Sung is too close to be passed over. For the mixture of power and corruption, grandeur and lack of imagination that characterized the Roman Empire is equally marked in the Ming Dynasty, which took as its model not the weak and dreamy Sung, whom they despised, but the splendour, the vigour — and, be it said, the occasional vulgarity — of T'ang. In the early fifteenth century Ming China was immensely powerful. Her navies roamed the southern seas under the remarkable Admiral Cheng Ho. But he was, characteristically, not bent on conquest; himself a eunuch in high favour with the emperor, his five expeditions between 1405 and 1433 were carried out for the express purpose of collecting curiosities for the entertainment of the court. China had no other interest in the outside world. Before the end of the century, however, Vasco da Gama had rounded the Cape of Good Hope; by 1509 the Portuguese were in Malacca, by 1516 in Canton, and China was finally forced to take account of the existence of the Western barbarians by reason of their atrocious conduct around her own shores.

The splendour of the Ming court concealed a creeping paralysis. Officials, selected by civil service examinations which centred round the stultifying complexities of the 'eight-legged essay', became correspondingly conservative and conventional in outlook. The energies of savants at court were devoted less to original scholarship than to the preparation of such vast works as the *Yung-lo ta-tien*, an encyclopaedia in 11,095 volumes compiled between 1403 and 1407. The Sung emperors had been men of taste and education, able to inspire the best in their scholars and painters; the Ming emperors were for the most part ruffians, usurpers, or weak victims of court intrigue. As a result, the palace tradition in painting petered out in a frozen academicism, and for significant developments we must look not to the court, but to the scholars, collectors and amateurs, many of them men of independent means, who carried on the tradition of the *wen-jen* of the Yüan Dynasty. This is the age of the gentleman's country estate, of garden-designing as a pastime for scholar and painter, of connoisseurship and of the great private collections such as those of Hsiang Mo-lin (1525–90) and of Liang Ch'ing-piao (1620–91), whose seal on a painting — if genuine — is often all that the modern collector requires to attest to its authenticity. It was these and other private collectors rather than the Ming emperors who preserved the remaining masterpieces of Sung and Yüan, which were to find their way into the Imperial Collection in the eighteenth century. Bibliophiles also collected paintings, repaired, remounted and annotated them, while the association between literature and painting became even closer with the publication of the first books with wood-block illustrations in colour. Of these one of the earliest was a monograph on ink sticks, *Ch'eng-shih mo-yüan*, published in 1606 with woodcuts in five colours executed after drawing by the painter Ting Yün-p'eng. The art of colour printing reached its peak in the exquisite *Treatise on the Paintings and Writings of the Ten Bamboo Studio, Shih-chu-chai shu-hua-p'u*, published in 1633. Thereafter handbooks on the art of painting as a pastime were to proliferate, the most famous being the *Painting Manual of the Mustard Seed Garden (Chieh-tzu-yüan hua-chuan)* first published in five parts in 1679, and still used as a technical handbook by Chinese artists and students today.

At the Ming court there was no personality of the stature of Chao Meng-fu to mediate between the academicians and the literati, who kept their distance and made no attempt to influence court art for the better. The Ming Emperors, following the T'ang model, made the Bureau of Painting a subdivision of the Hanlin Academy, but it was no longer the centre of culture and art that it had been in former times. It was set up in the Jen-chih Palace within the Imperial City, and a special office under the Directorate of Palace Eunuchs was established to control it. Painters were honoured with high military titles — (to distinguish them from civil officials!) — and treated with great favour. This favour, however, depended upon absolute obedience to a paralysing code of rules and regulations. Even though several of the emperors set out to rival Hui-tsung as patrons, and one, the Hsüan-te emperor

(Hsüan-tsung 1426–36), was a gifted painter himself, the task of the academicians was simply to establish a new nationalistic art on the T'ang model. They lived, moreover, literally in terror of their lives. Chou Wei, a gentleman-painter, was executed through the slander of his colleagues, Sheng Chu because in a wall-painting he inadvertently insulted the emperor, while Tai Chin was dismissed, to die in poverty, because he had painted the garment of a fisherman red, the colour reserved for officials. Under such circumstances it is astonishing that any good work was produced at all.

The most talented of the court painters was Pien Wen-chin (c. 1400–40), who specialized in painting birds and flowers in the careful, decorative outline-filled-with-colour style of the Five Dynasties master Huang Ch'üan. In his day he was considered one of the three greatest artists living, and indeed his works have a delicacy and perfection of drawing and colour which link him rather to Hui-tsung than to any of the host of decorators who turned out paintings by the hundred to adorn the endless rooms of the Palace. Of these the most gifted was the late-fifteenth-century painter Lü Chi, whose magnificently decorative compositions, rich in colour, definite and precise in form, conservative in style, were exactly suited to the taste of his Imperial patrons. In landscape, the models for the academicians were Ma Yüan and Hsia Kuei, partly because they too had been academicians, partly because the basis of their work, like that of the flower painters, was not self-expression but technique, and technique could be learnt. Ni Tuan, for example, modelled himself on Ma Yüan, Chou Wen-ching on both Ma Yüan and Hsia Kuei, Li Tsai — who is said to have taught the great Japanese landscape painter Sesshū — on Ma Yüan and Kuo Hsi. In their works the element of mystery in the Sung romantics has hardened into a brilliant eclecticism.

Among the court painters in the early years of the fifteenth century was Tai Chin (Tai Wen-chin), who like his colleagues based his style on that of the Southern Sung Academy. But he was too gifted and independent a spirit to submit to official dictatorship, and retired to his native Chekiang where he remained for the rest of his life, and where his influence was so wide as to give the name of his province to a very loosely connected group of professional landscape painters. The Che School, as it was called, embodied the forms and conventions of the Ma-Hsia tradition but treated them with a quite unacademic looseness and freedom, as is shown for instance in the detail from Tai Chin's handscroll of Fishermen in the Freer Gallery in Plate 57a. Other outstanding artists of the Che School — who, however, had no connection with Tai Chin himself — were Wu Wei and Chang Lu, both of whom specialized in figures in a landscape setting. At the very end of the dynasty, the Che School enjoyed a brief final flowering in the elegant art of Lan Ying (1578–1660).

Meanwhile, as in the Yüan Dynasty, the amateur tradition continued to flourish among the scholarly gentlemen of Kiangsu, notably those of Wu-hsien, which gave its name to an important school of landscape painting, the Wu School. Although by no means the first of this group, Shen Chou (1427–1509) and Wen Cheng-ming (1470–1559) were its greatest ornaments. Shen Chou, who came of a family of scholars and painters, lived out his life in comfortable retirement, the very embodiment of the *wen-jen* ideal. He steeped himself in the spirit of the Northern Sung masters, but modelled his own style more particularly on Huang Kung-wang and Ni Tsan, whom he copied assiduously. His well-known landscapes in the manner of Ni Tsan are extremely revealing of the change that was coming over the literary men's art during the Ming Dynasty; for while Ni Tsan is almost forbiddingly plain and austere, Shen Chou is something of an extrovert, who cannot help infusing a human warmth into his paintings. He also worked with superb ease and confidence in the manner of Wang Meng and Wu Chen. But Shen Chou was no mere copyist. He distilled a style that is uniquely his own. Whether in long panoramic landscapes, tall mountain scrolls, or small album paintings, his brushwork, seemingly so casual, is in fact firm and confident, his detail crystal clear yet never obtrusive, his figures — like those of

Canaletto — reduced to a kind of shorthand yet full of character, his composition open and informal yet perfectly integrated; and when he uses colour he does so with an exquisite freshness and restraint. It is not surprising that he became so popular, not only with the literati of his own time but also with modern connoisseurs. His debt to Huang Kung-wang is subtly evoked both in the style of the album-leaf illustrated in Plate 58, and in the subject, a self-portrait, 'Returning Home from the Land of the Immortals', with as his companion a crane who might be the spirit of Crazy Old Huang himself. Above, Shen Chou writes:

> Bearing a crane and my lute I am homeward bound across the lake;
> White clouds and red leaves are flying together.
> My home lies in the very depths of the mountains,
> Among the bamboos, the sound of reading, a tiny couch and a humble gate.[1]

Such album-leaves are full of a very human charm, and it is only when we compare Shen Chou with Huang Kung-wang or Wu Chen that we realise that something of their grandeur and breadth of vision is lost. But it was Shen Chou who transformed their lofty style into a language which other less gifted painters could use, and his influence is still at work today.

We cannot, unfortunately, linger over the many gifted painters in the new 'literary' style who followed in his footsteps, though we must not neglect his pupil Wen Cheng-ming, who sat for the civil service examinations regularly for twenty-eight years in the hope of becoming an official. He was for some time *tai-chao* in the Hanlin Academy but later returned to Soochow, where during his declining years he painted a remarkable series of gnarled pine trees, in pure monochrome ink, which in their rugged, twisted forms seem to symbolize the noble spirit of the aged *wen-jen* himself. His son Wen Chia and his nephew Wen Po-jen were also gifted

[1] Adapted from Richard Edwards, *The Field of Stones: A study of the Art of Shen Chou* (Washington, 1962), p. 40.

painters in the Wu tradition, while among his numerous pupils and followers were Lu Chih (1496–1576) and Ch'en Shun (Ch'en Tao-fu, 1483–1544), both specialists in landscapes and in flower painting, and Ch'ien Ku (1508–after 1574), who also worked in the manner of Tai Chin.

Two painters active in the first half of the fifteenth century cannot be classified as belonging to either the Che or the Wu school. T'ang Yin (1479–1523), ruined a promising career when he became involved in a scandal over the civil service examinations; he could thus no longer be considered a gentleman, and spent the rest of his life between the brothels and wine-shops of Soochow on the one hand and the seclusion of a Buddhist temple on the other. A pupil of Chou Ch'en, his true teachers were Li T'ang, Liu Sung-nien, Ma Yüan and the great Yüan masters. He was also associated with Shen Chou, and because of this is often classed with the Wu school. But his towering mountains painted in monochrome ink on silk are a recreation of the forms and conventions of the Sung landscapists, though with a hint of mannerism and exaggeration. It is these conflicting qualities in his style and social position that make him so hard to place and have caused a Japanese scholar to label him 'neo-academic'. Into the same class falls Ch'iu Ying (*fl.* 1520–40), a man born also in Wu-hsien of lowly origins, who was neither court painter nor *wen-jen*, but a humble professional, idealising in his pictures the leisurely life of the gentry whose equal he could never be (Plate 57b), and happiest if one of the great literati would condescend to write an eulogy on one of his paintings. He is also famous for his long handscrolls on silk depicting with exquisite detail and delicate colour such popular themes as the 'Peach Blossom Garden', life at the court of Ming Huang, or the multifarious activities of the ladies of the palace. As a landscapist he was the last great exponent of the green and blue style, though he worked also in the ink washes of the Wu school. His delightful pictures are widely appreciated both in China and in the west, and next to Wang Shih-ku he is probably the most-forged painter in the history of Chinese art.

In the development of the literary school no man played a more significant part than the scholar painter Tung Ch'i-ch'ang (1555–1636), who rose to high office under Wan-li. For not only did he embody, in his paintings, the aesthetic ideals of his class, but he also gave them theoretical formulation through his critical writings. Tung Ch'i-ch'ang was himself a noted calligrapher and a painter of landscapes in monochrome ink, but though he worked freely in the manner of the great masters of the past he was not content merely to paraphrase. His landscapes are raised above the level of eclecticism by a dryly intellectual cast of mind which gives them a somewhat cold distinction. They can seldom move us, but they command respect (Plate 59a). But it is as a critic that he is most famous; for it was he, borrowing an idea first put forward by the poet-painter Tu Ch'iung in the fifteenth century, who formulated the theory of the northern and southern schools for the express purpose of demonstrating the superiority of the *wen-jen* tradition above all others. It was primarily through land-scape painting, he maintained, that the scholar and gentleman expressed his understanding of the working of the moral law in nature, and hence his own moral worth. The *wen-jen*, indeed, was the only kind of man who could do this successfully, for only he was free both from the control of the academy on the one hand and the necessity to make a living on the other; moreover being a scholar his wide reading in poetry and the classics gave him an understanding of the nature of things combined with an epicurean nobility of taste which the lower orders of professional painters could never hope to acquire. In the spontaneous play of ink and brush, in his freedom to select, omit, suggest, the *wen-jen* had at his command a language capable of conveying the loftiest and subtlest concepts.

The tradition of the independent scholar painter Tung Ch'i-ch'ang called the 'southern school', because he saw in it an analogy to the southern school of Ch'an Buddhism in the T'ang Dynasty which held that enlightenment came of itself, spon-taneously and suddenly, as opposed to the northern or gradual school which had maintained that it could only be attained by degrees, after a lifetime of preparation and training. To Tung Ch'i-ch'ang all the great gentleman-painters were members of the southern school, beginning in the T'ang Dynasty with his hero Wang Wei — for a genuine work from whose hand he spent a lifetime in searching — and passing down through the great Northern Sung masters Tung Yüan, Chü-jan, Li Ch'eng and Fan K'uan, via Mi Fei (another ideal 'southern' type) to the four great masters of Yüan, ending in his own time with Shen Chou and Wen Cheng-ming. To the northern school he relegated all academic and court painters, beginning with Li Ssu-hsün and his followers in the green and blue style, including among them Li T'ang and Liu Sung-nien, Ma Yüan and Hsia Kuei. He had some difficulty over Chao Meng-fu. As a scholar, calligrapher and landscapist Tung admired him greatly, but he could never bring himself to include Chao among the 'southern' painters because he had compromised himself in the eyes of the literati by taking office under the Mongols.

This arbitrary scheme has dominated, and bedevilled, Chinese art criticism for three centuries, while its obvious inconsistencies have caused endless confusion. Moreover it has been extended to cover not only landscape but also bamboo and bird and flower painting as well. What Tung Ch'i-ch'ang objected to in the painters he dubbed 'northern' was on the one hand a careful academic realism making use of clearly defined forms and strong decorative colour such as we see in the work of the followers of Chao Po-chü, and on the other the tendency towards brilliant mannerist effects and a conventional romanticism latent in the style of Ma Yüan and Hsia Kuei. We may discount Tung Ch'i-ch'ang's prejudices and refuse to accept his classification in individual cases, but his division into northern and southern schools (which, as must by now be obvious, has nothing whatever to do with geography), does in fact represent a just division between two kinds of painting — the one in its purest manifestations academic, eclectic, precise and decorative, the other free, calligraphic, personal, subjective. At the same time, the doctrine of the two schools is a reflection of the feelings of the scholars themselves at this time. The corrupt Ming Dynasty was approaching its downfall, and men of integrity were once again withdrawing from public service into obscurity. Amateur painters and poets (for they applied the theory to literature as well) found comfort and reassurance in the belief that they were the élite, upholding the Confucian virtues, while painters and scholars in the service of the Emperor were prostituting their talents. However vague or inaccurate it might be as an interpretation of the history of Chinese painting, the doctrine is important as a symptom of the predicament of the late Ming literati — a predicament that is also reflected in their own painting. The almost painful distortions which we see in their landscapes — not least in those of Tung Ch'i-ch'ang himself — bear witness to their insecurity and pessimism. Even so humorous and urbane a character as Ch'en Hung-shou (1599–1652) shows, in the perceptible twist that he gives to the ancient figure-painting tradition derived from Ku K'ai-chih and Li Lung-mien, something of the restless spirit of the times (Plate 59b).

To many people 'Ming' means not painting — for it is only recently that Ming painting has come to be appreciated outside China — but the decorative arts. Before we discuss them, however, we should say a word about sculpture. As, during the Sung and Yüan Dynasties, Buddhism gradually loosed its hold over the mind and heart of China, so did Buddhist sculpture decline. Under the Ming 'revival', what it lacks in spiritual content it makes up for in vigour — a vigour shown, for example, in the colossal guardian figures of officials, warriors and animals which line the 'spirit way' leading to the tombs of the Ming emperors outside Nanking and Peking. The casting of large figures in iron had developed during the Sung Dynasty, as a substitute for more precious bronze. The finest of these figures have a simplicity and compactness of modelling that makes them extremely impressive. Far greater freedom of movement was possible in ceramic sculpture, which now lent an air of gaiety and splendour to the roof-ridges of palaces and temples, already glittering with yellow, blue and green tiles. The boldly conceived figure of a man in green and brown terracotta in Plate 60 is a splendid example of the confident manner in which Ming craftsmen revived and transformed the style of the T'ang Dynasty.

The Ming love of colour and of all that made for luxurious living was satisfied by the cloisonné enamel, the lacquer, and the richly-woven textiles which were worn both by officials and by the wealthier members of the middle class. Figured silks, embroideries and brocades have a long history in China: examples of all types going back to the T'ang Dynasty have been found in the dry desert sand of Chinese Turkestan, and are more perfectly preserved in the Shōsōin Repository at Nara. Many T'ang motifs were still in use in the Sung Dynasty, to be revived once again in the Ming and continued, with some modifications, in the Ch'ing. The great achievement of the Sung weavers had been the perfecting of *k'o-ssu*, a form of tapestry woven from silk, using a needle as a shuttle. This technique had been invented in Central Asia, possibly by the Sogdians, improved by the Uighurs, and finally passed on to the Chinese early in the eleventh century. The term *k'o-ssu*, translatable as 'cut silk', is descriptive of the vertical gaps between adjacent areas of colour visible when it is held up to the light, but other variants suggest that *k'o-ssu* is probably a transliteration of the Persian *qazz* or Arabic *khazz* referring to silk and silk products. After the débacle of 1125-7 the art was taken to the Southern Sung court at Hangchow where a historian records that *k'o-ssu* was used for mounting paintings and binding books in the Imperial collection. It was also used for robes, decorative panels and, most astonishingly, for translating paintings and calligraphy into the weaver's art (Plate 61a). We can form some idea of its microscopic fineness when we realize that whereas the finest Gobelins tapestry has 8 to 11 warp threads to the centimetre, Sung *k'o-ssu* has up to 24, and 116 weft threads per centimetre of warp as against the 22 of Gobelins. In the Yüan Dynasty, when trade across Central Asia was probably easier than at any other period in history, panels of *k'o-ssu* were exported at enormous expense to Europe, where they were incorporated into the vestments of the cathedrals in Danzig, Vienna, Perugia and Regensburg, while splendid examples have also been found in Egypt. Hung-wu, the spartan and ferocious first emperor of the Ming, forbade its manufacture, but it was revived early in the fifteenth century under Hsüan-te.

Little Sung *k'o-ssu* has survived until today, but we may get an impression of the splendour of the weaver's art from the court robes of the Ming Dynasty. These include both the ceremonial robes made for the Imperial sacrifices and decorated with the Twelve Emblems — sacred symbols which go back to hallowed antiquity and are described in the early Chou *Classic of History* (*Shu-ching*) — and the so-called 'dragon robes', a term used to describe a long semi-formal robe worn by courtiers and officials from Ming times onwards, embroidered with a number of motifs of which the chief, and most conspicuous, was the dragon. If we are to judge from surviving paintings, dragons with three claws had been a principal motif on T'ang robes, and became an established institution under the Yüan. Strict sumptuary laws introduced in the fourteenth century permitted a robe with four-clawed dragons (*mang-p'ao*) to lesser nobles and officials, while restricting to the emperor and royal princes dragons with five claws. The Ming emperors wore robes decorated with both the dragons and the Twelve Symbols. Dragon robes became extremely popular under the Ch'ing, when the regulations of 1759 confined the Twelve Symbols, at least in theory, to the emperor's personal use.

The Ming and Ch'ing official robes were further embellished with 'Mandarin squares', badges of rank which had already been used decoratively in the Yüan Dynasty and were first prescribed for official dress in the sumptuary laws of 1391. The Ming squares were broad, and made in one piece generally from *k'o-ssu* tapestry. The Manchus, who were content with embroidery, used them in pairs back and front, splitting the front panel down the centre to fit the open riding jacket. Official regulations prescribed bird motifs (symbolizing literary elegance) for civilian officials, animals (suggesting fierce courage) for the military; the emblems were precisely graded from the fabulous monster *ch'i-lin* (for dukes, marquesses and imperial sons-in-law), through white crane or golden pheasant (for civil officials of the first and second ranks), down to the silver pheasant for the fifth to ninth; military ranks had a corresponding animal scale. Though these magnificent woven and embroidered garments vanished from the official world with the parsing of the Manchus, they may still be seen today lending their glitter and pageantry to the traditional theatre.

Lacquer, as we have seen, was already a highly developed craft in the Warring States and Han. At that time, decoration was restricted to painting on a ground of solid colour or incising through one colour to expose another beneath it. In the Yüan Dynasty, however, there started the practice of applying lacquer very thickly and then, before it had completely hardened, carving it in rich floral designs. Genuine Sung pieces (mostly in unadorned ceramic shapes) are extremely rare; but by the Ming Dynasty this new art had become very popular, and the names of several master craftsmen are recorded. Nevertheless lacquer is easy to imitate, and many of the 'signed' pieces of the fifteenth century, and those bearing Ming reign titles (*nien-hao*) may well be later Chinese or Japanese forgeries. Indeed by the fifteenth century the Japanese had become so expert in lacquer work that Chinese craftsmen were journeying to Japan to learn the art. While lacquer might be painted, decorated with gold leaf, or inlaid with mother-of-pearl, it was most frequently carved in red with rich floral or pictorial designs (*ti-hung*): these were either modelled in full relief or the background was cut away leaving the design in flat relief as on many Han engraved stones. By the Chia-ching period two styles of carving, one sharp-edged, the other more rounded, can be identified. The early Ming also saw the introduction of *guri* lacquer, a Japanese name for carving the design through layers of contrasting colours. The cup-stand shown in Plate 61b is a richly-carved example of Ming *ti-hung*; it was evidently a palace piece through two dynasties, for in addition to the reign-mark of Yung-lo (1403–24) it carries round the inside an inscription by Chien-lung dated 1781.

The earliest known reference to cloisonné enamel in China occurs in the *Ko-ku yao-lun* ('Discussion of the Principal Criteria of Antiquities'), published in 1387, which states that this so-called 'Arabian ware' (*Ta-shih yao*), resembling the inlaid work of Fo-lang (i.e. Byzantium) was then being made by Yunnanese craftsmen established at factories in the capital. No authetic examples of fourteenth-century Chinese enamel-work can now be identified, though it is quite possible that pieces were being made for ritual use in the Lama temples of Peking during the latter part of the Yüan Dynasty.[1]

This art, which permits of such rich and vibrant colour effects, came into its own in the Ming Dynasty, and the earliest positively datable pieces have the Hsüan-te reign mark (1426–35). They include incense burners in archaic shapes (Plate 62a), dishes and boxes, animals and birds, and pieces for the scholar's desk. In the early Ming pieces the *cloisons* are not perfectly filled and the surface has a certain roughness; but the designs are bold, vigorous and endlessly varied. Unfortunately, as the technique improved these qualities were lost, till we come to the technically perfect yet lifeless and mechanical enamel-ware of the time of Ch'ien-lung. Identical shapes and designs were produced through the nineteenth century, while today the reappearance of these same designs bears eloquent witness to the archaistic revival of traditional arts under the People's Republic.

It used to be thought that the ceramic art in China declined, if it did not actually come to a standstill, in the Yüan Dynasty. The Yüan rulers in Peking were not men of refined taste, and their patronage must have been a sad anti-climax after the challenge set

[1] See Sir Harry Garner, *Chinese and Japanese Cloisonné Enamels* (London, 1962) pp. 28-36.

by the Sung emperors. A splendid jar in the British Museum, decorated with the 'baby among floral scrolls' design in brown reserved on a white slip is dated 1305 and shows that the Tz'u-chou tradition was still vigorous, though it was never to recapture the beauty of form and drawing of the Sung pieces. But now the focus of the ceramic industry shifts permanently to the centre and south. The kilns at Lung-ch'üan and Li-shui in Chekiang continued to produce celadons on a large scale — indeed, production must have increased to keep pace with the demand for exports to the Near East which the *Pax Tartarica* had stimulated. A baluster vase dated 1327 in the Percival David Foundation is typical of the more baroque preferences of the period, being elaborately and somewhat tastelessly decorated with floral scrolls moulded in relief under the glaze. Sometimes the flower scrolls were separately modelled and then luted on. A similar taste is reflected in the technique of leaving the central decorative motif on a dish, such as a dragon, unglazed in relief. Sometimes these reliefs were modelled by hand, but the presence in the Percival David Foundation of a celadon dish and a flask bearing identical dragons (the former unglazed and the latter glazed) indicates that moulds were also used. It is possible that spotted celadon (*tobi-seiji*) may also have been a Yüan innovation. There are signs, however, that by the mid-fourteenth century the quality of Lung-ch'üan wares was beginning to fall off, the probable reason being the competition from the factories at Ching-te-chen in Kiangsi.

During the Sung Dynasty the finest products of the Ching-te-chen kilns had been white porcelains, chiefly *ch'ing-pai* ware and an imitation of the northern Ting-yao. But by the beginning of the fourteenth century new techniques were already being explored. The *Annals of Fou-liang*, written before 1322, notes that at Ching-te-chen 'they have experts at moulding, painting and engraving'. Painting we will consider in a moment. Moulding and engraving can be seen in the so-called *shu-fu* (privy council) wares. The Yüan put the Imperial factory (*Yü-ch'i-ch'ang*) under a Mongol Commissioner — whose extortions, incidentally, caused them to lose much business to other ceramic centres — and it seems likely that the *shu-fu* was the first ware to be made at Ching-te-chen on official order. It comprises chiefly bowls and dishes with incised, moulded or slip decoration — generally consisting of flower sprays, lotus leaves, or phoenixes amid clouds — under a bluish-white (*ch'ing-pai*) glaze. Sometimes the characters *shu-fu* are included, or other auspicious words such as *fu* (happiness), *shou* (long life) or *lu* (emolument). Closely related to these are the stemcups, ewers, bottles and jars whose decoration consists of applied reliefs often in zones separated by pearl-beading. Another of the innovations at Ching-te-chen which may have occurred before the middle of the fourteenth century was painting in copper red under the glaze. It is not known where this technique was invented. It is certainly not Near Eastern and may possibly, as some Japanese scholars have suggested, have originated in Korea in the Koryŏ period at the end of the twelfth or beginning of the thirteenth century. Some of the most convincing early Chinese examples are the bottles with graceful pear-shaped body and flaring lip decorated with sketchily-drawn flower-sprays or clouds. During the Ming Dynasty the designs become more elaborate, but the copper red had a dull colour and a tendency to run, and was consequently abandoned in the fifteenth century in favour of the more manageable underglaze cobalt blue. This defect is very apparent in a superb fourteenth-century jar decorated with flower-sprays in an underglaze red so intense that it is almost black, which is believed to have been taken from one of the Thirteen Imperial Tombs (*Shih-san Ling*) of the Ming emperors outside Peking, and is now in a private collection in Japan. The decoration is very similar to that of Yüan blue and white, and indeed the two families are intimately related.[1]

In the whole history of ceramics probably no single ware has

[1] It is illustrated in colour in *Sekai Tōji Zenshū* (Catalogue of World's Ceramics), Vol. II (Tokyo, 1955), Plate 6. Another jar, evidently from the same set but in much poorer condition, is now in the British Museum (formerly Eumorfopoulos Collection). See Soame Jenyns, *Ming Pottery and Porcelain* (London, 1953), Plate 18.

been so much admired as Chinese blue-and-white. It has been imitated in Japan, in Indo-China and Persia, and it was the inspiration of the pottery of Delft and other European factories; its devotees have ranged from the head-hunters of Borneo and New Guinea to Whistler and Oscar Wilde, and its enchantment is still at work. Perhaps Chinese potters had begun to paint in cobalt under a transparent glaze in South China late in the thirteenth century, but there is no written record of the art before the slighting reference in the *Ko-ku yao-lun* (1387) which, speaking of the products of the Jao-chou factories, says 'there were blue-and-white and five-colour wares but they were very vulgar'. Painting in underglaze blue and black was already practised in Persia during the thirteenth century, while in Mesopotamia painting in cobalt on a tin glaze goes back to the ninth century. We have already noted crude underglaze painting in Changsha in the T'ang Dynasty, and more advanced techniques in the Tz'u-chou wares of the Sung Dynasty, so the application of underglaze painting to the white porcelain of Ching-te-chen in the Yüan Dynasty is not at all surprising. In some of the earliest pieces underglaze blue painting is combined with relief or incised decoration of the *shu-fu* type, and there is no doubt that an intimate relationship existed between them. Cobalt had been one of the coloured glazes used on the splashed T'ang wares, but as these went out of fashion in the Sung Dynasty, when the Near Eastern sources of cobalt were no longer accessible, there is no historical connection between these T'ang coloured glazes and painting in blue under a transparent glaze. The idea of painting in cobalt came from the Near East; but the shapes of the vessels, the technique of painting and the motifs employed were for the most part Chinese.

The pieces which can now be put with confidence in the first half of the fourteenth century are mostly stemcups, pear-shaped vases with flaring lip, and small covered jars, decorated with dragons, with lotus or chrysanthemum scrolls and narrower bands of petals. The famous dated temple vases of 1351 in the Percival David Foundation mark the transition to decoration on a bolder and more confident scale. By the time these monumental pieces were made, the potters and painters at Ching-te-chen had fully mastered their art, and the vases and dishes of the next hundred years are unequalled for their splendour of shape and beauty of decoration. The drawing is free and bold, yet delicate, the blue varying from almost pure ultramarine to a dull greyish colour, and with a tendency to clot and turn black where it runs thickest — a fault which was eradicated by the sixteenth century and cleverly imitated in the eighteenth. The climax was reached in the Hsüan-te period (1426–35) to which belong the earliest pieces bearing genuine reign marks. In addition to dishes there are stemcups, jars and flattened 'pilgrim-flasks', in which an earlier tendency to crowd the surface with flowers, waves, tendrils and other motifs set in ogival panels has given way to a delicate play of lotus scrolls, vines or chrysanthemums over a white surface. The influence of courtly bird-and-flower painting on porcelain decoration is very evident in the lovely blue-and-white flask illustrated in Plate 62b.

The blue-and-white of each reign has its own character, which the connoisseur can readily recognize. The Hsüan-te style continued in the Ch'eng-hua era, though beside it there now appeared in the so-called 'palace bowls' a new style more delicate and less sure in its drawing and consequently easier for the eighteenth-century potter to imitate. In the Cheng-te period (1506–21) there was a great demand among the Moslem eunuchs at court for the so-called 'Mohammedan wares' consisting mostly of brush-rests, lamps, boxes and other articles for the writing-table whose decoration incorporated inscriptions in Persian or Arabic. The pieces of the reign of Chia-ching (1522–66) and Wan-li (1573–1620) show a change from the old floral decoration to more naturalistic scenes, while in the former reign the Taoist leanings of the court made popular such auspicious subjects as pine-trees, immortals, cranes and deer. The 'imperial' wares of the Wan-li period closely follow those of Chia-ching — but now begins a general decline in quality, the result of mass production, rigidity in the requirements of the Palace, and the exhaustion of the fine quality clay-beds at Ching-te-chen. The most pleasing and vigorous blue-and-whites of the last hundred years of the Ming are wares made in the numerous commercial kilns. These are of two kinds: those made for domestic consumption (*min*: literally 'people's'), and the even more roughly modelled and painted export wares, made for sale or barter to the countries of Southeast Asia, to which I shall refer again. Soon after 1600 a particular type of thin, brittle Wan-li export blue-and-white began to reach Europe. This ware, called *kraak* porcelain because it had formed part of the cargo of two Portuguese carracks captured on the high seas by the Dutch, caused a sensation when it appeared on the market in Holland, and was soon being imitated in the painted faience of Delft and Lowestoft. In spite of intense efforts on the part of European potters, however, it was not until 1708 that the Dresden potter Böttcher, an alchemist in the service of Augustus the Strong of Saxony, succeeded for the first time in making true porcelain — a thousand years after it had been perfected in China.

By the middle of the fifteenth century Ching-te-chen had become the greatest ceramic centre in China. It was ideally situated near the Poyang Lake, whence its products could go by lake and river to Nanking and by the Grand Canal to Peking. An apparently inexhaustible supply of china-clay lay in the Ma-ch'ang hills near by, while just across the river at Hu-t'ien was to be found the other essential ingredient in the manufacture of porcelain, namely 'china-stone' (*pai-tun-tzu*). By this time there had evolved out of the nearly white *ch'ing-pai* and *shu-fu* wares of Sung and Yüan a true white porcelain, which was perhaps already being made at the Imperial factory for the Hung-wu emperor. The most beautiful pieces, however, were those made in the Yung-lo period (1403–24), most of which are decorated with motifs incised or painted in white slip under the glaze — a technique aptly called *an-hua*, 'secret decoration', for it is scarcely visible unless the vessel is held up to the light. From the technical point of view, the eighteenth-century white glaze is perhaps more perfect, but it lacks the luminous warmth of the Ming surface. In some Yung-lo bowls the porcelain body is pared down to paper thinness so that the vessel appears to consist of nothing but glaze: these are the so-called 'bodiless' (t'o-t'ai) pieces. Almost as beautiful are the other monochromes produced at Ching-te-chen, notably the dishes and bowls decorated with imperial dragons under a yellow or blue glaze.

Ching-te-chen, though the largest, was by no means the only Ming factory producing monochrome wares. A white porcelain was being made at Te-hua in Fukien as early as the Sung Dynasty. The Fukien wares, indeed, form a race apart. They never bear reign marks, and are extremely difficult to date accurately, while they range in quality from the finest porcelain with a luminous, warm and lustrous glaze with a brownish tint where it runs thick, to the more metallic products of the last hundred years. In addition to vessels and ceremonial objects such as incense burners and other bronze shapes, the Te-hua potters modelled figurines in white porcelain, a lovely example being the Kuanyin from the Barlow Collection illustrated in Plate 63. Here the subtle turn of the body and the liquid flow of the drapery show how much ceramic modelling was influenced by the sweeping linear rhythms of figure painting. From the seventeenth century onwards Te-hua ware was shipped from Amoy to Europe where, as 'blanc-de-Chine', it had a considerable vogue and was widely imitated.

Robust Ming taste is more typically expressed in the so-called san-ts'ai, 'three-colour' wares (Plate 70a). The exact origin of this family is not known, though there is reason to believe that it may have been produced in stoneware at Chün-chou in Honan, where the kilns were still active in the sixteenth century, while it was also, and more perfectly, made in porcelain at Ching-te-chen. The colours are generally more than three in number, but the ware takes its name from the rich turquoise, dark blue and aubergine which predominate. They are thickly applied in bold floral motifs, and separated by raised ridges which perform the same function as the cloisons on Ming enamels. Occasionally the turquoise glaze was used alone, as on a magnificent vase in the

Percival David Foundation inscribed on the shoulder 'For general use in the Inner Palace'. Although this ware follows the range of shapes earlier made in Chün ware — storage-jars, flower-pots and bulb-bowls — the vigour of the shapes and the strong, rich-coloured glazes show how much closer in feeling Ming art often comes to that of the T'ang Dynasty than to the Sung.

Another important Ming family comprises the five-colour wares (*wu-ts'ai*), a name given to the white porcelain painted with enamel colours, an art which was perfected by Chinese potters, possibly in the reign of Hsüan-te or slightly earlier. The colours were prepared from the materials of lead glaze, applied over the glaze or directly 'on the biscuit', and the vessel fired at a low temperature. These pieces are generally small and often of the 'bodiless' variety, the painting — chiefly vines, flower sprays and flowering branches — disposed with perfect taste and a subtle balance over the white ground. Sometimes, as in the *tou-ts'ai* ware, the enamels were combined with underglaze blue, but this phrase, which means 'fighting colours', hardly does justice to their delicate harmony. The five-colour enamels of the Ch'eng-hua period were never surpassed for their purity of form and decoration; they were already being copied in the Wan-li period, while even to the expert the finest of eighteenth-century copies are almost indistinguishable from them. However, beside these exquisite enamels the sixteenth century saw the appearance of a more full-blooded style, often decorated with genre scenes chiefly in red and yellow; this style was to be echoed in the *wu-ts'ai* wares made for export in the South China kilns — known generally by the misleading term 'Swatow' ware. No pottery was made at Swatow itself, but some of these rough and vigorous porcelains (both blue-and-white and five-colour enamels) were made up-river at Chao-chou and probably at Shih-ma in Fukien, while a kiln producing blue-and-white export ware has recently been found in Ch'üan-chou, Marco Polo's Zayton. Swatow, however, was most probably the main port of despatch.

China's export trade to the *Nan-hai* ('South Seas') was already flourishing in the Sung and Yüan Dynasties. A wide range of early Ming wares, including Lung-ch'üan celadon, Ching-te-chen white porcelain, Tz'u-chou, *ch'ing-pai* and Te-hua have been found in huge quantities over an area extending from the Philippines to East Africa. These export wares had a profound influence on the native pottery of Southeast Asia: blue-and-white was not only successfully imitated in Japan (Imari ware), but also in Annam and, less successfully because they lacked the cobalt, by the Thai potters at Sawankalok, although the Siamese kilns succeeded in producing a beautiful celadon of their own. Before the end of the Ming Dynasty, the Chinese factories were also making porcelain on order for European customers, notably through the Dutch 'factory' established at Batavia (Jakarta) in 1602; but this trade, which was to play so great a part in the contacts between Europe and China, we must leave to the next chapter.

CHAPTER TEN

From 1644 to the Present Day

The Ming Dynasty was brought down by the same inexorable laws of decay which had operated on previous occasions in Chinese history: corruption and the power of the eunuchs at court, leading to breakdown of the administration, large-scale banditry in the provinces, and an enemy on the northern frontier patiently awaiting their opportunity to pounce. In 1618 the Manchu nation had been founded on the banks of the bleak Sungari river. Seven years later the Great Khan, Nurhachi, set up his capital in Mukden, calling his new dynasty Ch'ing (clear) to parallel the Chinese Ming (bright). Their moment came when in 1644 the Chinese General Wu San-kuei appealed to them for held to expel the rebel leader Li Tzu-ch'eng who had forced his way into Peking. The Manchus promptly accepted, drove Li out of the city and, while Wu San-kuei was pursuing him into the west, quietly occupied the capital and proclaimed the rule of the Ch'ing Dynasty. Their unexpected success left the Manchus momentarily exposed, but Wu San-kuei waited ten years before attempting to dislodge them, and then it was too late. But for nearly four decades he and his successors held South China, which was not finally secured for the Manchus until the capture of Kunming in 1682. As a result of this long civil war there grew up a bitter hostility between north and south. Peking became increasingly remote and suspicious, the south ever more rebellious and independent.

It would be wrong to picture the Manchus as barbarous and destructive. On the contrary, they felt an intense admiration for Chinese culture and leaned heavily on the Chinese official class, reserving to themselves only the senior military posts — an arrangement with which the Chinese for their part were well content. But it had its dangers. The Manchu trust of the literati did not extend to a sympathetic consideration for the 'new thought' of the eighteenth century. Having no cultural traditions of their own they clung to the most reactionary forms of Confucianism, becoming more Chinese than the Chinese themselves, and strenuously resisting up to the end every one of the attempts at reform which were made by the literati, some of whom were responsible and far-seeing men. This hidebound refusal to recognize the inevitability of change eventually brought about the collapse of the dynasty. But for the first century and a half, China basked in the sunlight of her restored power and prosperity, which was due largely to the work of the second emperor, K'ang-hsi (Sheng-tsu), who ruled from 1662 to 1722. It was he who pacified all China and restored her, after decades of chaos during which the empire had been truncated and her foreign trade lost, to a paramount position in Asia.

During the seventeenth century and the first half of the eighteenth China was treated with enormous respect by the European powers; admiration for her principles of government filled the writers of the Enlightenment, while her arts gave birth to two waves of *chinoiserie*, the first late in the seventeenth century, the second at the height of the eighteenth. During this period, indeed, China had far more influence upon the thought, art, and material life of Europe than had Europe on China. Western influence was confined to court, where, ever since the arrival of the Jesuit missionary Matteo Ricci in 1601, the Emperors and their immediate entourage of officials and savants had been in close touch with western art and learning. But apart from Adam Schall's reform of the calendar and Verbiest's ordnance factory, the arts and techniques brought by the Jesuits were treated by all but a tiny minority of scholars as mere curiosities. This was not true of painting, however. For while the literati completely ignored European art, some academicians at court made strenuous efforts to master western shading and perspective in the interests of greater realism.

The most characteristic intellectual achievement of the Ch'ing Dynasty was, like that of the Ming, not creative so much as synthetic and analytical; indeed, in the production of such works as the anthology *Ku-chin t'u-shu chi-ch'eng* (1729), and the *Ssu-k'u ch'üan-shu*, a gigantic encyclopaedia in 36,000 volumes begun in 1773 and completed nine years later, the Ch'ing scholars far surpassed their Ming forbears in sheer industry. Characteristically, also, the latter work was compiled not primarily in the interests of scholarship, but as a means of seeking out all books whose contents might reflect upon the legitimacy of the Manchu Dynasty. Nevertheless this enormous compilation contains many otherwise unknown texts and the fruits of much scholarly research. For this was an antiquarian age when, as never before, men looked back into the past, burrowing into the Classics, dabbling in archaeology, forming huge collections of books and manuscripts, paintings, porcelain and archaic bronzes. Most famous among the collectors of paintings were Liang Ch'ing-piao, whom we have already referred to, and An I-chou (*c.* 1683 to *c.* 1740), many of whose treasures were later acquired by the Ch'ien-lung Emperor. Ch'ien-lung, who had succeeded the able but ruthless Yung-cheng in 1736, possessed a prodigious enthusiasm for works of art, and in his hands the imperial collection grew to a size and importance it had not seen since the days of Hui-tsung.[1] His taste, however, was not always equal to his enthusiasm, and he could not resist the temptation to write indifferent poems all over his most treasured

---

[1] The catalogue of the Ch'ien-lung collection, *Shih-ch'ü Pao-chi*, was compiled in three volumes between 1745 and 1817; only the first part has been published. Buddhist and Taoist works were catalogued separately. A survey made by the Palace Museum authorities in 1928–1931 showed the vast scale of the collection: 9,000 paintings, rubbings and specimens of calligraphy, 10,000 pieces of porcelain; over 1,200 bronze objects (including mirrors), and a large quantity of textiles, jades, and minor arts. Some of the finest pieces had been sold or given away by the last Manchu emperor P'u-i during the twenty years following the Revolution of 1911. All but a fraction of the remainder were taken to Taiwan by the Kuomintang when they quit China in 1949.

paintings and stamp them with large and conspicuous seals. His abdication in 1796 (because he considered it unfilial to occupy the throne longer than his illustrious grandfather), marks the end of the great days of the Ch'ing Dynasty. To the familiar story of internal dissolution was added the aggressive advance of the European powers, whose original admiration had now given way to hostility, provoked by impatience at irksome trade restrictions. We need not linger over the tragic history of the nineteenth century, the shameful Opium Wars, the failure of the Taiping rebels to regenerate China, and her final abasement after 1900. This was not a time for greatness either in politics or in the arts. Though a few of the literati maintained a certain independence of spirit, the educated class as a whole took its lead more and more from the reactionary attitude of the Manchus.

The architecture of the Ch'ing Dynasty was, in the main, a tame and cautious continuation of the style of the Ming— with one notable exception. To the north of the capital the K'ang-hsi Emperor laid out an extensive park, the 'Summer Palace', in emulation of the great hunting parks of the Han and Liang emperors. It was enlarged by Yung-cheng, who gave it the name Yüan-ming-yüan, and again by Ch'ien-lung who added to the palaces already built in it a huge assembly of pleasure pavilions designed by the Italian Jesuit missionary and court painter Guiseppe Castiglione (1688–1766) in a somewhat chinesified version of Italian eighteenth-century baroque. These extraordinary buildings were set about with elaborate fountains and water-works devised by Father Benoit, a French Jesuit who had familiarized himself with the fountains at Versailles and Saint-Cloud. Every detail down to the furniture was specially designed (much of it copied from French engravings) and the walls hung with mirrors and Gobelins tapestries sent out by the French court in 1767. The total effect must have been bizarre in the extreme. But the heyday of the Yüan-ming-yüan was brief. Before the end of the eighteenth century the fountains had long ceased to play, and Ch'ien-lung's successors so neglected their transplanted Versailles that by the time the Western allies destroyed the palace and looted its treasures in 1860, it had already fallen into a sad autumnal state of disrepair. But we can obtain some idea of what it looked like in its prime from the engravings made by Castiglione's Chinese assistants in 1786. The last great architectural achievement — if indeed it deserves the name — of the Manchus was the Summer Palace built outside Peking by the Dowager Empress Tzu-hsi with funds raised by public subscription to construct a navy. Although she was condemned at the time for her extravagance, it has since been observed that had she built a fleet it would certainly have been sunk by the Japanese in the war of 1895, while the Summer Palace will endure for centuries.

Less pretentious and far more appealing is the Ch'i-nien-tien, Hall of Annual Prayers, erected near the altars of Heaven and Earth in the Southern quarter of the city late in the nineteenth century (Plate 64a). Its gleaming marble terraces, its richly painted woodwork and the deep blue of its tiles dazzle the eye. But we need only to glance at the poverty of its detail, its reliance upon paint rather than imaginative carpentry, to realize that, fairy-like as is its total effect, the Hall of Annual Prayers marks the final exhaustion of a great tradition.

In a corner of the Forbidden City, K'ang-hsi set aside a courtyard known as the Ch'i-hsiang-kung as a studio and repair-shop where Chinese and Jesuit artists and mechanics worked side by side, painting, engraving, repairing clocks and musical instruments. The court painter Chiao Ping-chen studied perspective there under the Jesuits and embodied what he had learned in forty-six illustrations to the famous agricultural work *Keng-chih-t'u*, while his pupil Leng Mei was noted for delightful but over-elegant paintings of court ladies, generally in a garden setting and showing some knowledge of western perspective. Castiglione, who had arrived in Peking in 1715, was already an accomplished painter. He soon mastered the academic manner of his Chinese colleagues, and proceeded to create a synthetic style in which a Chinese medium and technique are blended with western naturalism, aided by a subtle use of shading (Plate 66a). He was a favourite at court, where his still-life paintings, portraits and long handscrolls depicting horses in a landscape or scenes of court life signed, very carefully, with his Chinese name Lang Shih-ning, were greatly admired. He had numerous pupils and imitators, for the decorative realism of his style was particularly suited to the kind of 'furniture painting' which the palace required in such huge quantities to decorate its endless apartments. Castiglione, however, no more affected the general trend of Chinese painting in his time than did the Chinese artists working for the Europeans in Canton and Hongkong. Tsou I-kuei (1686–1772), a court artist to Ch'ien-lung noted for the painstaking realism of his flower paintings (an art in which he probably influenced the style of his colleague Castiglione) — much admired western perspective and shading. 'If they paint a palace or a mansion on a wall,' he wrote, 'one would almost feel induced to enter it.' But he makes it clear that these are mere technicalities, to be kept in their proper place. 'The student should learn something of their achievements so as to improve his own method. But their technique of strokes is negligible. Even if they attain perfection it is merely craftsmanship. Thus foreign painting cannot be called art.'[1]

The most interesting and neglected of the Ch'ing professional painters, however, was the group centred round Li Yin and Yüan Chiang, both of whom were working in prosperous Yangchow between about 1690 and 1725, after which the latter, like his son(?) Yüan Yao, became a court painter. They are chiefly noted for having given a violent twist to the long moribund 'northern' tradition by applying to the style and composition of early Sung

[1] Europe, at this time, felt much the same way about China. 'In *Painting*', wrote Alvarez de Semedo in 1641, 'they have more curiositie, than perfection. They know not how to make use of either *Oyles* or *Shadowing* in the Art. . . . But at present there are some of them, who have been taught by us, that use *Oyles*, and are come to make perfect pictures.' Sandrart, in his *Teutsche Akademie* (1675) expressed a similar view. Cf. my article 'Sandrart on Chinese Painting', *Oriental Art*, I, 4 (Spring, 1949), 159–61.

masters such as Kuo Hsi the fantastic distortions of the late Ming expressionists. The blend of fantasy and mannerism in their work can be seen in the detail from Li Yin's landscape in the Freer Gallery illustrated in Plate 66b.

The literati, who carried on the lofty intellectual and aesthetic ideals of Tung Ch'i-ch'ang, shared none of the academicians' grudging admiration for European painting. They simply ignored it. Nevertheless, in the hands of the 'Four Wangs' and their followers, the free, unfettered style of the Ming scholar painters became itself a new kind of academicism. The earliest of the four was Wang Shih-min (1592–1680), who had learned to paint from the hand of Tung Ch'i-ch'ang himself. Like Tung, he deeply admired the broad, relaxed manner of Huang Kung-wang, and his great series of landscapes in the manner of the Yüan recluse, painted in his seventies, are among the noblest achievements of the Ch'ing literati. Wang Chien (1598–1677), his close friend and pupil, was an even more conscientious follower of the Yüan masters. More gifted was Wang Hui (1632–1717), who as a young and impecunious student had been introduced by Wang Chien to Shih-min, whose pupil he too became. He devoted much of his talent to imitations of early masters, and the Palace Museum and other collections contain a number of 'tenth century' and 'Northern Sung' landscapes which are almost certainly his work.

Of the four Wangs, Wang Yüan-ch'i (1642–1715) was the most gifted and original. The grandson of Wang Shih-min, he rose to high office under the Manchus, becoming Chancellor of the Hanlin Academy and vice-president of the Board of Finance. He was a favourite of K'ang-hsi, who frequently summoned him to paint in his presence, and he was appointed one of the editors of the great anthology of painting and calligraphy *P'ei-wen-chai shu-hua-p'u* published on imperial order in 1708. But Wang Yüan-ch'i was no academician. Although he drew his themes from the Yüan masters and his curious angular forms and gaunt trees from Tung Ch'i-ch'ang, he had an obsession with form, unique in a Chinese painter, which has caused some Western writers to liken him to Cézanne. With deep concentration, he would as it were pull apart and reassemble the elements in his landscapes like a cubist, to achieve a semi-abstract order of reality of great purity and serenity that recalls Ni Tsan (Plate 67a) and is utterly different from the mannered distortions of Yüan Chiang and his school.

Chinese art historians like to classify painters in groups, and the Four Wangs, together with Wu Li and Yün Shou-p'ing (1633–1690) make up the 'Six Great Masters of the Ch'ing Dynasty'. Yün Shou-p'ing (commonly known as Yün Nan-t'ien) was the son of an ardent Ming loyalist and consequently had to live in partial obscurity in the Soochow-Hangchow region far from the capital, where he supported himself by his painting and calligraphy. He had aspirations as a landscape painter, but feeling himself unable to compete in this field with his close friend Wang Hui, he turned to flower painting in the 'boneless' style. At his best in the intimate art of painting fans and album leaves, his pictures have become deservedly popular for the beauty of their colour and the skill of their brushwork and arrangement. Wu Li, born in 1632, is of unusual interest because he came under the influence of the Jesuits, was baptized, spent six years studying theology in Macao where he was ordained in 1688, thereafter devoting the rest of his life to missionary work in Kiangsu. However his conversion in no way changed his style of painting. A pupil of Wang Chien and an intimate friend of Wang Hui, he called himself Mo-ching Tao-jen, the Taoist of the ink-well (in the literal sense of Alice's treacle-well), continuing to paint in the eclectic manner of the early Ch'ing *wen-jen*, without a hint of European influence, until his death in 1718.

A typical eighteenth-century example of this growing eclecticism is Hua Yen (1682–after 1755), or Hsin-lo Shan-jen, whose oeuvre included boneless flower paintings, echoes of the misty impressionism of Kao K'o-kung, landscapes in the literary style of Wang Hui and Shen Chou and in the old green-and-blue style. Hua Yen was one of the 'Eight Unusual Characters of Yangchow', who also included among their number Lo P'ing (1733–99), Huang Shen (1687–after 1768) the element of caricature in whose paintings made him especially popular in Japan, and Chin Nung (1687–1764) who did not begin to paint his odd, vigorous and highly individual little landscapes and bamboos until he was fifty.

No account of seventeenth-century painting should omit the name of Hung-jen, one of the 'Four Masters of Anhui', a Buddhist monk who died young in 1663 after painting a number of spare, dry, exquisitely sensitive landscapes closer in spirit to Ni Tsan than to any of his contemporaries. A third important group of the period was the 'Eight Masters of Nanking' who included several minor landscapists of great sensibility such as Kao Ts'en and Fan Ch'i, and one major figure — Kung Hsien (c. 1620–1689), one of whose still, silent landscapes is illustrated in Plate 67b. This strange stillness, produced by a brush that barely moves, this chiaroscuro and dense texture, suggest that Kung Hsien and his circle may have seen European engravings brought to Nanking by the Jesuits. Though a dour recluse, Kung Hsien was an influential teacher, and his pupil Wang Kai was the chief compiler of the *Painting Manual of the Mustard Seed Garden*, referred to above.

Painters such as Hua Yen, Hung-jen and Kung Hsien were by no means orthodox members of the literary school. They belong rather in the company of the Individualists, whose achievement made the first century of the Ch'ing Dynasty one of the most creative periods in the history of Chinese painting. The greatest of the early Ch'ing Individualists were Chu Ta (1625–c. 1705), K'un Ts'an (c. 1610–c. 1670) and Shih-t'ao (1641–c. 1717).

Chu Ta (or Pa-ta Shan-jen, as he generally signed himself), was a distant descendant of the Ming royal house who with the advent of the Manchus became a monk, turning his back not only upon the world but upon the whole art of painting as practised in his time. He was an eccentric character whose brush style appears at first glance to be careless and slapdash and yet, like that of the Zen masters who were his spiritual ancestors, it is incredibly sure and precise. His remarkable landscape compositions are executed in a brilliant shorthand, with the aid of a highly personal repertoire of brushstrokes, dots and hatchings that would have shocked an orthodox disciple of Tung Ch'i-ch'ang. Perhaps his peculiar genius is most evident in his swift album sketches, in which small angry-looking birds perch on a rock or twig amid an infinity of space (Plate 68a), or in larger studies of rock-like fishes and fish-like rocks, drawn in a few brilliant sweeping lines. This is 'ink-play' at its purest; yet it is no mere virtuosity, for Pa-ta Shan-jen's deceptively simple style contains the very essence of the life and form of the flowers, plants and creatures he portrays. In a few strokes he had made a complete statement.

Shih-t'ao and Shih-ch'i are linked together by Chinese art historians as the Two Stones (*Erh Shih*), yet there is no positive evidence that they were close friends. Shih-ch'i (K'un-ts'an) was a devout Buddhist who spent all his life as a monk, his later years as abbot of a monastery at Nanking. The texture of his landscapes, painted with a dry, scrubby brush, has the groping, almost fumbling, quality that we find in Cézanne, and as in Cézanne this very awkwardness, this refusal to make concessions to the viewer, are witness to the painter's integrity. Yet the final effect — in the beautiful autumn landscape in the British Museum, for example (Plate 69) — gives an impression of grandeur and serenity. He, of all the Individualists, comes closest to the expressionism of the early Ch'an painters. Shih-t'ao, whose family name was Chu Jo-chi, was a lineal descendant of the founder of the Ming Dynasty, which fell when he was a boy of fourteen. He thereupon joined the Buddhist community on Lu-shan, taking the monastic name Tao-chi. But he was no recluse. In 1657 he went to live in Hangchow, and thereafter spent much of his life wandering about China, visiting sacred mountains in the company of monks and scholars, spending three years in Peking (where he and Wang Yüan-ch'i collaborated on a picture of Bamboo and Rocks), finally settling in Yangchow, where he often painted in company with Pa-ta Shan-jen till the latter's death in 1705. He himself died perhaps twelve years later. A chronicle of Yangchow, a city famous for its gardens, says that one of his favourite hobbies was 'piling up stones' — i.e. designing gardens, among which his 'Garden of Ten Thousand Rocks' laid out for the Yü family was considered his masterpiece. We may be sure that a number of his little album landscapes — and indeed those of such men as Yün Shou-p'ing and Li Liu-fang — were actually suggestions for garden designs.

Though Shih-t'ao was a Buddhist by training, he was a Taoist at heart. His aesthetic philosophy is contained in the *Hua-yü-lu*, a series of notes on painting written at different times, put together and published after his death. Like Kung Hsien, he has no doubts about his own powers, though, unlike Kung Hsien, we may be sure he had his tongue in his cheek when he wrote, 'If it happens that my work approaches that of some old painter, it is he who comes close to me, not I who am imitating him.' The core of his doctrine is the supreme importance of the *i-hua*, literally the 'one line'. There has been much speculation as to what this means, but perhaps it had already been explained by the Sung writer Kuo Jo-hsü, commenting on a remark of Chang Yen-yüan's about Lu T'an-wei. 'His meaning,' wrote Kuo, 'was not that a whole page of writing or the depiction of an entire object can be carried out with a single brush-stroke; but rather that from beginning to end the brush is kept responsive, with continuity and interrelationship, and no "break in flow of spirit".'[1] It is by means of the *i-hua* that form is made to emerge out of undifferentiated chaos, and only when he understands this can the painter begin to represent nature. It is essential, moreover, that he be deeply versed in the old masters, though this does not mean that he should imitate their methods for, as Shih-t'ao said in the *Hua-yü-lu*, 'The method which up till now has not been a method is the painter's best method.' Shih-t'ao's concept of the ecstatic union of the artist with nature is not new, but nowhere in the whole of Chinese art will we find it expressed with so much spontaneous charm.

[1] See Soper, *Kuo Jo-hsü's Experiences in Painting*, p. 16.

Whether in a long handscroll such as the extraordinary, swirling panorama in the Sakuragi collection, or in a towering landscape such as the magnificent view of Mount Lu in the Sumitomo collection, or in any of his innumerable album leaves (Plate 68b, and frontispiece), his forms and colours are ever fresh, his spirit light, his inventiveness and wit inexhaustible.

The art of Shih-t'ao, and indeed that of all the Individualists, represents a private protest against the new academicism of the literati. But as the Ch'ing settled deeper into that stagnation which seems to have been the fate of every long-lived dynasty in Chinese history, the lamp of individualism burned more and more dimly. During the nineteenth century the growing foreign menace produced not action but paralysis at the centre, and patronage shrank to almost nothing. A handful of literati kept the tradition alive, however, until in the twentieth century there took place a revolution in Chinese painting over which the artists themselves had little control.

The astonishing work of the seventeenth-century Individualists was produced during a long period of confusion, banditry and civil war which began after the death of the Wan-li Emperor in 1620 and was not finally resolved until the time of K'ang-hsi. These years of political and economic chaos had a serious effect upon the gigantic ceramics industry at Ching-te-chen. Already before the end of the Ming Dynasty the imperial wares had sharply declined both in quality and quantity. The reign of T'ien-ch'i is noted for a coarse, brittle blue-and-white prized in Japan as *tenkei* ware, but marked pieces of his successor Ch'ung-cheng are very rare and of poor quality. During these years China lost to Japan the great market she had built up in Southeast Asia and Europe, and did not fully recover it again till Wu San-kuei had been defeated and South China brought once more under the control of the central government. Consequently the so-called 'transitional wares' of the mid-seventeenth century, being for the most part continuations of earlier styles, are not always easy to identify. The most characteristic of them are strongly-built blue-and-white jars, bowls and vases decorated with figures in landscapes, rocks and flowers (especially the 'tulip', possibly based on a European motif) in a thick violet glaze which Chinese collectors call 'ghost's-face blue' (*kuei-mien-ch'ing*) and western connoisseurs 'violets in milk'. Many of them were made primarily for export, and like the export blue-and-white of Chia-ching and Wan-li have a freedom of drawing that gives them considerable appeal.

No abrupt change at Ching-te-chen followed the establishment of the new dynasty. The imperial factory was still functioning after a fashion in the 1650's and pieces produced during these unsettled years represent, as we would expect, a continuation of the style of the Wan-li period. Between 1673 and 1675 Kiangsi was laid waste by Wu San-kuei's rebels and in the latter year the imperial factories at Ching-te-chen were destroyed. They were rebuilt a few years later. In 1682 K'ang-hsi appointed as Director of the Imperial Kilns Ts'ang Ying-hsüan, a Secretary in the Imperial Parks Department. Ts'ang, who arrived at Ching-te-chen early in the following year, was the first of three great directors whose names are linked to this supreme moment in the history of Ching-te-chen. It is not known precisely when Ts'ang retired. In 1726 Yung-cheng appointed Nien Hsi-yao, who in turn was succeeded in 1736 by his assistant T'ang Ying, who held the office until 1749 or 1753. Thus Ts'ang's directorship corresponds roughly to the K'ang-hsi period, Nien's to Yung-cheng, and T'ang Ying's to the first years of Ch'ien-lung.

Two Chinese works give us useful information on the Imperial kilns and their output, though both were written after the factory had begun to decline. Chu Yen published his *T'ao-shuo* in 1774, while the *Ching-te-chen t'ao-lu* written by Lan P'u did not appear till 1815. The most valuable description however is that contained in two letters written by the French Jesuit Père d'Entrecolles who was in China from 1698 to 1741, and not only had influential friends at court but also many converts among the humble artisans in the factories at Ching-te-chen. These letters, dated 1712 and 1722, give a vivid picture of the whole process of manufacture, of which he was an intelligent observer.[1] He recounts how the *petuntse* (china stone) and *kaolin* (china clay) are quarried and prepared, and the enormous labour involved in kneading the clay. He describes a degree of specialisation among the decorators so minute that it is a wonder the painting has any life at all: 'One workman does nothing but draw the first colour line beneath the rims of the pieces; another traces flowers, while a third one paints. . . . The men who sketch the outlines learn sketching, but not painting; those who paint (i.e., apply the colour) study only painting, but not sketching,' all in the interests of absolute uniformity. Elsewhere he says that a single piece might pass through the hands of seventy men. He speaks of the hazards of the kiln and of how a whole firing is often lost by accident or miscalculation. He tells how the emperor would send down Sung Dynasty *kuan*, Ju, Ting, and Ch'ai wares to be copied, and of the gigantic fish-bowls ordered by the palace which took nineteen days to fire. The greatest challenge however was set by the agents of the European merchants at Canton who demanded open-work lanterns, table-tops, and even musical instruments in porcelain. These orders were dreaded, because they were often rejected for the smallest flaws, and were quite impossible to dispose of in the local market. As early as 1635 the Dutch were forwarding, via Formosa, wooden models of the shapes of vessels required. We can get some idea of the extent of the foreign trade from the fact that in 1643 no less than 129,036 pieces of porcelain were sent via Formosa to the Dutch Governor-General of Batavia for shipment to Holland. Most of it must have been produced at Ching-te-chen.

The most beautiful of K'ang-hsi wares, and those which have been most admired both in China and the west, are not the oddly-shaped and extravagantly-decorated pieces made for the export market, but the small monochromes, which in their classic

[1] They were originally published in the Jesuit miscellany *Lettres édifiantes et curieuses*, Vols. XII and XVI (1717 and 1724), reprinted in S. W. Bushell's *Description of Chinese Pottery and Porcelain* (Oxford, 1910), and translated in part in Bushell's *Oriental Ceramic Art* (New York, 1899). Some interesting passages are quoted by Soame Jenyns in his *Later Chinese Porcelain* (London, 1951), 6–14.

perfection of form, surface and colour recapture something of the subtlety and restraint of the Sung. The *T'ao-lu* says that Ts'ang Ying-hsüan's clays were rich, his glazes brilliant, his porcelain thin-bodied, and that he developed four new colours — eel-skin yellow, spotted yellow, snake-skin green and turquoise-blue. He also perfected a mirror black which was often decorated with gold, an exquisite soft red shading to green known as 'peach-bloom' and used, it seems, for a very small range of vases and vessels for the scholar's desk, an 'Imperial yellow', and a clear powder-blue, blown on through a bamboo tube and then often painted with arabesques in gold. The latter were especially admired in France where it was the fashion to mount them in *ormolu*. The most splendid effect was a rich red produced from copper, known in Europe as *sang-de-boeuf* (ox-blood) and in China as Lang-yao (Plate 70b); several members of the Lang family have been suggested as possible candidates for the honour of having this ware named after them — the most likely being Lang T'ing-chi who, as governor of Kiangsi from 1705 to 1712, took an active interest in the kilns at Ching-te-chen. The glaze was probably applied by spraying and ran down the sides of the vase, stopping miraculously short of the foot — a degree of control which was lost in the Ch'ien-lung period and has only recently been recovered; while a beautiful effect appears around the rim where the colour has failed to 'develop' and the glaze has a pale greenish tinge. The K'ang-hsi potters also copied the beautiful white 'egg-shell' bowls of Yung-lo, their versions being more flawless than the Ming originals, and made a fine imitation of the classical Ting ware of the Sung period.

These monochromes appealed chiefly to cultivated taste. Much more widely appreciated were the underglaze blue and enamelled wares, for which there was a huge demand both in China and abroad. Most K'ang-hsi blue-and-white was produced by the mass-production methods of which Père d'Entrecolles gives so depressing a picture, and as a result has a technical perfection combined with dead uniformity only partly redeemed by the magnificent quality of the cobalt itself which has a vivid, intense luminosity never equalled before or since (Plate 71a). It had a great vogue in Europe in the first half of the eighteenth century, particularly popular being the 'ginger jars' decorated with blossoming prunus on a blue ground reticulated with lines suggesting ice-cracks. Thereafter it was largely replaced in favour by the brightly coloured enamelled wares. Between 1667 and 1670 an Imperial edict had been issued forbidding the use of the K'ang-hsi *nien-hao*. It is not known how long the ban remained in force, but there are comparatively few genuine pieces with the K'ang-hsi mark, and a correspondingly large number to which the potters added the fictitious marks of the Ming Emperors Hsüan-te and Ch'eng-hua.

The great achievement of the potters working under Ts'ang Ying-hsüan, however, was in the enamels, of which two kinds had been developed by the end of the Ming Dynasty: *wu-ts'ai* (five colours) enamelled over the glaze, and *san-ts'ai* (three colours) applied directly 'on the biscuit'. In the K'ang-hsi *wu-ts'ai*, over-glaze violet-blue replaces the underglaze blue of Wan-li, but the dominating colour is a transparent jewel-like green which led its European admirers in the nineteenth century to christen it *famille verte*. Most of these pieces are vases and bowls, made purely for ornament, and decorated with birds or butterflies amid flowering branches, disposed with an exquisite and subtle sense of balance which strongly suggests that these designs were inspired by paintings. Some of the loveliest are the small bowls and 'chicken-cups' which are almost indistinguishable from the Ch'eng-hua *tou-ts'ai* enamels they imitate. The revived *san-ts'ai* enamel-on-biscuit was used chiefly for reproductions of archaic bronzes, and for figurines of Buddhist and Taoist divinities, children, birds and animals. Also enamelled directly on the biscuit is the so-called *famille noire*, whose polychrome floral decoration is set off against a background of a rich black made almost iridescent by being washed over with a transparent green glaze. Until recently this spectacular ware had an enormous vogue among foreign collectors, and, like certain other Ch'ing enamels, still commands prices out of all proportion to its aesthetic worth. Examples of both *famille verte* and *famille noire* were sometimes adorned with Ch'eng-hua reign marks to show how highly their makers regarded them. Towards the end of the K'ang-hsi period the robust vigour of the *famille verte* began to yield to a new style dominated by a delicate rose-pink, which is known in Europe as *famille rose* and which the Chinese call *yang-ts'ai* (foreign colour). It had been invented, about 1650, by Andreas Cassius of Leyden, who succeeded in producing a rose-red from gold chloride. A saucer dish in the Percival David Foundation dated 1721 must be one of the earliest Chinese examples of the use of this colour, which was probably introduced by the Jesuits.

The feminine elegance of *famille rose* came to its full flowering with the appointment of Nien Hsi-yao as director of the Imperial factories in 1726. Nien's directorship is chiefly famous for its 'imitation of the antique and invention of novelties'. As a typical example of the former we have his exquisite copies of classical Sung wares, so perfect that a Ju ware bottle now in the Percival David Foundation was for many years accepted as a genuine Sung piece by the Palace Museum authorities, until its carefully concealed Yung-cheng mark was discovered. Indeed many Yung-cheng pieces had the reign-mark ground away so that they might be passed off as Sung when they were illicitly sold out of the Palace collection. Nien's 'novelties' included the 'tea-dust' glaze, made by blowing green enamel on to an iron yellow-brown glaze, an improvement on the exquisite pale blue glaze known in Europe as *clair-de-lune*, and such rococo effects as painting in ink-black flecked with gold or in greenish-blue flecked with red. Already in 1712 d'Entrecolles had been asked by the officials at Ching-te-chen for curious European objects which might be copied in porcelain and sent to court, and during the Yung-cheng period — and increasingly under Ch'ien-lung — this taste for extravagant forms and new effects was to absorb the energies of the potters at the cost of real refinement of taste. Its most lamentable results can be seen in the decline of *famille rose*, which early in the Yung-cheng period had had an exquisite, feminine delicacy; it was spoilt by the foreign demand for rich and garish decoration, finally degenerating into the livid salmon-pink of the nineteenth century.

In point of sheer craftsmanship the Ch'ien-lung period is supreme, and the finest of the enamelled wares produced under the directorship of T'ang Ying are unsurpassed (Plate 65b). T'ang, who has himself described how he lived and worked with his potters, had complete mastery of their techniques and was continually experimenting with new effects, reproducing the colour and texture of silver, grained wood, lacquer, bronze, jade, mother-of-pearl and even cloisonné. He copied Italian faience drug pots, Venetian glass, Limoges enamels and even Delft painted pottery and Japanese 'old Imari' ware which were themselves copies of late Ming blue-and-white. T'ang Ying also reproduced all the familiar Sung wares (his rather glassy copies of Lung-chüan celadon being particularly fine), while his versions of the robust Canton wares were considered a great improvement on the originals. But the most beautiful of the porcelains produced under his direction are the enamelled egg-shell vessels and bowls such as the lovely lavender vase decorated with mallow flowers and chrysanthemums and bearing a poem believed to be by T'ang Ying himself, which forms the frontispiece to Soame Jenyns' *Later Chinese Porcelain*. In recent years fashion has swung away from these exquisite objects to the more free and vital wares of T'ang and Sung, in which we can see and feel the touch of the craftsman's hand, but nothing can surpass the finest of these Ch'ien-lung pieces for sheer perfection of craftsmanship.

The influence of European taste on the decoration of Ching-te-chen porcelain, which had been growing since the end of the K'ang-hsi period, is nowhere more clearly seen than in a small and choice group of *famille rose* enamelled pieces known as *Ku-yüeh-hsüan*. Of several suggested explanations for this term, which was first used in the mid-nineteenth century, the most ingenious is that it is a disguised form of the phrase *hu-hsien* 'fox-fairy' — the guardian spirit of the seals of some high official, who perhaps had glass objects painted in enamels for his private use, in imitation of a fine enamelled ware which, in the eighteenth century, had been decorated in the palace workshops by well-known court painters.[1] Chiang T'ing-hsi, Ts'ai Kung, and even Castiglione himself, it has been suggested, may have taken a hand in painting these exquisite pieces. Indeed, many of them are decorated with European scenes, and even the Chinese flower motifs have a foreign quality in the realistic drawing, shading and handling of perspective. They generally bear poems followed by red seals, while the *nien-hao* on the base is in embossed enamel.

A few words should be said on the subject of the porcelain made for the European market during the seventeenth and eighteenth centuries. Already in the sixteenth century the South China potters were decorating dishes with Portuguese coats-of-arms, and the Dutch trade vastly increased the demand in the seventeenth century. It was the Dutch who chiefly furnished the 'porcelain rooms' in the great houses of France and Germany, of which the unfinished 'Japanese Palace' of Augustus the Strong, King of Prussia and Elector of Saxony, was the most ambitious. Augustus is reputed to have bartered a regiment of grenadiers for a set of *famille verte* vases, while it was he at whose order Johannes Böttger made the first European porcelain at Meissen near Dresden in 1708. During the seventeenth century European enthusiasts had been quite content to receive Chinese shapes decorated in the Chinese taste, but by the end of the century the practice was growing of sending out to Canton not only specimen shapes but also subjects for decoration, in response to which Ching-te-chen sent huge quantities of white porcelain 'in the blank' down to Canton, where it was painted under the supervision of the European agents. The motifs included armorial bearings, genre scenes, figure subjects, portraits, hunting scenes, pictures of ships taken chiefly from engravings, and religious subjects such as the Baptism, Crucifixion and Resurrection — the so-called 'Jesuit China'. Towards the end of the eighteenth century however, the

[1] The mystery of *Ku-yüeh-hsüan* is discussed fully by Soame Jenyns in Appendix I of his *Later Chinese Porcelain*, 87–95.

enthusiasm for things Chinese began to wane, as Europe was beginning to supply her needs from her own porcelain factories. The great days of the export trade were over, and the so-called 'Nankeen ware' (enamelled porcelain) of the nineteenth century bears eloquent witness to its decay.

Although the Imperial factory continued to flourish until the end of the eighteenth century, its great era ends with the departure of T'ang Ying. Thereafter the decline was slow but steady. At first we see an even greater ingenuity and elaboration in the manufacture of such freakish objects as boxes with porcelain chains and perforated and revolving vases. But after the beginning of the nineteenth century the decay is more rapid, and though some of the wares of the reign of Tao-kuang (1821–50) are of fine quality, the industry suffered a crippling blow when Ching-te-chen was sacked by the Taiping rebels in 1853. Thereafter there was a revival under T'ung-chih (1862–74), and a further revival has taken place in the twentieth century. Today the factories at Ching-te-chen are run on modern industrial lines, but care is being taken to preserve the skills and techniques of the traditional potters.

While the Imperial kilns were concentrating on an ever greater technical perfection, it was the provincial factories in the South which most successfully maintained their vigour and vitality. Of the scores of these kilns we can only mention a few. I-hsing in Kiangsu specialized in the production of little vessels, made of red stoneware, for the scholar's table, most ingeniously fashioned in the form of plants, tree trunks, beetles, rats and other creatures, and in the manufacture of teapots. Te-hua continued to make the fine white porcelain developed in the Ming Dynasty. Other provincial wares were made either for local use or for shipment to regions less exacting in their demands than the Europeans. This applies particularly to the vigorous brown stonewares made at Shekwan, near Fatshan in Kwangtung, consisting chiefly of large jars decorated with a thick blue glaze streaked and flecked with grey and green, which since the Ming Dynasty had been exported in quantity to the *Nan-hai*.

About the year 1680 K'ang-hsi set up workshops in the Palace precincts for the manufacture of porcelain, lacquer ware, glass, enamel, furniture, jade, and indeed all the pretty things which palace life required. The porcelain project, intended to replace distant Ching-te-chen, was found impracticable and soon abandoned, but the other workshops continued in production for the rest of the dynasty and turned out a variety of decorative arts of superb technical quality. Other factories supplied the needs of the wealthy middle class and of the export market. Peking and Soochow, for example, specialized in carved lacquer, Foochow and Canton in the painted sort. The Canton products were considered inferior both in China and abroad because they were often made hastily to meet the demands of European merchants who were only permitted to reside in Canton for a few months in the year. The Foochow lacquer folding screens and cabinets, with their bold carving and soft colours embellished with powdered gold, were exported not only to Europe, but also to Russia, Japan, Mecca and India. K'ang-hsi's glass factory turned out a wide variety of coloured glass bottles and vases, the speciality being an opaque glass laminated in layers of several contrasting colours, through which the designs were carved by the intaglio method — a technique probably copied from lacquer-ware. 'Snuff bottles' (originally made for medicine in the Sung and Yüan Dynasties), were carved in glass and painted with enamel colours. They were also made in an endless variety of semi-precious substances such as lacquer, jade, crystal, coral, agate and enamel, all of which were imitated in porcelain at Ching-te-chen. In the eighteenth century the art of 'back-painting' on glass was introduced from Europe into China. It was said to have been practised by Castiglione in Peking, and soon became popular for painting delightful genre scenes on the backs of mirrors. The application of this technique to the decoration of the inside surface of transparent snuff-bottles, first attempted about 1887, represents the last pathetic effort of the dying arts of the Ch'ing Dynasty to venture into new fields.

It is the general custom for books on Chinese art to end with the pious abdication of Ch'ien-lung in 1796, as though from that moment until today nothing of the least significance had occured. If we glance at the decorative arts, there is indeed enough depressing evidence to support such a view. The porcelain, lacquer, carved jade and other crafts of the late nineteenth and the first half of the twentieth century are derivative and uninspired. Although the level of workmanship has always remained high, and has even improved since 1949, the aesthetic problems that arise during the transition from handicraft to industrial mass-production have yet to be solved. But this should cause no surprise when one considers how long this process took in Europe.

In architecture, the first half of the twentieth century produced many uneasy compromises between traditional and Western styles, and a very few successful ones. In the first fifteen years after 1949 the impact of the official Soviet wedding-cake style saddled Peking with a group of monumental buildings that are neither modern nor Chinese. There are signs, however, that Chinese architects have at last been freed from this disastrous influence and are discovering the truth — which their Japanese colleagues have never lost sight of — that the essence of the traditional style is not the curved roof, beautiful as it is, but the frame structure, which, unlike the roof, is easily adaptable to the modern idiom and modern needs.

The painting of the last fifty years provides a more subtle illustration of the conflicting forces that have been at work in shaping modern China. By the end of the nineteenth century the court painters, once so highly honoured, had sunk to a status hardly higher than that of palace servants. Even their names are not known.

In recent years the palace tradition flickered once more into life in the work of three members of the former Manchu imperial family, P'u Ju, P'u Chin and P'u Hsieh, who between them practised a wide range of academic and literary styles. But, as before, it was only the literati who were able to infuse any life into a slowly petrifying tradition. Typical of nineteenth-century taste was the Shanghai artist Jen Po-nien (1840–1895). He painted some interesting portraits of scholars and merchants, but his landscapes and bird and flower paintings were for the most part executed in a vigorous, and somewhat tasteless, manner which had a marked influence on his twentieth-century admirer Hsü Pei-hung. The literary tradition is better represented by his contemporary Chao Chih-ch'ien (1829–1884), a distinguished scholar who was noted for his paintings of flowers and vines amid rocks, and whose 'boneless' technique and composition were to be much imitated by the modern master Ch'i Pai-shih. Wu Ch'ang-shih (1846–1927) was an extremely prolific painter of every subject in the traditional repertoire, and especially of bamboo, in combination with which his power as a calligrapher shows to special advantage.

Twentieth-century China has produced, among scores of minor masters, two outstanding traditional painters. Huang Pin-hung (1864–1955) was the last of the great scholarly landscape painters of the old Wu School in Chekiang, while Ch'i Pai-shih dominated the art world of Peking. A man of humble origins, Ch'i Pai-shih was apprenticed to a carpenter as a boy, and remained a wood-carver, and carver of seals, all his life. He began to paint when he discovered a copy of the *Painting Manual of the Mustard Seed Garden*, but his uniquely powerful and spontaneous style did not emerge until he was in his sixties. Although he became a devoted admirer of Shih-t'ao and Pa-ta Shan-jen, he was a true individualist. In his sixties he painted some remarkably bold and original landscapes, but he is best known for his late paintings of birds and flowers, crabs and shrimps, of which the little album leaf illustrated in Plate 71b is typical.

More significant historically — if not always so satisfying aesthetically — is the work of those painters who have responded to the challenge of the twentieth century. Many modern Chinese artists have wrestled, consciously or unconsciously, with the problem of how to preserve Chinese traditional painting and yet make it a true reflection of modern life. The first concerted move in this direction was launched by Kao Chien-fu and his brother Ch'i-feng, who in 1912 started an art school in Kwangtung for the express purpose of revitalizing the traditional style, by incorporating into it such modern western devices as perspective, shading and chiaroscuro, and by using it to depict modern urban life realistically. The movement, known as the *Ling-nan p'ai* (Cantonese School) was however too self-conscious, and too much influenced by modern Japanese 'decorative realism' to be an unqualified success. However, during the 'twenties and 'thirties it had a considerable influence upon the artists of South China, while since the People's Republic came to power in 1949 its combination of visual realism with traditional technique has brought it into high favour with the authorities.

The first modern art school in the Orient had been founded in Tōkyō in 1876, but no developments took place in China till Nanking High Normal School opened a Department of Fine Arts on western lines in 1906, soon to be followed in Shanghai by several private studios modelled upon romantic visions of the typical Paris *atelier*, acquired, very much at second hand, from Japanese artists who had studied in France. Soon after the end of the First World War art schools were being opened in Peking and Hangchow, Nanking and Shanghai, and students were flocking to Paris where they came under the influence of the Post-Impressionists. By the middle 'twenties, Hsü Pei-hung had returned to Nanking, Liu Hai-su to Shanghai, Lin Feng-mien to Hangchow, and there was beginning to flourish in the big cities an art which was just as academic as that of the traditional painters — the only difference being that now the medium was not Chinese ink but oil paint. The French Concession in Shanghai became a little Montmartre, the centre for a transplanted bohemianism the more grotesque because it was so sincere. Inevitably the modern movement was completely out of touch with the feelings and aspirations of the mass of the Chinese people.

In the early 'thirties, however, as the menace of Japanese aggression rose on the eastern horizon, the atmosphere began to change. In Shanghai, for example, the cosmopolitan Société des Deux Mondes founded by the modern painter P'ang Hsün-ch'in was dissolved, and the Storm Society took its place. The names are significant. Artists and writers became involved in bitter controversies regarding their responsibility to society, the Bohemians proclaiming a doctrine of art for art's sake, the Realists urging a closer identity with the people. Finally, all doubts about the place of the artist in modern China were resolved by the Japanese attack on Peking in July 1937. Three years of steady retreat brought the painters and intellectuals close to the real China, and the later work of P'ang Hsün-ch'in, of the Realists such as Hsiao Ting, and of the best of the wood-engravers, is full of a sense of discovery — not only of their own people, but also of their own land; for they were driven by the war far into the interior, to come face to face for the first time with the beauty of the western provinces, as yet untouched by the cosmopolitan culture of the treaty ports. As the war dragged on, however, artists with a social conscience became increasingly disturbed by decay and corruption on the home front. Some joined the woodcut movement which had been founded by the great writer Lu Hsün in the nineteen-twenties and was now being promoted by the Communists at Yenan for political ends; others turned in protest to political cartooning or to an elaborate and indirect form of social symbolism.

The Japanese surrender in 1945 left China exhausted and longing for peace. But hardly had the firing died away when this unhappy land was plunged into civil war, and all hopes of peaceful reconstruction were shattered. The art of the last years before the fall of the Kuomintang was marked by an even deeper bitterness on the part of the Realists, or an almost defiant lyricism in the work of P'ang Hsün-ch'in, the wood-engraver Huang Yung-yü, and Chao Wu-chi (Zao Wou-ki), a young student of Lin Feng-mien at the Hangchow Academy who had emerged from the obscurity of the Japanese occupation with a highly sensitive and original style which seemed to point the way to a new direction in

Chinese painting. In 1948 Chao Wu-chi went to Paris, where he has since acquired an international reputation. Perhaps the most remarkable metamorphosis occurred in the art of Tseng Yu-ho who, from being a competent academic painter in the manner of her master P'u Chin, has, since she went to live in Honolulu, come under the influence of some of the most recent developments in western art.

These and other Chinese painters living abroad, such as Lü Shou-k'un in Hong Kong, Liu Kuo-sung in Taiwan, and Cheong Soo-pieng in Singapore, are making a significantly Chinese contribution to the international movement in modern art; for even when their work appears most abstract it is, like that of the late T'ang eccentrics, never entirely divorced from the natural world, and the fact that we can 'read' their abstractions as landscapes gives them an added dimension. At the same time, recent developments in Western art, notably abstract expressionism, seem to be exploring for the first time ground that has long been familiar to the Chinese painter and calligrapher. East and West are learning from each other, and what this portends for the eventual development of art in a more unified world, we can only guess.

Meantime, in China itself the total mobilisation of hands and minds for the task of transforming the sleeping giant into a great modern power has left little room for the individualist. Painters are discouraged from moving too far ahead of the masses, while abstract expressionism is condemned not merely because it is linked with Western bourgeois ideology, but on the more subtle grounds that the Chinese brush technique, in both painting and calligraphy, already has an abstract expressionist element, and hence the Chinese artist has no need to depend upon a foreign style. The strength and freedom that painters still find within the tradition can be seen in a painter such as Li K'o-jan (born in Soochow in 1907) whose work (Plate 72) combines a spontaneity recalling Ch'i Pai-shih and, more remotely, Shih-t'ao and Pa-ta Shan-jen, with a vigour and realism that well reflect the spirit of present-day China.

FROM 1644 TO THE PRESENT DAY

When the new régime came to power in 1949 many people feared that the art of the past would be swept away in the surge of 'socialist realism'. The latter has its place certainly, but the sense of history innate in the Chinese has led China to reject nothing from her past but what was considered socially obstructive or ethically wrong. Far from destroying her cultural heritage, she has, at least until the Cultural Revolution began in 1966, devoted more care to revealing and preserving it than ever before in her history. Changes in her leaders' policy towards the arts reflect their estimate of the world situation, and there is little doubt that the more secure China feels, the more liberal will be their attitude to art and artists.

For over fifty years the long river of Chinese history has been passing through the rapids; its surface has been tossed and broken, its banks strewn with the wreckage of empty forms and outworn traditions. But now, as she emerges into deep water once more, the flood of Chinese civilization resumes its steady flow into the future. The landscape has changed; but it is the same majestic river whose course we have been tracing down the centuries.

Huang Yung-yü; Harvest (Woodcut, 1948.)

BOOKS FOR REFERENCE
AND FURTHER READING

GENERAL WORKS ON CHINA

Raymond Dawson (*ed.*) *The Legacy of China* (Oxford, 1964)
Wolfram Eberhard, *A History of China* (London, 1950)
C. P. Fitzgerald, *China, A Short Cultural History* (London, 1950)
L. Carrington Goodrich, *A Short History of the Chinese People* (*rev. ed.*, London, 1950)

GENERAL WORKS ON CHINESE ART

S. Howard Hansford, *A Glossary of Chinese Art and Archaeology* (*rev. ed.*, London, 1961)
Sherman E. Lee, *A History of Far Eastern Art* (London, 1964)
Laurence Sickman and A. C. Soper, *The Art and Architecture of China*, a volume in the Pelican History of Art (*rev. ed.*, London, 1968)
Michael Sullivan, *Chinese Art in the Twentieth Century* (London, 1959); *Chinese and Japanese Art*, Volume IX in Great Art and Artists of the World (New York, 1966)
William Willetts, *Foundations of Chinese Art* (London, 1965)

EXHIBITIONS AND GENERAL COLLECTIONS

Royal Academy of Arts, *The Chinese Exhibition, A Commemorative Catalogue of the International Exhibition of Chinese Art in 1935–36* (London, 1936)
S. Howard Hansford, *The Seligman Collection of Oriental Art; Volume I: Chinese, Central Asian and Luristān Bronzes and Chinese Jades and Sculptures* (London, 1957)
R. L. Hobson and W. P. Yetts, *The George Eumorfopoulos Collection*, nine volumes (London, 1925–32)
Sherman E. Lee and Wai-Kam Ho, *Chinese Art under the Mongols: The Yüan Dynasty (1279–1368)* (Cleveland, 1969)

BOOKS FOR REFERENCE

Nils Palmgren, *Selected Chinese Antiquities from the Collection of Gustav Adolf, Crown Prince of Sweden* (Stockholm, 1948)

Michael Sullivan, *Chinese Ceramics, Bronzes and Jades in the Collection of Sir Alan and Lady Barlow* (London, 1963)

ARCHAEOLOGY

J. G. Andersson, *Children of the Yellow Earth* (London, 1934)

Kwang-chih Chang, *The Archaeology of Ancient China* (New Haven and London, revised ed., 1968)

Cheng Te-k'un, *Archaeology in China*: Vol. I, *Prehistoric China* (Cambridge, 1959); Vol. II, *Shang China* (Cambridge, 1960); Vol. III, *Chou China* (Cambridge, 1966)

H. G. Creel, *The Birth of China* (rev. ed., New York, 1954)

Li Chi, *The Beginnings of Chinese Civilisation* (Seattle, 1957)

William Watson, *China Before the Han Dynasty* (London, 1961); *Early Civilisation in China* (London, 1966)

BRONZE

Noel Barnard, *Bronze Casting and Bronze Alloys in Ancient China* (Canberra and Nagoya, 1961)

Bernhard Karlgren, *A Catalogue of the Chinese Bronzes in the Alfred F. Pillsbury Collection* (Minneapolis, 1952); and many important articles in the *Bulletin of the Museum of Far Eastern Antiquities* (Stockholm)

J. E. Lodge, A. Wenley, and J. A. Pope, *A Descriptive and Illustrative Catalogue of Chinese Bronzes* (Washington, 1946)

Max Loehr, *Chinese Bronze Age Weapons* (Ann Arbor, 1956); *Ritual Vessels of Bronze Age China* (New York, 1968)

J. A. Pope and others, *The Freer Chinese Bronzes,* II vols., (Washington, 1968)

Mizuno Seiichi, *Bronzes and Jades of Ancient China*, in Japanese with English summary (Kyoto, 1959)

William Watson, *Ancient Chinese Bronzes* (London, 1962)

PAINTING AND CALLIGRAPHY

James Cahill, *Chinese Painting* (New York, 1960)

BOOKS FOR REFERENCE

Chiang Yee, *The Chinese Eye* (London, 1936), *Chinese Calligraphy* (London, 1954)

William Cohn, *Chinese Painting*, Phaidon Books (2nd ed., London, 1957)

Richard Edwards, *The Field of Stones: A Study of the Art of Shen Chou* (Washington, 1962)

Basil Gray and John B. Vincent, *Buddhist Cave Paintings at Tun-huang* (London, 1959)

Roger Goepper, *The Essence of Chinese Painting* (London, 1963)

R. H. van Gulik, *Chinese Pictorial Art as Viewed by the Connoisseur* (Rome, 1958)

Kuo Hsi, *An Essay on Landscape Painting*, tr. Sakanishi (The Wisdom of the East Series, London, 1936)

Sherman E. Lee, *Chinese Landscape Painting* (rev. ed., Cleveland, 1962)

Chu-tsing Li, *The Autumn Colors on the Ch'iao and Hua Mountains; a Landscape by Chao Meng-fu* (Ascona, 1965)

S. Sakanishi, *The Spirit of the Brush* (Wisdom of the East Series, London, 1939)

Osvald Sirén, *The Chinese on the Art of Painting* (Peking, 1936); *Chinese Painting, Leading Masters and Principles* (London, 1956 and 1958)

A. C. Soper, *Kuo Jo-hsü's Experiences in Painting, T'u-hua chien-wen chih* (Washington, 1951)

Laurence Sickman ed., *Chinese Painting and Calligraphy in the Collection of John M. Crawford Jr.* (New York, 1962)

Michael Sullivan, *The Birth of Landscape Painting in China* (Berkeley, Los Angeles and London, 1961)

Arthur Waley, *An Introduction to the Study of Chinese Painting* (London, 1923, reprinted 1958)

SCULPTURE

Leroy Davidson, *The Lotus Sutra in Chinese Art* (New York, 1954)

Mizuno Seiichi and Nagahiro Toshio, *Unko Sekkutsu: Yun-kang, The Buddhist Cave Temples of the Fifth Century A.D. in North China*, sixteen volumes, in Japanese, with English summary (Kyoto, 1952–55); *Chinese Stone Sculpture* (Tokyo, 1950); *Bronze and*

Stone Sculpture of China: from the Yin to the T'ang Dynasty, text in Japanese and English (Tokyo, 1960)

Alan Priest, *Chinese Sculpture in the Metropolitan Museum of Art* (New York, 1954)

Richard Rudolf, *Han Tomb Art of West China* (Berkeley and Los Angeles, 1951)

Osvald Sirén, *Chinese Sculpture from the Fifth to the Fourteenth Centuries*, four volumes (London, 1925)

A. C. Soper, *Literary Evidence for Early Buddhist Art in China* (Ascona, 1959)

Michael Sullivan and Dominique Darbois, *The Cave Temples of Maichishan* (London, Berkeley and Los Angeles, 1969)

ARCHITECTURE

Andrew Boyd, *Chinese Architecture and Town Planning* (London, 1962)

J. Prip-Møller, *Chinese Buddhist Monasteries* (Copenhagen and London, 1937)

Osvald Sirén, *The Walls and Gates of Peking* (London, 1924); *The Imperial Palaces of Peking*, three volumes (Paris and Brussels, 1926); *Gardens of China* (New York, 1949)

CERAMICS

John Ayers, *The Seligman Collection of Oriental Art, Vol. II: Chinese and Korean Pottery and Porcelain* (London, 1964)

Stephen W. Bushell, *Description of Chinese Pottery and Porcelain, Being a Translation of the T'ao Shuo* (Oxford, 1910)

Sir Harry Garner, *Oriental Blue and White* (London, 1954)

G. St G. M. Gompertz, *Chinese Celadon Wares* (London, 1958)

A. L. Hetherington, *Chinese Ceramic Glazes* (London, 1948)

R. L. Hobson, *Chinese Pottery and Porcelain* (London, 1915); *The Wares of the Ming Dynasty* (London, 1923); *A Catalogue of Chinese Pottery and Porcelain in the Collection of Sir Percival David* (London, 1934)

W. B. Honey, *The Ceramic Art of China and Other Countries of the Far East* (London, 1945)

BOOKS FOR REFERENCE

Soame Jenyns, *Ming Pottery and Porcelain* (London, 1953); *Later Chinese Porcelain* (rev. ed., London, 1965)

John A. Pope, *Fourteenth-century Blue and White: A Group of Chinese Porcelains in the Topkapu Sarayi Musesi, Istanbul* (Washington, 1952); *Chinese Porcelains from the Ardebil Shrine* (Washington, 1956)

G. D. Wu, *Prehistoric Pottery in China* (London, 1938)

JADE AND MINOR ARTS

Schuyler Cammann, *China's Dragon Robes* (New York, 1952)

Martin Feddersen, *Chinese Decorative Art* (London, 1961)

Sir Harry Garner, *Chinese and Japanese Cloisonné Enamels* (London, 1962)

S. Howard Hansford, *Chinese Jade Carving* (London, 1950); *Chinese Carved Jades* (London, 1968)

Soame Jenyns and William Watson, *Chinese Art: The Minor Arts* (London, 1963)

George N. Kates, *Chinese Household Furniture* (London, 1948)

Berthold Laufer, *Jade, A Study in Chinese Archaeology and Religion* (New York, 1912)

Alfred Salmony, *Chinese Jade through the Wei Dynasty* (New York, 1963)

Pauline Simmons, *Chinese Patterned Silks* (New York, 1948)

PERIODICALS

Archives of Asian Art (formerly *Archives of the Chinese Art Society of America* (New York, 1945–)

Ars Orientalis (Washington and Ann Arbor, 1954–)

Artibus Asiae (Dresden, 1925–, Ascona, 1947–)

Bulletin of the Museum of Far Eastern Antiquities (Stockholm, 1929–)

China Reconstructs (Peking, 1950–)

Far Eastern Ceramic Bulletin (Boston, 1948–50, Ann Arbor, 1951–60)

Oriental Art (Oxford, 1948–51, New Series, 1955–)

Ostasiatische Zeitschrift (Berlin, 1912–43)

Revue des Arts Asiatiques (Paris, 1924–39)

Transactions of the Oriental Ceramic Society (London, 1921–)

Index

Academia Sinica, 35, 39, 42–3
Academy, Imperial, *see Han-lin Yüan*
Academy of Painting, Imperial, *see Yü-hua Yüan*
Acker, William, cited, 123
Admonitions of the Instructress to the Court Ladies, 126–7
aesthetic theory, 121–4, 160–1, 179 *passim*, 224–6
Amitābha, 156–7
an hua ('secret decoration'), 235
An I-chou, collector, 241
An Lu-shan, General, 148
Anau, 33, 35
Andersson, J. Gunnar, 31, 32, 33, 34, 37
ang ('bracket arm'), 151, 173, 208
Ang-ang-hsi, 32
animal style, 57, 82, 110
Annals of Fou-liang, 231
Anyang, Honan, 37, 39 ff.
Ao, Shang capital, 43
Architecture: Shang, 45, 47; Chou, 64–7; Han, 98–102, 116; Six Dynasties, 132–3; T'ang, 149–52; Sung, 172–4; Yüan and Ming, 205–8; Ch'ing, 242–3; 20th. cent., 260
Aśoka, King, 130
Augustus the Strong, King of Prussia, 235
Avalokiteśvara, 131

bamboo painting, 215–16
Bāmiyān, Afghanistan, 133
bell (bronze), 80–1
belt hooks, *see* garment hooks

Benoit, Father, 242
black pottery, 36
'blanc de Chine', 236
bodhisattva, 131
Book of History, see Shu-ching
Book of Songs, see Shih-ching
Böttger, Johannes, 235
bronze casting, 51
bronze inscriptions, 50, 63, 67–8
bronze weapons, 56–7, 82, 110
bronzes, ritual: types, 50, 51–2, 53, 68–9; Shang, 47 ff., 54 ff.; Chou, 67–9; Warring States, 88–90; Han, 109–10
Buddhism, 95–6, 120 ff., 128 ff., 146–9, 176

calligraphy, 123, 209–12
Cammann, Schuyler, cited, 112, 163
Canton, 148
Castiglione, Guiseppe, 242–4, 257
celadon ware, 117–18, 143–4, 201–2, 231
Ch'a-ching (Tea Classic), 166
Ch'ai ware, 197
Ch'an Buddhism, 154, 176–7, 224
Ch'an painters, 176–7, 193–5
Chang Ch'ien, Han general, 94, 113
Chang Heng, Han poet, 96, 98
Chang Hsüan, 159, 177
Chang Lu, 221
Chang Seng-yu, 140, 190
Chang Ta-ch'ien, 141 n. 1
Chang Tao-ling, 120, 125
Chang Tse-tuan, 186
Chang Yen-yüan, 152, 154, 155, 156, 159

INDEX

Ch'ang-an, 98, 146

Ch'ang-chih, Shansi, 84

Ch'ang-p'ing, nr. Peking, 84

Ch'ang-sha, Hunan, 64, 85 ff., 108

Ch'ang Shu-hung, 141 n. 1

Ch'iang-chia-p'o, Shensi, 64

Chao-hun (The Summons to the Soul), 99–100

Chao Chih-ch'ien, 261

Chao-ku-chen, Honan, 77

Chao Meng-fu, 208–9, 212, 216, 224

Chao Po-chü, 191–2

Chao Wu-chi, 263–4

Che School, 193, 220–1

Chen-yen (Shingon) Sect, 159

Ch'en Hung-shou, 225

chen-jen (Shang diviner), 44

Ch'en Jung, 195

Ch'en Shun (Ch'en Tao-fu), 222

Ch'en Yung-chih, 155

Chengchow, Honan, 37, 43, 44, 48, 52, 54, 59–60

Cheng Ho, Admiral, 218

Cheng-ting (Shang king), 43

Ch'eng-shih mo-yüan, 219

Ch'eng-tzu-yai, Shantung, 35

ch'i (axe), 56

Ch'i-chia-p'ing, Kansu, 36

Ch'i-chou kilns, Kiangsi, 167, 197, 200

Ch'i-nien-tien (Hall of Annual Prayers), Peking, 205–6, 243

Ch'i Pai-shih, 261

ch'i-yün ('spirit consonance'), 122–3

Chia-ting, Szechwan, 96

Chiang T'ing-hsi, 257

Chiao Ping-chen, 243

Chiao-t'an ('Suburban Altar') kilns, Hangchow, 200

Chiao-tso kilns, N. Honan, 199

Chieh-tzu-yüan hua-chuan (Painting Manual of the Mustard Seed Garden), 219, 247, 261

Chien-an kilns, Fukien, 200

Chien-tz'u-ts'un kilns, Hopei, 166 n. 1, 196

Ch'ien Hsüan, 191, 214–15

Ch'ien Ku, 222

Ch'ien-lung, emperor, 241–2

Chin Nung, 246

Chin-ts'un, Honan, 64, 76, 78, 81, 82, 83, 90

chinoiserie, 240

Ch'in Shih-huang-ti, 49, 92–3, 104

Ch'in state, 74–5, 92–3

Chinese Academy of Sciences, *see* Academia Sinica

Ching Hao, 179–80

Ching-te-chen kilns, Kiangsi, 167, 203, 231–6, 250–8

Ching-te-chen t'ao-lu, 251, 253

Ch'ing-chiang, Kwangsi, 48

ch'ing-lü (green and blue) style of painting, 162

ch'ing-pai ware, 167, 202–3, 231–2

Ch'ing-t'u, *see* Pure Land sect

ch'ing-tz'u, *see* celadon

Chiu-yen kilns, Chekiang, 117–18

Ch'iu Ying, 223

Chou Ch'en, 223

Chou Dynasty, 41

Chou Fang, 159, 177

Chou-k'ou-tien, Hopei, 31, 32

Chou Kung, Duke of Chou, 62

Chou-li, cited, 64–5, 70–1, 97

Chou Tun-i, 172

Chou Wei, 220

Chou Wen-ching, 220

Chou Wen-chü, 177

Chu Hsi, 172

Chu-p'u hsiang-lu Manual of bamboo painting), 216

Chu Ta (Pa-ta Shan-jen), 247–8

Ch'u state, 64–6, 75–6, 102

Ch'u Tz'u (The Elegies of Ch'u), 82, 84 ff.

Chü-jan, 180, 185–6

Chü-lu-hsien, Hopei, 197

Ch'ü Yüan (poet), 75

Chuang, Duke of Lu, 66

Chuang Tzu, 75, 90

Chün ware, 167, 196–7

Ch'üan-chou, Fukien, 148

ch'üeh (watch-tower), 99

Ch'un-ch'iu (Spring and Autumn Annals), 63–4

Ch'un-ch'iu Tso-chuan, cited, 55

clair-de-lune glaze, 255

272

cloisonné enamel, 227, 230
coin-tree, 117
coinage, 75
collections of art: imperial, 99, 109, 127, 172, 188-9, 194, 241; private, 144, 219, 241
colour printing, 219
Confucianism, 95, 96-7, 146, 172
Confucius, 63, 75, 80
connoisseurship, 178-9, 194, 241-2
copying of paintings, 179

Darel, Afghanistan, colossal Buddha, 135
Djalai-nor, 32
Dongson culture, 87-8
Dowager Empress Tzu-hsi, 243
dragon painting, 194-5
'dragon robes', 228

'Eight Masters of Nanking', 247
'Eight Unusual Characters of Yang-chow', 246-7
d'Entrecolles, Father, 251-3, 255
export wares, 165-6, 202-3, 235-6, 257-8

famille noire, 254-5
famille rose, 255
famille verte, 254-5
Fan Ch'i, 247
Fan K'uan, 180, 184-5
Ferghana, horses from, 94
figurines, tomb, 87, 116-17, 167-8
flower painting, 155, 189-91, 220
Fo-kuang-ssu, Wu-t'ai-shan, 149-50, 151-2
'Forbidden City', 205-8, 243
'Four Wangs', 245-6
Fu Hsi (legendary emperor), 41
Fung Yu-lan, cited, 75

Gandhāra, 130, 131
gardens, 248
garment hooks, 82-3, 110

Genghis Khan, 169, 171, 204
Gigantopithecus, 31
glass, 83, 86, 163, 259
glaze, early use of, 49, 72-3, 115, 143-4, 165
goldsmith's work, 77, 79-80, 110, 163
Grand Canal, 145
Great Wall, 76, 92, 217
guri lacquer, 229-30

Han Hsi-tsai, 177-8
Han Kan, 160
Han-lin Yüan (Imperial Academy of Letters), 97, 147, 188, 219
Hangchow, 170 passim
Hansford, S. Howard, cited, 49
Hao-pi-chi kilns, Honan, 196, 198, 199
Hawkes, David, quoted, 76 n. 1
Hentze, Carl, cited, 58
hill-jar, 109-10
Hinayāna, 130
Ho Ch'ü-ping, General, 102
Ho-lu, King of Wu, 66
Ho-lung, Kwangsi, 32
'Honan temmoku', 199-200
Hou-chia-chuang, Anyang, 48
Hsi-ching fu, 96
Hsi Wang Mu, 94
Hsia Dynasty, 41
Hsia Kuei, 192-3
Hsia Nai, cited, 36, 72
Hsiang Mo-lin, 219
Hsiang Yü, Ch'u general, 93
Hsiao-t'ang-shan, Shantung, 104
Hsiao Ting, 263
Hsiao-t'un, 39, 46
Hsiao T'ung, 121
Hsieh Ho, 121-3, 179, 180
hsien steamer, 36
Hsien-yang, Ch'in capital, 92-3
Hsin-cheng, Honan, 64, 70, 76, 77
Hsin-tien, 36
Hsin-yang, Honan, 87
Hsing ware, 166
Hsing-p'ing-hsien, Shensi, 79
Hsiu-nei-ssu ('Surveyor's Office') kilns, Hangchow, 201-2

INDEX

Hsiu-wu kilns, Honan, 199
Hsiung-nu, 82, 94, 119
Hsü Hsi, 190–1
Hsü Pei-hung, 261, 262
Hsü Shen (author of *Shuo-wen chieh-tzu*), 59
Hsü Tao-ning, 180
Hsüan, King of Ch'i, 75
hsüan-chi (jade disc), 60
Hsüan-ho hua-p'u, 194
Hsüan-te, Ming emperor, 219–20
Hsüan-tsang, 147, 153
Hu-shu, Nanking, 36
hua-kung (craftsman), 97
Hua shan-shui hsü, 124
Hua shan-shui lu, 180
Hua Yen, 246
Hua-yen-ssu, Tatung, Shansi, 173–4, 175
Hua-yü-lu, 249
Huai Nan Tzu, 94, 109
Huang Ch'ao, 148
Huang Chü-ts'ai, 191
Huang Ch'üan, 190
Huang Kung-wang, 213–14, 222
Huang-men ('Yellow Gate'), 97
Huang Pin-hung, 261
Huang Shen, 246
Huang Ti (Yellow Emperor), 41
Huang T'ing-chien, 187
Huang Yung-yü, 263
Hui-hsien, Honan, 43, 76–7, 83–6
Hui-tsung, Sung emperor, *see* Sung Hui-tsung
Hundred Schools of Philosophy, 75
Hung-jen, 247
Hung-shan-hou, Jehol, 32

I-hsien, Hopei, 65
I-hsing kilns, Kiangsu, 258
i-hua ('one line') technique in painting, 249
Imperial Academy, *see* Han-lin Yüan
'Individualists', 226, 247–50
I-nan, Shantung, 81, 100–1, 105
i-p'in ('untrammelled class' of painting), 177
Ishiyamadera, Japan, 152

ivory, 60

jade, 37, 56, 58–9, 70–2, 83, 86, 90–91, 112–13, 260
Japan, early contacts with, 93, 95
Java Man, *see Pithecanthropus erectus*
Jen Po-nien, 261
'Jesuit china', 257
Jesuits in China, 240, 255
Ju Péon, see Hsü Pei-hung
Ju ware, 197–8

K'ang-hsi emperor, 240
K'ang Seng-hui, 140
Kanishka, 130, 132
Kao Chien-fu, 262
Kao K'o-kung, 214
Kao Ts'en, 247
Karasuk, Siberia, 57
Karlgren, Bernhard, 52, 67–8, 111
Keng-chih-t'u, 243
'Kian ware', 200
kinuta celadon, 202
ko (dagger-axe), 37, 56
Ko-ku yao-lun, 230, 233
'*ko* ware', 202
k'o-ssu tapestry, 227–8
Koenigswald, Dr. G. H. R. von, 31
Korea, 95
kou-le t'ien-ts'ai ('clear outline filled with colour') style of painting, 190–191
Koyama, Fujio, 165, 196
Kozlov expedition, 114–15
'*kraak* porcelain', 235
Ku-chin t'u-shu chi-ch'eng, 241
Ku-hua p'in lu, 121–2
Ku Hung-chung, 177
Ku K'ai-chih, 121, 125–7, 137
Ku-wei-ts'un, Honan, 77, 83
ku-yüeh-hsüan, 256–7
Kuan T'ung, 187
Kuan Tzu, 80, 86
kuan ware, 196–8, 200–1
Kuang-tse kilns, Fukien, 48, 200
Kuanyin, 131, 175
Kubilai Khan, 204–8

INDEX

K'un-lun, Mount, 94, 96, 98
K'un Ts'an, *see* Shih-ch'i
Kung Hsien, 247
kung-kuan (agency for decorative arts), 97
Kuo Hsi, 180–1, 184
Kushan Dynasty, 95

lacquer-ware, 88, 96, 107–9, 227, 229–30, 259
Lan-t'ien, Shensi, 31
Lan Ying, 221
landscape painting: Han, 105–9, 116; Six Dynasties, 124 ff.; T'ang, 160–162; Sung, 179–88, 191–4; Yüan, 212–15; Ming, 220–6; Ch'ing, 243–50
Lang Shih-ning, *see* Castiglione, Guiseppe
Lang-yao, 253
Lao Tzu, 75
Legalists, 75
lei-wen ('thunder pattern'), 48, 55
Leng Mei, 243
Li Chao-tao, 160–2
Li Chen, 159
Li Ch'eng, 179–82
Li Chi, cited, 58
Li Chiai, architect, 173
Li-fan, Szechwan, 36 n. 1
Li Hou-chu, 'emperor' of S. T'ang, 177
Li K'an, 216
Li K'o-jan, 264
Li Kung-lin, 178
Li Lung-mien, *see* Li Kung-lin
Li Shih-min, *see* T'ang T'ai-tsung
Li Ssu, Ch'in minister, 92
Li Ssu-hsün, 160–2
Li-tai ming-hua chi (847), 127, 152, 154
Li T'ang, 192
li tripod, 36, 49, 51
Li Tsai, 220
Li Yin, 244–5
Li-yü, Shansi, 64, 77, 78
Liang Ch'ing-piao, 219, 241
Liang K'ai, 193
Liang Yüan Ti, 127

Liao Kingdom, 170–1, 174
Liao wares, 199
Liao-yang, Manchuria, 106–7
Lieh-nü t'u (Scroll of Virtuous Women), 126
Lin Feng-mien, 262, 263
Lin-hsi, Jehol, 32
Lin-tzu-hsien, Shantung, 65
ling-chih (spirit fungus), 94–5
Ling-kuang Palace, 104–5
Ling-nan p'ai, 262
Liu Hai-su, 262
Liu Kuo-sung, 264
Liu-li-ko, Hui-hsien, Honan, 43, 77
Liu Pang, first Han emperor, 93
liu-po, 111–12
Liu Ying, Prince of Ch'u, 96
Lo Chen-yü, 39
Loehr, Professor Max, cited, 52
Lo-lang, Korea, 108
Lo P'ing, 246
Lo-shen Scroll, 125–6
Lotus Sūtra (*Saddharmapundarika Sūtra*), 137, 153
Loulan, Mongolia, 114
Loyang, Honan, 64, 90, 98, 135
Lu Chi, poet, 121
Lu Chih, 222
Lu Hsün, writer, 263
Lu Yü, writer, 166
Lü Chi, 220
Lü shih Ch'un-ch'iu, cited, 55
Lü Shou-k'un, 264
Lung-ch'üan kilns, Chekiang, 201–2, 231
Lung-hsing-ssu, Cheng-ting-hsien, Hopei, 173
Lung-men, Honan, 136–7, 152–3
Lung-shan, Shantung, 35, 36
Luristan, Persia, 57

Ma-chia-yao, Kansu, 35
'Ma-Hsia school', 191–4
Ma Yüan, 192–3
Mahāyāna, 130, 146, 153–4
Mai-chi-shan, Kansu, 133, 137–8, 141
mandala, 154, 174

mang-p'ao (dragon robe), 228
Manichaeans, 147, 163–4
Mañjuśrī, 131
maps, early, 309
Marco Polo, 148, 205–6
Mei-hua Tao-jen, *see* Wu Chen
Mencius, 75
Meng-ch'i pi-t'an, quoted, 181–2
mesolithic, 32
Mi Fei, 187–8
Mi Yu-jen, 188
Miao-ti-kou, 35
microliths, 32
ming-ch'i (funerary furniture), 86, 101, 115–17, 143, 162, 167–8
Ming Huang, *see* T'ang Hsüan-tsung
Ming-t'ang ('Bright Hall'), 67
Ming Ti, Han emperor, 96
mirrors, 89–90, 110–12, 163–4
Mizuno, Sei-ichi, cited, 55
mo-ko-hua ('boneless' painting), 190–1
Mongols, 204–6
Moslems in China, 147, 148
Mu-ch'i, 193–4
Mu Wang (Chou king), 63
music, 80–1

Nan-ch'an-ssu, Wu-t'ai-hsien, Shansi, 149
'Nankeen ware', 258
Nanking, 120 ff.
Nanyang, Honan, 59
Nara, Japan, 149, 152, 156–7
Neo-Confucianism, 172
neolithic culture, 32–8
Nestorians, 147
Ni Tsan, 213, 216
Ni Tuan, 220
Nien Hsi-yao, 251, 255
Ning-yang, Shantung, 37
Noin-Ula, Siberia, 114–15
'northern celadon', 197
Northern and Southern schools of landscape painting, 160–2, 224–6
'northern *kuan*' ware, 197
Nurhachi, Khan, 239

O-fang Kung, 93

Okakura, Kakuzo, quoted, 195
oracle bones, 39, 41, 42, 44
'Ordos' art, 57, 82, 83, 110

Pa-i kilns, Shansi, 199
pa-kua (eight trigrams), 41, 124
Pa-ta Shan-jen, *see* Chu Ta
Pa-ts'un kilns, Honan, 199
pagoda, 132–3, 151–2, 173
pai-miao ('plain line') technique of painting, 178
painted pottery, 32, 33, 34–5, 37
painting: Shang, 58; Warring States, 88–9; Han, 103–9; Six Dynasties, 121–7, 140–2; T'ang, 153–62; Sung, 178–95; Yüan, 212–16; Ming, 219–226; Ch'ing, 243–50; XXth cent., 260–5
palaeolithic, 31, 32
pan-chu ('plank building'), 45
Pan-p'o, Shensi, 34, 35, 115
Pan-shan, Kansu, 34
P'an-keng (Shang king), 42
P'an Ku, 29
P'ang Hsün-ch'in, 263
paper, invention of, 109
P'ei-wen-chai shu-hua-p'u, 245
P'ei Wen-chung, 31
Peking, 204–8, 217
Peking Man, *see* Sinanthropus pekinensis
Pelliot, Paul, 141 n. 1
P'eng-lai, Mount, 93, 94, 98
perspective, treatment of, 181–2, 183–184
Phoenix Hill kilns, Hangchow, 201
pi (disc), 37, 60, 71, 90–1
Pi-fa-chi (Record of Brush Methods), 180
pi-hsieh (guardian spirit), 133
Piao clan bells, 81
Pien Wen-chin, 220
pin-hsiang (master of ceremonies), 63
P'ing-ling-ssu, Kansu, 133, 141
Pithecanthropus erectus (Java Man), 31
Po-shan hsiang-lu, 109–10
porcelain, 115–18, 165–7, 195 ff., 231 ff., 250 ff.
portrait painting, 159

INDEX

pottery: neolithic, 33–8, 47, 48; Shang, 47–8; Chou, 72–3; Warring States, 83–5; Han, 113, 115–17; Six Dynasties, 143; T'ang, 164–7; Sung, 195

printing, 154 n. 1, 171–2

'proto-porcelain', 115–18

P'u Chin, 260

P'u Hsieh, 260

P'u Ju, 260

P'u-tu-ts'un, Shensi, 64, 73

Pure Land sect of Buddhism, 153–4

relief sculpture: Han, 102–6; Six Dynasties, 127–8, 135–8

Ricci, Father Matteo, 240

roof, curved, 173

Śakti, 154

Śākyamuni, 128–30

Samarra, 166

San-men Gorge dam site, Honan, 64

San Ta Tien, Peking, 205–7

san-ts'ai (three-colour) wares, 236–7, 254

sang-de boeuf (ox-blood) glaze, 253

Sawankalok ware, 238

Schall, Adam, 240

screen painting, 180

sculpture: Shang, 47; Chou, 67; Han, 102–6; Ming, 226

sculpture, Buddhist: Six Dynasties, 132 ff.; T'ang, 152–3; Sung, Liao, Chin, 173–6

Shan-hai-ching, 94, 109

shang-fang (imperial workshop), 111

Shang-lin Hu kilns, Chekiang, 118, 143, 165

Shang-ts'un-ling, Honan, 70, 90

Shekwan kilns, Kwangtung, 258

Shen Chou, 213, 221–2

Shen Kua, writer, cited, 181–2, 185, 191

Shen Nung (legendary emperor), 41

Shen pillar, Szechwan, 103

Sheng Chu, 220

Shih-chai-shan, Yunnan, 87–8

Shih-ch'i (K'un Ts'an), 247, 248

Shih-ching (Book of Songs), 63, 65–6

Shih-chu-chai shu-hua-p'u, 219

Shih-ch'ü pao-chi, 241 n. 1

Shih-hu-wan kilns, Kiangsi, 167, 203

Shih K'o, 177

Shih-shuo hsin-yü, 125 n. 1

Shih-t'ao, 247, 248–50

Shōmu, Emperor, 162

Shōsōin Repository, 162–3

Shou-chou, Anhui, 64, 82, 84 ff., 110

Shu (Szechwan), 77, 169

Shu-ching (Book of History), 63

shu-fu ware, 231–2, 233

Shun (legendary emperor), 41, 55

Shuo-wen chieh-tzu, 59

Sickman, L., quoted, 175

silk, 58, 94, 114–15

Sinanthropus pekinensis (Peking Man), 31, 32

Six Principles (of painting), 121–3

snuff bottles, 254

Société des Deux Mondes, 263

Soper, A. C., cited, 122, 173

Ssu-k'u ch'üan-shu, 241

Ssu-ma Hsiang-ju, poet, 98

Stein, Sir Aurel, 114, 141 n. 1, 158

stoneware, 115–17, 165

Storm Society, 263

stūpa, 130, 132–3

Su Tung-p'o, 178, 187, 216

Sulaiman, Arab traveller, 166

Summer Palace, Peking, 243

Sung Hui-tsung, 49, 159, 170, 188–190, 194, 197

Sung Yü, 75

Susa, 35

'Swatow ware', 237

Ta-ming Kung, Changan, 146, 150

Ta-ssu-kung-ts'un, Anyang, 46, 60

Ta-yi kilns, Szechwan, 166

tai-chao (official in attendance), 97, 188

Tai Chin (Tai Wen-chin), 193, 220–1

Tai K'uei, 137

Tan-t'u, Kiangsu, 67

Tan-yao, Overseer of Monks, 135

INDEX

T'ang-ch'ao ming-hua-lu, quoted, 155

T'ang Hsüan-tsung, 147–8, 162

T'ang-shan, Hopei, 7

T'ang T'ai-tsung, 145–7

T'ang Yin, 223

T'ang Ying, 251, 256

Tao-chi, see Shih-t'ao

Taoism, 75, 93–5, 106, 120–1, 123–5

T'ao-shuo, 251

t'ao-t'ieh (monster mask), 54–5, 58, 60–1, 68, 72, 77, 115

T'ao Yüan-ming, poet, 121

Te-ch'ing, Chekiang, 118, 143

Te-chou kilns, Shantung, 199

Te-hua kilns, Fukien, 236, 258

temmoku, 200

'Temple of Heaven', see Ch'i-nien-tien

tenkei ware, 250

Tepe Hissar, Iran, 35

textiles, 114–15, 163, 227–9

Ti (supreme deity), 44–5, 62

T'ien (Heaven), 62

T'ien-lung-shan, Shansi, 153

T'ien-t'ai sect, 153

Ting-ts'un, Shansi, 32

Ting ware, 166, 196–7

Ting Yün-p'eng, 219

'TLV' mirror design, 110–12

t'o-t'ai (bodiless) porcelain, 236

Toba Wei, 119 ff., 133–5

tobi-seiji (spotted celadon), 231

tombs: Shang, 46–7; Chou, 64, 70; Warring States, 76–7, 85–7; Han, 100–2, 118; Six Dynasties, 142–3; T'ang, 152, Ming, 208

'transitional wares', 250–1

Ts'ai, feudal state, 85

Ts'ai Kung, 257

Ts'ang Ying-hsüan, 251, 253, 254

Ts'ao Chung-ta, 155

Ts'ao Pu-hsing, 140, 195

Tseng Yu-ho, 264

Tso-chuan, 64, 89

Tso Ssu, poet, 126

Tsou I-kuei, 244

Tsou Yen, 111

Ts'ui Po, 216

ts'un (texture stroke), 185, 192, 213

Tsung Ping, 123–4

ts'ung (symbol of Earth), 37, 60, 90–1, 111

Tu Ch'iung, 224

Tuan Fang, 39

Tung Ch'i-ch'ang, 213, 224–6, 245

Tung Wang Kung, 94, 112

Tung Yu quoted, 156, 157

Tung Yüan, 179–80, 185–6

T'ung-kou, Korea, 127

Tunhuang, Kansu, 133, 141–2, 157–8

Tze-yang, Szechwan, 32

Tz'u-chou ware, 198–9

Udayana, King, Buddha image made for, 153

underglaze blue, 232–5, 250–1, 253–5

underglaze red, 232

Vasco da Gama, 218

Verbiest, Father, 240

Waley, Arthur: cited, 76 n. 1; quoted 65–6, 105

wall-painting, 99, 103–7, 127, 141–2, 152–8

Wang Chien, King of Former Shu, tomb of, 169, 176, 188, 190

Wang Chien (painter), 245, 246

Wang Hsi-chih, 123

Wang Hui, 245, 246

Wang Kuo-wei, 39

Wang Mang, 95

Wang Meng, 213–14

Wang Shih-ku, see Wang Hui

Wang Shih-min, 245

Wang Wei, fifth-century poet, 124

Wang Wei, T'ang poet-painter, 161, 225

Wang Yen-shou, quoted, 104–5

Wang Yüan-ch'i, 245, 248

Wang-tu, Hopei, 106

Wei-ch'ih I-seng, see Yü-ch'ih I-seng

Wen Cheng-ming, 221, 222

Wen-chi, palace of, 113

Wen Chia, 222

INDEX

Wen-hsüan, 121

wen-jen-hua ('literary men's painting'), 187, 208, 212–16, 224–6, 245–51

Wen Po-jen, 222

Wen Ti, Han emperor, 93

Wen T'ung, 187, 216

Wen Wang, Chou king, 62

woodcut movement, 263

Wright, Arthur, cited, 135 n. 1

Wu Ch'ang-shih, 261

Wu Chen, 214, 216

Wu Chin-ting, 35

Wu family shrines, Shantung, 100–1, 104, 105

Wu Li, 246

Wu-kuan-ts'un, Anyang, 46, 60

Wu San-kuei, 239, 251

Wu school of landscape painters, 221–223

Wu Tao-tzu, 155–7

Wu Ti, Han emperor, 94, 95, 97, 98, 106

Wu Ti, Liang emperor, 120, 142

wu-ts'ai (five-colour) wares, 237, 254

Wu Tse-t'ien, T'ang empress, 49, 147

Wu Wang, Chou king, 62

Wu Wei, 221

ya-hsing, 50

Yang Hui-chih, sculptor, 152

Yang Kuei-fei, 148

Yang Lien-sheng, 111–12

Yang-shao, Honan, 33, 34, 37

yang-ts'ai (foreign colour), 255

Yang-tzu-shan, Szechwan, 77, 91

yang-yin, 110–11

Yao, legendary emperor, 41

Yao-yao kilns, Shensi, 198

Yen Li-pen, 152, 158–9

Yen Wen-kuei, 180

ying-ch'ing ware, *see* ch'ing-pai ware

Ying-tsao fa-shih, 172–3

Ying Yü-chien, 194

Yü, founder of Hsia Dynasty, 41, 49

Yü Hao, master builder, 173

Yü-hua-yüan, Imperial Academy of painting, 188–93, 219, 243

Yu Wang, Chou ruler, 63

Yü-ch'i-ch'ang (imperial factory), 231

Yü-ch'ih I-seng, 155–6

Yü-ch'ih Po-chih-na, 155

Yüan Chiang, 244

Yüan-ming-yüan, 242–3

Yüan Ti, Liang emperor, 127

Yüeh-chih, 94, 95

Yüeh peoples, 42, 60

Yüeh ware, 85, 117–18, 165–6, 167, 198

Yün-kang, Shansi, 135–7, 174

Yün Shou-p'ing, 246

Yün-t'ai-shan (Cloud Terrace Mountain), 120, 125

Yung-lo-ta-tien (Ming encyclopaedia), 218

Zau Wou-ki, *see* Chao Wu-chi

Zen Buddhism, *see* Ch'an Buddhism

Zoroastrians, 147

1a. Funerary vase; pottery, painted in purple and black. From
Yangshao, Honan. Ht. 42·5 cm. Neolithic.

1b. Stem-dish; black Lungshan-type pottery. Neolithic.

2a. Anyang; tomb at Wu-kuan-ts'un after excavation. Length 10 m. Shang Dynasty.

2b. Ox-head; marble. Excavated at Hou-chia-chuang, Anyang. Length 29·2 cm. Shang Dynasty.

3a. Jar; white
stoneware with
impressed
decoration. From
Anyang. Ht. 33 cm.
Shang Dynasty.

3b. Wine container of type *kuang*; bronze. Ht. 24 cm.
Shang Dynasty.

4. Vessel of type *chia*; bronze. Ht. 34·2 cm. Shang Dynasty.

5a. Dagger-axe of type *ko*; bronze haft and jade blade. From Anyang.
Length 28 cm. Shang Dynasty.

5b. Executioner's axe of type *ch'i*; bronze. From
Anyang. Length 23·5 cm. Shang Dynasty.

6a. Tiger; bronze. Length 75·2 cm. Chou Dynasty.

6b. Knife with animal-head handle; bronze. Length 26·3 cm. Shang Dynasty.

7a. Vessel of type *bu*; bronze. From Hsin-cheng. Ht. 52 cm. Late Middle Chou.

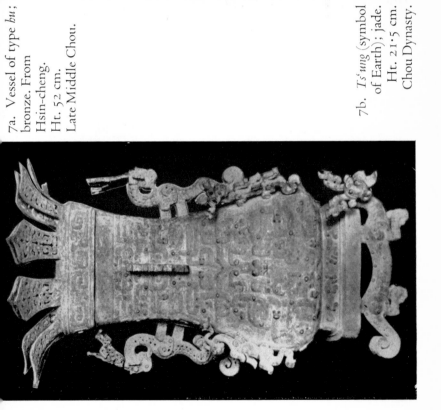

7b. *Ts'ung* (symbol of Earth); jade. Ht. 21·5 cm. Chou Dynasty.

8. Vessel of type *hu*; bronze. Ht. 60·6 cm. Middle Chou period (ninth century B.C.).
Inscription dated equivalent to 862 or 853 B.C. "it was in the 26th year, 10th moon, 1st quarter, in the day *chi-mao*, when Fan Chü Sheng had this bridal *Hu* cast as a bridal gift for his first child, Meng Fei Kuai. May sons and grandsons forever treasure and use it" (tr. Loehr).

9a. Vessel of type *ting*, with cover; bronze inlaid with silver. Probably from Chin-ts'un, Loyang. Ht. 15·2 cm. Warring States.

9b. Bell of type *chung*; bronze. Ht. 54·5 cm. Warring States.

10a. Plaque depicting two animals fighting; bronze.
Length 11·5 cm. Han Dynasty.

10b. Garment hook; gilt bronze, inlaid with jade and glass.
Length 15·7 cm. Warring States.

11a. Gong-stand formed of addorsed phoenixes and tigers; lacquered and painted wood. From Hsin-yang, Honan Ht. 134 cm. Warring States.

11b. Top of container for cowrie-shells, decorated with modelled sacrificial scene; bronze. From Shih-chai-shan, Yünnan. Diam. 34 cm. Late Warring States, or early Han Dynasty.

12b. Mirror; bronze. Diam. 14 cm.
Warring States.

12a. Bowl; painted lacquer. From Changsha.
Diam. 25·4 cm. Warring States.

13b. Woman, phoenix and dragon; painting on silk. Excavated at Changsha. Ht. 30 cm. Warring States.

13a. *Pi* disc; jade. Diam. (of disc) 16·5 cm. Warring States.

14a. Horse trampling upon a barbarian; stone sculpture standing before the reputed tomb of Ho Ch'ü-ping (died 117 B.C.), Shensi. Ht. 188 cm.? Han Dynasty.

14b. Pillar of Shen; stone sculpture. Ch'ü-hsien, Szechwan. Han Dynasty.

15a. The attempt to assassinate Ch'in Shih-huang-ti; rubbing from engraved stone in Wu family shrine at Chia-hsiang, Shantung. Ht. 23 cm. Han Dynasty (second century A.D.).

15b. Shooting birds on a lake shore; rubbing from relief on pottery tile from a tomb at Kuanghan, Szechwan. Ht. 42 cm. Han Dynasty.

16a. The guests arrive for the funeral feast; wall-painting in a tomb
in Liao-yang, N.E. China. Ht. 109 cm. Han Dynasty.

16b. Detail of a painted tomb tile. Ht. 19 cm. Han Dynasty.

17. Hill-censer, *po-shan hsiang-lu*; bronze, inlaid with gold, silver, turquoise and carnelian. Ht. 17·9 cm. Early Han Dynasty.

18a. Paragons of filial piety; lacquer painting on basket-work box from Lolang, North Korea. Ht. (of panel) 5 cm.

18b. TLV-type mirror; bronze. Diam. 20·3 cm. Han Dynasty.

19a. Head and shoulders of a horse; green jade. Ht. 18·9 cm. Han Dynasty.

19b. Figured silk fabric from Noin-Ula, Mongolia. Han Dynasty.

20a. Model of a house; painted pottery. Ht. 132 cm. Han Dynasty.

20b. Stand for a 'coin-tree', decorated with a procession of elephants in relief; pottery. From a tomb at Neichiang, Szechwan. Ht. 33·9 cm. Han Dynasty.

21a. Basin; Yüeh stoneware, covered with a grey-green glaze.
Diam. 28·8 cm. Third or fourth century.

21b. Seated watchdog; red-glazed pottery, from
Changsha. Ht. 36·8 cm. Han Dynasty.

22. After Ku K'ai-chih (c. 344–406); The bedroom scene, from the handscroll illustrating the *Admonitions of the Court Instructress* by Tso Ssu; ink and slight colour on silk. Ht. 25 cm. Ninth or tenth century?

23. The story of the Filial Yüan Ku; engraved on the side of a stone sarcophagus. Ht. 56 cm. First half of sixth century.

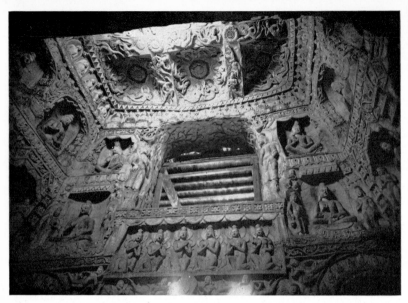

24a. Yünkang, interior of Cave VII. Late fifth century.

24b. The Wei Empress and her attendants; restored relief panel from
Pin-yang Cave, Lungmen. Ht. 198 cm. About A.D. 522.

25. Stele illustrating scenes from the Life of the Buddha and the teachings of the Lotus Sutra; stone. In Cave 133, Maichishan, Kansu. First half of sixth century.

26b. Colossal Buddha; stone. Yünkang, Cave XX. Ht. 13·7 m. Late fifth century.

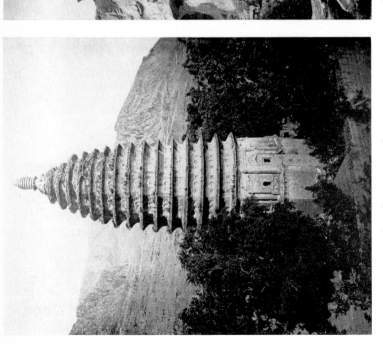

26a. Stone pagoda of Sung-yüeh-ssu, on Mount Sung, Honan. About A.D. 520.

27a. Standing Buddha; gilt bronze. Ht. 61 cm. Dated A.D. 536.

27b. Buddha preaching the Law; wall-painting in Cave 249 (Pelliot 101), Tunhuang. Northern Wei Dynasty.

28a. Bodhisattva; stone. Ht. 188 cm. Northern Ch'i Dynasty.

28b. Kuanyin bearing a vase; stone. Excavated at Chengtu, Szechwan. About seventh century.

28c. The Buddha incarnate in a golden gazelle (the *Rūrū Jātaka*); wall-painting in Cave 257 (Pelliot 110), Tunhuang. Northern Wei Dynasty.

29. Jar; Yüeh stoneware with moulded decoration under olive-green glaze. Ht. 51·6 cm. Six Dynasties.

30a. Winged lion; stone. Length 152 cm. Sixth century.

30b. A charger and his groom; stone relief from the tomb of
T'ang T'ai-tsung (died 649). Length 206 cm. T'ang Dynasty.

31a. 'Udyāna type' Buddha image; white marble. From Ch'ü-yang-hsien, Hopei. Ht. 145 cm. Seventh century.

31b. Nursemaid with a baby; partly glazed and painted pottery. Ht. 36·8 cm. T'ang Dynasty.

32a. The Paradise of Amitābha; detail of a wall-painting in the Kondō of Hōryūji, Nara. About A.D. 700.

32b. Yen Li-pen (died 673): The Emperor Hsüan of the Ch'en Dynasty. Detail of the handscroll of the Thirteen Emperors; ink and slight colour on silk. Ht. 51 cm. T'ang Dynasty.

33. Seated Buddha; stone. From T'ien-lung-shan, Shansi.
(head restored) Eighth century.

34. Sung Hui-tsung (r. 1101–25); Court ladies preparing silk. Handscroll after Chang Hsüan; ink and colour on silk. Ht. 37 cm. Sung Dynasty.

35a. Han Kan (active 740–60); 'Night White', a favourite horse of T'ang Ming Huang. Handscroll; ink on paper. Ht. 29·5 cm. (Detail.)

35b. Style of Wang Wei (698–759)?; Riverside under snow. Part of a handscroll(?); ink on silk. About tenth century.

36. Anon; The Emperor Ming Huang's Journey to Shu. Hanging scroll; ink and colour on silk. Ht. 55·9 cm.

37. Attributed to Tung Yüan; Scenery along the Hsiao and Hsiang Rivers. Part of a handscroll; ink and slight colour on silk. Early Sung Dynasty.

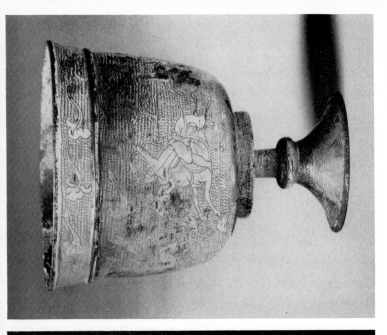

38b. Miniature stem-cup, engraved with hunting scene; gilt bronze. Ht. 6·4 cm. T'ang Dynasty.

38a. 'Sea-horse and Grape' mirror; bronze. Diam. 24·1 cm. T'ang Dynasty.

39a. Pottery jar decorated with splashed polychrome glaze. Ht. 17·8 cm. T'ang Dynasty.

39b. Ewer with stopper in the shape of a pheasant's head; white-glazed porcelain. Ht. 30·5 cm. T'ang Dynasty.

40a. Interior of the Buddha Hall of Upper Hua-yen-ssu, Tatung, Shansi.　Dedicated 1140. Chin Dynasty

40b. Lohan; modelled in pottery with three-colour glaze. Ht. 105 cm. Liao-Chin Dynasties.

41. Kuanyin; wood and plaster, painted and gilded. Ht. 225 cm. Sung Dynasty.

42a. After Shih K'o (active mid-tenth century); Two minds in harmony. Part of a handscroll; ink on paper. Ht. 44 cm.

42b. Attributed to Ku Hung-chung; The night entertainments of Han Hsi-tsai. Part of a handscroll; ink and colour on silk. Ht. 29 cm. Sung Dynasty.

3. Chang Tse-tuan (early twelfth century); Life along the river on
the eve of the Ch'ing-ming festival. Detail of a handscroll; ink and
slight colour on silk. Ht. 25·5 cm. Sung Dynasty.

44. Fan K'uan (active 990–1030); Travelling amid mountains and gorges. Hanging scroll; ink and slight colour on silk. Ht. 233 cm. Sung Dynasty.

45. Attributed to Su Tung-p'o (1036–1101); Bare tree, bamboo and rocks. Handscroll; ink on paper. Ht. 23·4 cm. Sung Dynasty.

46. Sung Hui-tsung (r. 1101–25); The five-coloured parakeet. Handscroll; ink and colours on silk. Ht. 53 cm. Sung Dynasty.

47. Hsia Kuei (c. 1180–1230); Clear distance over mountains and streams. Part of a handscroll; ink on paper. Ht. 46·5 cm. Sung Dynasty.

48. Li T'ang (*c.* 1050–1130); Whispering Pines in the Mountains, dated 1124. Hanging scroll; ink and colour on silk. Ht. 139·8 cm. Sung Dynasty. (Detail.)

49a. Mu-ch'i (*c.* 1200–70); Shrike on a pine-trunk. Detail of a hanging scroll; ink on paper. Sung Dynasty.

49b. Ch'en Jung (active 1235–*c.* 1260); The nine dragons. Part of a handscroll; ink on paper. Ht. 46 cm. Sung Dynasty.

50b. Vase with lobed sides; *ch'ing-pai* ware. Ht. 13 cm. Sung Dynasty.

50a. Deep bowl with incised design of ducks amid water plants; Ting ware. Diam. 20 cm. Sung Dynasty.

51a. *Mei-p'ing* vase; Honan black-glazed stoneware. Ht. 25·4 cm. Sung Dynasty. 51b. *Kinuta* vase; Lung-ch'üan celadon. Ht. 16·9 cm. Sung Dynasty. 51c. Traveller's flask, with cockscomb ornament in green enamel over white glaze. Ht. 37·5 cm. North China, Liao Dynasty.

52a. Covered jar; stoneware decorated with black flowers on a white glaze. Tz'u-chou ware. Ht. 11·7 cm. Sung Dynasty.

52b. Tea bowl; dark stoneware with black 'hare's fur' glaze. Fukien *temmoku*. Diam. 13 cm. Sung Dynasty.

居角東舂風多客花小蕭容膝
庚年峯金梭躍水池魚戲彩鳳
栖林澗竹斜橐清疎霏玉屑
蕭々白髮岸烏紗而今不二辭
庚戍市上縣盡未之辭甲寅三
月望即劉復攜竹嵩表素
鹿詩贈寄仁仲醫師且錫山
不次玆鄉玉答膝齋則仁燃
居之玉徳月搏琿玖鄉登斯齋
持己滴我其属為仁巾野當
與吾志也雲林子識

53. Ni Tsan
(1301–74); The
Jung-hsi Studio.
Dated 1372. Hanging
scroll; ink on paper.
Ht. 73·3 cm. Yüan
Dynasty.

54. Chao Meng-fu (1254–1322); Autumn Colours on the Ch'iao and Hua Mountains. Dated 1295. Part of a handscroll; ink and slight colour on paper. Ht. 28·4 cm. Yüan Dynasty.

55. Huang Kung-wang (1269–1354); Living in the Fu-ch'un Mountains. Dated 1350. Part of a handscroll; ink on paper. Ht. 33 cm. Yüan Dynasty.

56a. Ch'ien Hsüan (c. 1235–after 1300); Sparrow on an apple-branch. Handscroll; ink and slight colour on paper. Ht. 22·2 cm. Yüan Dynasty.

56b. Wu Chen (1280–1354); Leaf from an album of studies of bamboo. Dated 1350. Ink on paper. Ht. 42·9 cm. Yüan Dynasty.

57a. Tai Chin (*c.* 1390–1460); Fishermen on the River. Detail of a handscroll; ink and colour on paper. Ht. 46·1 cm. Ming Dynasty.

57b. Ch'iu Ying (*c.* 1510–51); Fisherman's flute heard over the lake. Detail of a hanging scroll; ink and slight colour on paper. Diam. 84·9 cm. Ming Dynasty.

湖磐參翠竹橋
春冬傳盧影逢
凸雲飛濕亂山
冬多草評鋒荒
流死行程在上軒

58. Shen Chou (1427–1509): Returning home from the Land of the Immortals. Album-leaf mounted as a handscroll; ink and colour on paper. Ht. 38·9 cm. Ming Dynasty.

59a. Tung Ch'i-ch'ang (1555–1636); Leaf from an album dated 1601; ink and colours on paper. Ht. 42·8 cm.

59b. Ch'en Hung-shou (1599–1652); Portrait of the poet Po Chü-i, in the manner of Li Lung-mien. Dated 1649. Part of a handscroll; ink and colours on paper. Ht. 31·6 cm. Ch'ing Dynasty.

60. Ridge-tile in the form of a guardian figure; pottery, glazed green and dark brown. Ht. 80 cm. Ming Dynasty.

61a. Peony and rock. *K'o-ssu* tapestry. Detail. Diam. 27 cm. Ming Dynasty.

61b. Carved lacquer cup-stand. Yung-lo mark and Ch'ien-lung inscription dated 1781. Diam. 6·5 cm. Ming Dynasty.

62a. Incense-burner; cloisonné enamel. Ht. 12·7 cm. First half of fifteenth century. Ming Dynasty.

62b. Pilgrim-bottle; white porcelain decorated in underglazed blue. Ht. 30·4 cm. Hsüan-te period. Ming Dynasty.

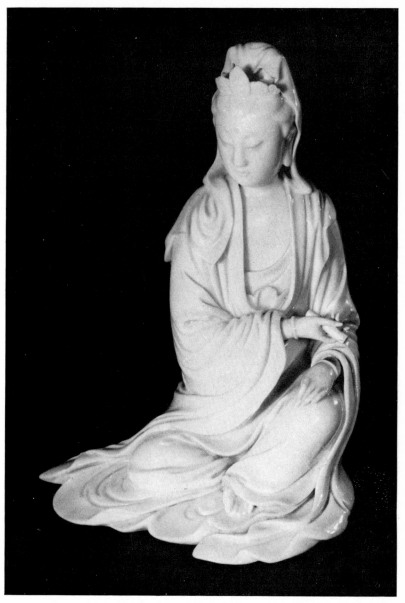

63. Kuanyin, modelled in white porcelain. Fukien Te-hua ware.
Ht. 21·6 cm. Early Ch'ing Dynasty.

64a. Peking; the Ch'i-nien-tien, Hall of Annual Prayers, in the Precinct of the Altar of Heaven. Late Ch'ing Dynasty.

64b. Peking; the Imperial Palace, looking north from the Wu-men to the T'ai-ho-men. A corner of the T'ai-ho-tien is visible beyond. Ming and Early Ch'ing Dynasties.

65a. Covered tripod; white jade. Ht. 15·3 cm. Early Ch'ing
Dynasty.

65b. Tea-pot of enamelled porcelain. Mark and period of Ch'ien-
lung. Ht. 12·9 cm. Ch'ing Dynasty.

66a. Lang Shih-ning (1688–1766) (Guiseppe Castiglione);
Horses in a landscape. Ink and colour on silk. Ch'ing Dynasty.

66b. Li Yin (active about 1690–1710); Landscape, dated
1694. Detail of a hanging scroll; ink and colour on silk.
Width 104·3 cm. Ch'ing Dynasty.

67a. Wang Yüan-ch'i (1642–1715); Landscape, dated 1706. Hanging scroll; ink and colour on paper. Ht. 106·4 cm. Ch'ing Dynasty.

67b. Kung Hsien (c. 1620–89); Landscape of Ch'i-hsia. Hanging scroll; ink on paper. Ht. 153 cm.

天不法容法五法人
法師倍人不有法無
自古不知便知法法
畫今能此乃法自
此之古畫必人立
非造能曾何有也
超化泥古如太法無
泥也古人也朴者法
古泥師末不一何之
塞之心嘗是散也法
高矣不破予也化也

68a. Chu Ta (Pa-ta Shan-jen, 1625–*c.* 1705); Two birds. Album leaf; ink on paper. Ht. 31·8 cm.

68b. Tao-chi (Shih-t'ao, 1641–*c.* 1717); Landscape. Album leaf; ink and colour on paper. Ht. 48 cm. Ch'ing Dynasty.

69. K'un-ts'an (Shih-ch'i, c. 1610–93); Autumn Landscape, dated 1666. Handscroll; ink and slight colour on paper. Ht. 31·5 cm. Ch'ing Dynasty.

70a. Vase; stoneware, decorated with aubergine, yellow and blue enamels. Ht. 30·7 cm.
Ming Dynasty.

70b. Porcelain vase with *lang-yao* (ox-blood)
glaze. Ht. 19·6 cm. Ch'ing Dynasty
(K'ang-hsi period).

71b. Ch'i Pai-shih (1863–1957); Cabbages. Leaf from an album dated 1934; ink on paper.

71a. Porcelain vase, decorated in underglaze blue. Ht. 26·7 cm. Ch'ing Dynasty (K'ang-hsi period).

72. Li K'o-jan (born 1907); Gorges of the Yangtse. Hanging scroll,
dated 1962; ink and colour on paper.